BART

BART

THE DRAMATIC HISTORY OF THE BAY AREA RAPID TRANSIT SYSTEM

MICHAEL C. HEALY

FOREWORD BY JOHN KING

HEYDAY, BERKELEY, CALIFORNIA

Library of Congress Cataloging-in-Publication Data
Names: Healy, Michael C., author.
Title: BART : the dramatic history of the Bay Area Rapid Transit system / Michael C. Healy.
Description: Berkeley, California : Heyday, 2016. | Includes index.
Identifiers: LCCN 2016025736| ISBN 9781597143707 (pbk. : alk. paper) | ISBN 9781597143813 (e-pub)
Subjects: LCSH: San Francisco Bay Area Rapid Transit District (Calif.)—History. | Local transit—California—San Francisco Bay Area—History.
Classification: LCC HE4491.S45 H43 2016 | DDC 388.4/2097946—dc23
LC record available at https://lccn.loc.gov/2016025736

Cover Image: Photo by Thomas Hawk.
Cover Design: Ashley Ingram
Interior Design/Typesetting: Rebecca LeGates
POD by Lightning Source

Image credits: All images courtesy of BART except p. 28, courtesy of John Harder, and p. 182, courtesy of David Lance Goines.

Published by Heyday
P.O. Box 9145, Berkeley, California 94709
(510) 549-3564
www.heydaybooks.com

10 9 8 7 6 5 4 3 2

This book is dedicated to the memory of Marvin E. Lewis, BART's early pioneer; to the memory of B. R. Stokes, who guided the building of the system; to my wife, Joan Van Horn, whose knowledge of some of the history was invaluable; and to all the men and women who make BART work each and every day.

CONTENTS

FOREWORD

The evidence of how well BART has shaped and served the Bay Area is that, these days, we take it for granted. We complain about having to stand. We complain about the crowded escalators. We grumble if the doors close before we can rush on, and we grouse if someone blocks the door to keep them from closing once we're inside. If there isn't a stop within an easy walk of where we're headed...why not?

In essence, we're disgruntled because we've come to rely on this constantly evolving system with forty-five stations and 107 miles of track—the real-life version of the original promise of "a mass transportation service that is at least as fast, as comfortable, and as cheap to ride as the private automobile." Those words are from the original consultant study presented to the state legislature in 1956, a rosy preamble to the convoluted and often confounding saga that Mike Healy tells so engagingly in the pages that follow.

Healy is the ideal raconteur to spin the yarn, having served BART as its spokesman for decades before retiring in 2005. He was there for the opening in 1972 and the years of problem-solving that followed. His older coworkers were the bureaucrats who had pushed forward tenaciously through the prior decade of missed deadlines and budget strains, the hype of "space-age" design and the reality of old-school politics. Pick your anecdote from the abundance, starting with the incongruous scene at a Martinez breakfast counter in 1962 as the mayors of San Francisco and Oakland pitched woo to a tight-lipped Contra Costa County supervisor. The latter was the swing vote on whether residents of that county, then largely rural, would be presented with a ballot measure to finance the system. (Not even Healy knows exactly what was said, but the rest is history.)

Now look past the entertainment factor: this is an important story that Healy tells, and a timely one, too.

In today's California we like to think either that nothing large should be attempted because it might have troublesome side effects, or that nothing will get done because opponents can find too many ways to hobble progress. But the history of BART is a reminder that this has always been true. Big plans stir big opposition. Every bump in the road is portrayed as the beginning of the end. Long-term planning confronts short-term grandstanding. The same Oakland mayor who lobbied for the overall system later forced BART to reroute a portion of his downtown's subway around a popular hardware store. By the opening day, the hardware store already had gone out of business—and thanks to the tighter underground alignment, Healy tells us, riders for years endured "the screaming sound of wheel flanges scraping the rail as trains negotiated the curve."

In hindsight, obviously, the original alignment was better. Just as, in hindsight, San Mateo's board of supervisors made a bad call in 1961 when they pulled out of the proposed system and delayed service south of San Francisco for more than twenty years. But this is how the real world works when something ambitious is at stake: you keep moving forward any way that you can, rather than stop until everything is ideal. The reason we can put our ticket through the turnstile in Richmond or Pittsburg or Pleasanton or Fremont and step off the train at San Francisco International Airport is because hundreds of smart, determined people ignored headlines and lawsuits and technological strains to summon the system into existence and then get the trains to run (mostly) on time.

Why does this matter now? Simple. Try to imagine the Bay Area without BART, and I'll wager that you come up short. The system ties together communities and has allowed Bay Area residents the option of an expansive car-free lifestyle. Neighborhood centers such as Rockridge in Oakland were revived by BART's presence, exactly the opposite of the apocalyptic warnings from the political left that saw the system as nothing more than a corporate plot to funnel workers into San Francisco's Financial District. As for projections that trains would be vacant except during commute hours—not far from the truth early on—now it can seem crowded at most hours of the day. This is how we get around whenever we can, our mode of choice for outings and events. Outings and events that, often, choose their location so that BART is close by. The region and its rapid transit are inseparable, a bond that only grows stronger as once placid suburban cities add "transit villages" next to stops.

Yes, there were mishaps along the way. Test cars crashed and homeless people camped out in bicycle lockers. Some marketing forays were ill conceived, including a brief experiment in the early 1980s when trains could be chartered for private events, complete with food and beverages. The system also was put to the test by cultural changes; Healy is quietly eloquent in detailing how and why BART became the first transit system to provide elevator service to train platforms. The reason in large part was the crusade launched by Harold Willson, who had moved to the Bay Area after being paralyzed in a coal-mining accident in West Virginia and made it his mission to ensure BART was accessible to people like him. "Willson possessed not only a hardened determination but also an engaging charm," Healy writes, and in 1968, the board came around.

This is history that we need to remember. Not just for history's sake but for what might lie ahead.

We live in an era when map-altering endeavors are in the works, from high-density housing in suburban downtowns to the effort to link San Francisco and Los Angeles with high-speed rail. Without fail, they're attacked as destructive boondoggles sure to mar our quality of life. Sometimes we need to say no, to be sure. Other times, though, we need to dream. The legacy of BART is that large-scale audacity can succeed—and the Bay Area is better as a result.

John King,
urban design critic for the *San Francisco Chronicle*
and author of *Cityscapes* and *Cityscapes 2*

PREFACE

Over the past sixty or so years, the story of the iconic San Francisco Bay Area Rapid Transit system, known throughout the world simply as BART, has often played out like an old-fashioned melodrama. In many ways its story is a metaphor for the grit and resolute determination that built a nation out of the vast land we call America. But in this it is not alone, of course. Other great public works projects through the years have also been symbolic of our nation's constant striving to reach the other side of the rainbow, more often than not against great odds. It's the journey itself that tests our resolve as a people. The phenomenon of BART, however, coming along in the mid-twentieth century, was pivotal in the adoption of aerospace technology for advancing ground transportation. It led the way into a brave new world of circuit boards, microchips, and a new kind of signaling. When BART burst on the scene it became a catalyst for a renaissance in modern rail transit both nationally and internationally. But at one point, when it was still no more than a scribble of an idea on a piece of paper, it came within a gnat's eyelash of never leaving that piece of paper, of not happening at all.

Putting the BART story down in words and pictures came about as a result of a casual conversation I had with BART general manager Grace Crunican during the summer of 2012. We were having lunch at an Oakland restaurant and I was telling her some quirky anecdotes from the early days of the system, for which I was head of Media and Public Affairs and official spokesman for more than thirty years before retiring in 2005. She was fascinated and, because it was BART's fortieth anniversary, suggested that I should write its history. I kiddingly said I didn't write science fiction, and the conversation moved on. However, on the drive back to the BART offices at the Kaiser Center overlooking Lake Merritt in Oakland, Ms. Crunican continued to encourage me to consider writing down the system's history for publication. The more I thought about it, the more intrigued I became with the idea as I realized a great story was waiting to be told. As many BART employees and observers who were around in those early days can attest, the project was replete with chuckholes, hurdles, constant controversy, and political machinations, sometimes ascending to high drama. This may in part have been because the concept as sold to Bay Area voters was gargantuan and bold, and determined to go where no urban/suburban rail transit system had gone before, all in one fell swoop. The question raised by pundits at its inception was: would this space-age system work or be the biggest boondoggle in the country's history? Many doubted its viability as a concept. And, of course, there was a great deal of pushback. In words attributed to Mark Twain, "The secret of getting ahead is getting started." Without question, that was the underlying mantra of its early proponents—get it started. My only condition for getting the BART story down in black and white was that it would be with warts and all. Grace Crunican agreed that this was the only way the story should be told.

Michael C. Healy
Oakland, California

CHAPTER 1

SAN FRANCISCO, NOVEMBER 6, 1962

The old Flood Building stands on the northeast corner of Market and Powell Streets. Seen diagonally from across the street, it appears to be shaped a like a giant wedge of cheese, with Woolworths wrapping around its base. Built by James L. Flood in 1904, its twelve stories of gray Beaux-Arts architecture and sculptured exterior suggest a dark gothic fortress. This venerable structure is a San Francisco landmark, and at one time in its early history it was the second-tallest structure in the city—the old Call Building built by sugar king Adolph Spreckels in 1897 being the tallest at fourteen stories.

A great deal of lore is associated with the Flood Building. From 1907 to 1917 it was the headquarters of the old Southern Pacific Railroad. Back in the late 1920s, Dashiell Hammett, author of *The Maltese Falcon,* occupied an office on the third floor while working for the Pinkerton National Detective Agency. Below, on Powell Street, the muffled sounds of horns honking, mixed with clanking from the city's famous cable cars, can be heard. As the cable cars reach the end of their journey at Market Street, they reverse direction with the help of bystanders pushing them around on a turntable for a return trip up Powell to the top of the hill.

It is 11 P.M. on this day, November 6, 1962. The fall night is brisk and electric. In a small, marble-paneled office on the sixth floor of the Flood Building, two men wait with nervous anticipation as they continually check how the vote is going for rapid transit. The two men are B. R. (Bill) Stokes, the assistant general manager of the fledgling Bay

Area Rapid Transit District, and John E. (Jack) Everson of Parsons Brinckerhoff–Tudor–Bechtel, who is slated to coordinate the building of the transit project should it be approved by the voters today. Alameda and San Francisco Counties have been reporting favorable numbers. Contra Costa County is questionable. A great deal of opposition has been coming from that region and could drag the project down. Many community leaders have expressed concern that rapid transit will not only be costly but also bring crime to their tranquil suburban bedroom communities. Still others do not like the prospect of an *ad valorem* tax to service a long-term debt to pay the initial cost. The project has also been opposed by several of the county's newspapers serving the outlying areas, primarily because it might be decades before they will see a rapid transit train east of Concord.

Several years of planning and engineering have already been invested to get to this point. Yet, when it comes down to it, Bay Area Rapid Transit remains no more than the spark of a concept. This is all or nothing for the proposed project; the two men know if it doesn't get approved now, chances are it is not ever going to happen. If the proposal has to wait for the 1964 election, the cost to build it will likely escalate exponentially. Voter approval would in all probability be impossible to achieve, and the dream of regional rail transit would fall into that dark abyss where giant ideas sometimes go to die. By midnight all the votes still have not been counted. But one thing has been reported: as feared, the vote is behind in Contra Costa County. How much behind is uncertain. Approval for the financing requires 60 percent of voters saying yes to Measure A, the $792 million general obligation bond referendum.

It's after midnight. Jack Everson puts his head down on a table and dozes. Stokes stays up and paces the floor of his office, chewing on his trademark pipe. At 3 A.M. the final tally comes in. The registrar reports that Contra Costa has come in with less than the 60 percent required, but, when averaged out among the three counties, the project has been approved, with 61.2 percent of the voters in favor of taxing themselves and going forward. Though the vote was a squeaker, Stokes is jubilant nevertheless. With great excitement, he runs over and shakes the sleeping Everson.

"Jack, Jack, wake up!" Stokes says. "The project's been approved. We're in."

Everson, blurry-eyed, looks up.

"What?" he says. "You mean we actually have to build the damn thing?"

The two men look at each other and laugh, not really knowing what hurdles they would encounter in the coming years. All they can do in those early-morning moments of November 7, 1962, is ponder the formidable challenge of converting the vision of a regional rail transit system from an idea on a piece of paper to the reality of concrete and steel, a proposition of enormous magnitude. They also know that this is the dawn of a new era for the region, and perhaps for the transit industry at large. One thing is certain: the project will be the first rapid transit rail system with a subway west of Chicago.

WHAT CAME BEFORE PAVED THE WAY

The advent of the San Francisco Bay Area Rapid Transit system, which eventually became known worldwide simply as BART, did not, of course, occur in a vacuum. Its history is embedded in the history of America itself, of an indomitable people who invented themselves and have ever since been always on the move, always looking beyond the horizon, hungry for something more, constantly pushing the boundaries. In a journey that never really ends, great events often result in great challenges that shape the character of societies and also shape the world's urban centers, which in turn frame our history. Buildings and art reflect the unique characteristics and spirit of urban societies and visionary individuals who gather there to bring their dreams to the table. BART owes much to such events and individuals, and the changes they brought about, even going back as far as 150 years. In particular, the great eastern rail rapid transit systems, BART's direct ancestors, were built in cities, such as the one in Boston, whose initial subway line—the first subway in the nation—opened in 1897. But the prime example is one of the greatest public works projects in the nation's history: the building of the New York City subway, and the technology it pioneered. That technology, as well as other aspects of that system, would have a direct link to BART some sixty-five years in the future. In more ways than one, New York was the gateway to the promised land.

NEW YORK CITY'S POPULATION EXPLOSION

In 1800, New York City's population was estimated at a sparse 60,000. By 1820, immigrants, mostly from Europe, had begun arriving by the boatload, pouring tens of thousands of its people into the heart of the city. Many ended up in Boston or Philadelphia, but a preponderance of the new immigrants settled in Manhattan, with spillover into the four other districts, which became boroughs—Brooklyn, Queens, the Bronx, and Staten Island—creating the beginnings of a megalopolis. By 1899 the population had exploded to more than 3.5 million, reaching a critical mass. Even as early as 1860, the main challenge facing New York was the need for housing and infrastructure to support the influx of new residents. Development lagged behind as the building of brownstone tenements throughout Manhattan barely kept pace with the demand. Often in those days two or more families shared a flat while waiting for additional single-family accommodations to become available.

In addition to housing and commercial expansion as a result of the city's burgeoning population, another critical need became apparent: some form of mass transit to relieve the nightmare congestion that was beginning to hamper economic growth. But local government had a prevailing myopic view of just what that might entail. Some entrepreneurs were profiting from what transportation was already established along the city's bustling thoroughfares and did not want to see any significant change.

Around midcentury the primary modes of transport were horse-drawn wagons, cabs, and omnibuses, which were like elongated stagecoaches that required several horses for mobility. The carriers maintained a heated competition among themselves; sometimes pugnacious drivers ended up in street fights while customers stood by waiting to get to their desired destinations. At times coaches trying to pick up fares ran over people in the streets. Newspapers reported that customers were actually being, in their words, "shanghaied" by burly omnibus conductors in efforts to improve the bottom line of their operations. The victims would be ordered to pay some outrageous fare for the privilege of their trip when deposited at the other end. Such reports added to the growing pressure the city aldermen were feeling. In the final analysis, overall public transit was woefully inadequate.

FIRST SUBWAY PROPOSAL SABOTAGED

In 1864 the need for improved transportation in New York caught the attention of a businessman from Michigan named Hugh B. Willson. After observing firsthand the digging of the world's first subway transit system in London in 1863 (which would become the London Underground), Willson believed the concept could work in New York as well. In 1864 he proposed that a subterranean steam-powered rail line be built from the Battery in lower Manhattan to Central Park. Since it would be an exclusive right-of-way, trains would not be subject to street traffic, slow-moving carts, or pedestrians crossing the avenues. A subway would be clean and dust free, with luxurious transit cars that would have cushioned seats and could speed passengers to their destinations safely and cheaply. Willson formed the Metropolitan Railway Company, which he financed with mostly his own money. His goal, if he got the go-ahead from the state and the city, was to own and operate the system and seek private investors for capital.

Willson brought in a partner, A. P. Robinson, a civil engineer who called for tunneling under the streets of the city using a cut-and-cover method of construction. It was an ambitious scheme. The same method had been used for construction of the London subway, which began the work in 1861. On that initial demonstration line, train cars were hauled by steam-powered locomotives. A vexing issue Willson faced was that tearing up the streets was bound to cause enormous disruption for businesses, not to mention those just trying to get around. The owners of structures along the proposed route were concerned about cave-ins and possible damage to their buildings. Some officials also expressed safety concerns.

Willson's biggest obstacle, however, was a Scots Irishman named William Magear Tweed, better known in New York politics as "Boss Tweed." He was a large, barrel-chested figure and one of the most powerful men in the state. He headed New York City's Tammany Hall as if it were his personal fiefdom. Tammany Hall was the Democratic political machine that basically ran the city, from choosing candidates for political office and appointing police superintendents and other plum city jobs, to generally determining policy. One of the Hall's major functions, through shady backroom deals, was deciding who got contracts for publicly funded projects. More often than not, contracts went to relatives and friends and political supporters. Kickbacks

William Magear "Boss" Tweed was top dog of New York's Tammany Hall political machine in the mid-to-late 1800s. He eventually went to prison for forgery and larceny.

were routine. One of the major vendors with a very fat contract from the city was a printing and stationery supply company that later turned out to be owned by Tweed.

Officially, Tweed was the city's commissioner of public works, and he later became a state senator. Unofficially, Tweed and his select group of cronies firmly controlled just about everything that affected city life. Among his many enterprises was the collection of license fees from all of the privately owned street-transit businesses. They could not operate on the city streets without his okay, and that did not happen without a lot of money regularly crossing his palm. A subway presented potential competition for the cabs, wagons, and omnibus coaches, and thus a potential loss of revenue for Tweed. Since Willson made it clear that he was not going to make payoffs to Tammany Hall for approval, there would be no subway as far as Tweed was concerned.

Willson decided to fight on for his dream of an underground system to serve the citizens of New York. In that same year, 1864, he petitioned the state legislature to pass a bill that would allow him to go forward with his plan to build his proposed subway, but he was too late for a vote of the full legislature. The senate, however, did give him a thumbs-up with a 19 to 7 vote.

Encouraged, Willson in the following year presented his petition again to the full legislature, which passed a bill giving his company the go-ahead to build a rail system under the streets of New York. Still, Tweed got in the last word. Reuben E. Fenton, governor of the state of New York and a longtime friend and associate of Tweed, vetoed the bill at Tweed's insistence. Willson was back to square one.

ANOTHER RAIL CONCEPT GETS UNDER WAY

Two years later, in 1867, an entrepreneur named Charles T. Harvey came up with the idea to build an elevated line along the West Side that would operate on a cable system powered by steam engines. On paper it looked promising. He, too, went to the state legislature for approval and got it. On July 1, 1867, he began the construction of his line, which became known as "the elevated," or "el." Reportedly, Tweed did not oppose it because he was certain it would fail as an enterprise. Harvey completed a quarter mile of his el within six months, and soon after that he began passenger service.

A year later, another quarter mile had been completed, but in the following year, 1869, a nationwide depression hit, and the el's investors pulled out. The line was closed, and plans for expansion were put on hold. New investors in the form of Wall Street moneymen eventually came to the rescue, took control of Harvey's company, and ultimately booted him out. The el reopened in 1871 as the New York Elevated Railway Company. Eventually the new company expanded its cable line across the just-opened Brooklyn Bridge, of which Tweed was a director. As an interesting aside, Tweed and his pals had arranged the deal so that they had the voting stock in the New York Bridge Company while, ironically, Manhattan and Brooklyn, which put up most of the financing, had no vote. (Prior to the building of the bridge, Brooklyn had been an independent city.) As for the elevated line's effectiveness in relieving the city's ever-growing congestion, it helped but was not nearly strong enough to meet the demand.

THE SECRET SUBWAY

The very first subway on New York's Manhattan Island was more reminiscent of something out of Jules Verne than a functioning mass transit system. From the beginning, its construction was rife with intrigue.

Alfred Ely Beach, originally from Springfield, Massachusetts, and a partner, Orson Munn, published *Scientific American*, a successful magazine that popularized science and listed patents of new inventions. Beach's father owned the *New York Sun* newspaper, of which the younger Beach was an editor in his early days. Beach was also an inventor and, in addition to being a publisher, owned his own patent company. (One of his inventions in the mid-1800s was a typewriter for the blind.) Like Hugh Willson before him, he spent time in London and became interested not only in the big dig of the London Underground but also in the use of pneumatic technology for transportation. A demonstration pneumatic rail line had been built by the engineer Thomas Rammell and opened to the public in 1874. It was called the Crystal Palace Railway and carried passengers about 1,800 feet along a brick-lined tunnel. This was Rammell's answer to the steam-driven trains of the London Underground, which had caused numerous problems, including respiratory issues for passengers. Beach was more than intrigued. He was also greatly impressed with London's pneumatic-tube mail system; using large pneumatic tubes about 4 feet in diameter, the London postal system transported mail and small packages efficiently from point A to point B. Beach believed the concept of an underground pneumatic-driven rail system could work in New York.

In 1867, Beach applied to New York City for a permit to build a pneumatic subterranean transit system as a demonstration of its viability. He formed the Beach Pneumatic Transit Company to construct the proposed project. The concept called for forced air to be pushed through a tunnel behind a vehicle on a track. Earlier that year, he had displayed a similar concept at the American Institute Fair in the 14th Street Armory, located between 14th and 15th Streets in Manhattan. His demonstration involved a 100-foot tube, 6 feet in diameter, with a fan at one end that could use compressed air to push and pull a car carrying up to ten people.

Beach, like Willson, was denied approval by Tweed and his gang unless a payoff was in the offing. Beach was adamantly opposed to paying a bribe to Tweed. He did, however, manage to petition the state for a postal charter franchise to build small pneumatic tubes for the stated purpose of mail delivery. Later he amended his plan to build one large tunnel on the pretext that it would make it easier for a network of small pneumatic tubes to be installed. The amendment, of course, was a ruse to accomplish what he had originally set out to do: build the city's first subway. Now it would be done covertly.

In December 1869, Beach began his clandestine subway project by renting the basement of a well-known clothing store called Devlin's in downtown Manhattan. Located at the southeast corner of Warren Street and Broadway, the site, ironically, was directly across the street from City Hall. His work crew, sworn to secrecy, was ordered to begin

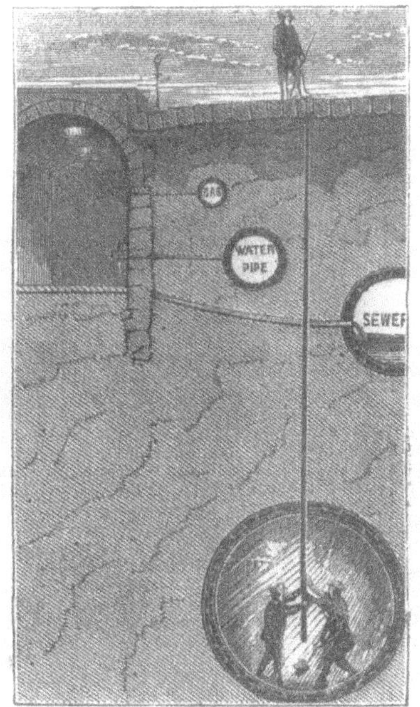

TESTING THE CORRECTNESS OF POSITION AT NIGHT.

Above, right: Alfred Ely Beach, publisher, inventor, visionary, and builder of the secret subway under New York in 1870.

Above, left: In October 1867, spectators at the American Institute Fair marveled at Beach's demonstration of a pneumatic train traveling through a tube with tight tolerances.

Left: This illustration depicts how Beach's subway tunneling stayed on course. Workers in the tube pushed a rod up through the ground while someone on top monitored.

digging using picks and shovels, with oil lanterns for light. A compass was used to guide the crew along the planned route. At night, when the digging was being done, steel rods were pushed up through the earth to the street above to verify the tunnel's direction. Initially the work was fraught with problems. The soft earth was dank and oppressive. The men had a constant fear of cave-ins from the street traffic looming about twelve feet above them. Some of them were beset with claustrophobia in the humid closeness of the dig and had to be replaced.

To solve the problem, Beach, putting on his inventor's cap, came up with an ingenious contraption: a hydraulic-driven shield, basically a cylinder with a series of blades and shelves to hold spoils. Beach's shield was actually a much-improved version of a shield designed in 1844 by the London engineer Marc Isambard Brunel to build a tunnel under the Thames. Brunel claimed in his writings that he had been inspired by a worm he once observed drilling its way through the wooden plank of a ship. The naval shipworm, a kind of saltwater termite, lines its tunnel with an excretion that hardens, the substance protecting the hole—and its digger—as work continues. Beach's 9-foot shield would bore about 20 inches of earth with each thrust forward, while protecting the workers just behind it. Sand and soft earth spoils were removed and carted away in wagons under the cover of darkness. Following the shield, other workers put the circular walls in place brick by brick, creating a foot-thick lining fixed by mortar. Rails were placed along the floor on each side of a shallow groove to guide the car.

The tunnel was 9 feet in diameter and 312 feet long (about one block) when completed. Beach had planned to go farther but, as the story goes, an enterprising reporter disguised himself as a worker one night to check out the project, which he later exposed in his newspaper. The story forced Beach to open before he could complete the full scale of what he had planned. The tunnel started under the corner of Warren Street, ran a short distance to Broadway, and then curved south under Broadway, ending at Murray Street.

The abridged project was completed in an astonishingly brief fifty-eight days and included two stations, one at each end, with the main entrance at Warren Street. A giant fan weighing 48 tons was installed. Nicknamed the Western Tornado, it was built especially to Beach's specifications by Roots Patent Force Rotary Blowers. A 100-horsepower steam engine provided the power. The fan was designed to push the transit car through the tunnel to one end and then reverse its blades and basically suck the car back for its return by creating powerful negative air pressure. The car could travel at a speed of 10 miles per hour. Building the car was done piece by piece inside the tunnel from prefabricated parts. It had to fit within very tight tolerances for maximum efficiency. Beach spent a total of $350,000 to complete what he envisioned would be an initial demonstration line.

BEACH OPENS HIS SECRET LINE

On February 26, 1870, Beach ceremoniously opened his pneumatic subway to the public, treating it as an extravaganza event complete with food and cocktails. Lore has it that Boss Tweed was absolutely flabbergasted at the unveiling and vowed to stop it. He had simply had no idea that Beach was in fact building an underground transit line. To add insult to injury, the project was right under Tammany Hall's nose, since it was across the street from City Hall. According to press reports at the time, pessimistic New Yorkers who came to see what the well-publicized opening of Beach's line was all about expected some dark, dismal underground display. Instead the curiosity seekers who came to see this strange marvel found something quite surprising: a clean, elegant, and well-lighted subterranean vault under Devlin's clothing store.

Though it was touted as a mass transportation demonstration line, most people viewed it more as a novelty than anything else. One thing no one could challenge, however, was the extent to which Beach outfitted his tiny line. The stations were adorned with paintings and other artworks, such as frescoes and statues, creating a pleasing aesthetic environment. The main station boasted a fountain with goldfish and a grand piano. Elaborate furniture was placed so passengers waiting for the transit car could sit comfortably. Chandeliers provided plenty of light. The single transit car was also elegantly appointed with cushioned seats, ornate woodwork, and decorative oil lamps on tables, giving the interior a comfortable brightness. The car could carry 22 passengers per trip. During the first year of operation, about 400,000 customers paid twenty-five cents a ride. The money was donated to charity.

The public had a great deal of skepticism about whether an air-driven system could be expanded, as Beach hoped to do. Meanwhile Tweed, outraged that he had been duped, had the city bring a lawsuit against Beach's company to enjoin it from any further development. The suit was based on the city's legal opinion that the state legislature did not have the authority to grant Beach's company a permit to dig under their streets. The question raised was, who owns Broadway? During a court-ordered halt to any further work by Beach, Tweed fell from grace. He was eventually convicted of stealing $25 to $45 million from the taxpayers of New York, although some reports said as much as $200 million may have been stolen during his reign. He eventually died in jail on April 12, 1878, at the age of fifty-five.

While continuing to operate the pneumatic line, Beach again petitioned the state legislature to amend his original franchise so as to

In 1912 workers and officials excavating the new BMT subway line were astonished to discover Beach's secret tube, by then long-forgotten.

allow further development of his system. His plan now was to convert to a steam locomotive operation. The legislature passed the bill, which was signed by the governor, but the matter never went any further. A bank crisis intervened, and Beach's potential investors walked away from his proposal, partly because of the financial risk and partly because of the public's skepticism that his plan was impractical. In 1873, after three years of operation, Beach closed up his tiny line. It was sealed off and forgotten until it was discovered fully intact forty years later, during the excavation of the Brooklyn-Manhattan Transit (BMT) tunnel. Workers at the time told the press that it was like opening a pharaoh's tomb. As a footnote to the history of Beach's secret subway dig, modified versions of his hydraulic tunnel-digging shield have been used through the years for numerous tunneling projects. One such project was BART, where a modern version from Sweden was called "the mole." But imagine, it all started in England with a humble shipworm.

NEW YORK'S CONTINUING STRUGGLE TO BUILD ITS SUBWAY

Over the years, New Yorkers saw numerous ideas and proposals to build a subway for their city materialize and then vanish. Because of politics, fear of what such a project might entail, or lack of investors, most ended up in an archival graveyard, all but forgotten. With Tweed dead and several of his minions dispersed, the political climate of New York City was ready once again to think about an underground rail mass transit system. Tammany Hall, still a factor, understood it was no longer a question as to whether or not such a system should be built; the pressure to do something was too great. On January 31, 1888, New York City mayor Abram Hewitt gave an impassioned speech to the city's aldermen that said building an advanced transit system was a paramount necessity. Without it the city would stagnate and strangle on its ever-growing congestion nightmare. He called on the city fathers to seize the moment.

Still, it took a few more years before city officials concluded that the extended el lines combined with street-level modes of transit just weren't able to meet the crushing demand. Over the long term, it was clear the city's social and economic growth was going to be stunted, and if something weren't done, the city as a center of commerce would eventually go into decline. The problem was agreeing on an approach.

A STRONG NUDGE FROM MOTHER NATURE

On March 12, 1888, a devastating event changed everything. The city was hit with a monstrous blizzard that buried the city in up to four feet of snow and ice, with thirty-foot drifts. Many horses froze where they stood. The city was paralyzed as all street transportation came to a halt. The pressure to do something—from citizens as well as the business community—was enormous and felt all the way to Albany. But still, two more years passed before action was taken.

The state legislature finally decided to pass the Rapid Transit Act of 1891. This may well have been a blueprint for what the California legislature passed years later. The new act created a Rapid Transit Commission to study the topography of Manhattan and the boroughs with a view to laying out potential routes for an underground railway and, where appropriate, elevated lines. In the latter half of 1892,

William Barclay Parsons, the builder of the New York subway system in the late 1800s, founded Parsons Engineering, which later became Parsons Brinkerhoff, part of the consortium that would eventually build BART.

the Rapid Transit Commission received its consultant's comprehensive report and recommendation, and in the following year the commission entertained bids for contracts that required private ownership and called for initial construction of lines in Manhattan. Unfortunately, the advertisement was ill timed. There were no bidders because the economy had taken a nosedive. Potential investors simply weren't interested. As a result, the transit commission folded.

A new board of rapid transit commissioners was formed in 1894. This time the leadership was in the hands of a well-respected thirty-five-year-old engineer by the name of William Barclay Parsons. He was the founder of the renowned engineering firm Parsons Brinckerhoff, which became one of the principal members of the consortium that would build BART some sixty-five years later. A tall, lean man with a stern demeanor and an intense disposition, Parsons gave off an aura of confidence and strength. He had a great deal of experience in design and structural engineering, and in addition to his work on the design of waterway projects, Parsons had also worked on the New York, Lake Erie and Western Railroad.

He had several major problems to deal with before anything concrete could take place. Among the key issues were the routes that had been laid out during the 1891 study, the parameters for how such a major undertaking would be financed, and who would own it. It would have to be privately financed and owned under a lease agreement with the city. Thus the project might be viewed as one of the first public-private partnerships.

Parsons meanwhile traveled to Europe to look at existing systems. He adopted various concepts based on the Budapest underground, which he greatly admired. Upon his return to New York, he re-charted the topography of Manhattan that the subway structure would follow. A particular objective was to ensure that the lines under Manhattan would be positioned for an eventual extension into the boroughs. He pulled together a group of talented engineers, each with a specialty, who together created the voluminous package of designs and specifications for the project, including cost estimates and a very precise plan for what construction would be done simultaneously at several sites. The estimated cost was $2 to $3 million per mile. Cut-and-cover would be the primary method of construction, and tunneling would be used where required. The initial project called for building approximately 21 miles of line.

A major decision was to use electricity instead of steam engines, as older systems had done. Direct current (DC) at 650 volts would be employed to power the trains and would be delivered by a third rail. Thomas Edison had built the first DC power plant at Pearl Street in lower Manhattan more than ten years earlier and, at about the same time, had taken out a patent on a third-rail design. Years later an African American inventor named Granville Woods took out a patent on an improved third rail that became the standard. The New York system would have its own power plants and substations strategically placed around the city. Alternating current (AC), which was developed for transit by George Westinghouse, would be used to operate streetcars with pole collectors running along overhead power lines.

Some additional key developments would shape the course of rail transit in the years to come. One of these was a system called multiple-unit train control, invented by a young engineer named Frank Sprague. This new system gave engineers or motormen working the lead car of a train the ability to control all of the motors of each car simultaneously, thus allowing for uniform speed control and braking. Another major development was George Westinghouse's railway air brake, which would be installed on the new steel-and-wood transit cars specially designed for the New York City subway and elevated systems.

BIDS COME IN

Two bids came in to build the first segment of the system. The accepted bid, for $35 million, came from a successful Irish contractor named John B. McDonald. As it turned out, he could not come up with the $7 million required under the contract to pay the city for rights to construct, and so he ultimately had to release the bid. McDonald did, however, end up as the contractor when a financier, August Belmont, took over the contract and became the backer and owner of what would be called the Interborough Rapid Transit Company (IRT). For Belmont, the business venture spanned the private and public sectors; under a lease agreement with the city, his private company would operate the system for fifty years. To that end, Belmont set up two companies: the Rapid Transit Construction Company to build the underground system and the Interborough Rapid Transit Company to operate it.

On March 24, 1900, ground was finally broken in a little park across from City Hall. The weather cooperated by presenting the city with a clear spring day. Mayor Robert A. Van Wyck drove in the first shovel, which had been specially made for the occasion by the silversmiths of Tiffany and Company. Suddenly fireworks filled the skies and John Philip Sousa's band began playing one of his famous marches. An estimated 30,000 people attended the ceremony.

The miracle is that the New York subway ever got built at all. Heavy excavation machinery was scarce at the time, so the subway was dug out primarily by thousands of unskilled workers wielding picks and shovels and getting paid $2 per day on average. A typical workday was ten hours long, and obstacles like old sewer pipes and high water tables were a constant challenge. The labor crews worked for pay, of course, but what they accomplished went beyond monetary compensation in terms of fulfilling what the dreamers envisioned, and so perhaps there was a prevailing sense of purpose, an indomitable spirit, among the men in the trenches. In any case, they got the job done.

Four years later, on October 27, 1904, the first completed Manhattan subway line was opened. It ran from downtown Manhattan up to 145th Street. It was a joyous occasion, but the official celebration almost turned into a disaster. The new mayor, George B. McClellan, opened the ceremony with a speech declaring the city's new subway ready for service, but what happened next was not in the script. The program called for McClellan to be presented with the motorman's control handle and to drive the first train, an eight-car consist, a short distance before turning it over to the trained motorman. (A *consist* is the linked group of rail cars that make up a train.) Instead, to everyone's horror, he accelerated the train to top speed and refused to give up control until 103rd Street. After all, he was the mayor; the way he saw it, it was his prerogative to drive the train if he so wished. The event was described by the officials in attendance as a very nervous and scary few minutes. After McClellan relinquished the control console to the motorman, the train completed its run at 145th Street. The sprawling subterranean network, which involved three separate systems with a combined 760 miles of track, would take another four decades to complete. By that time, it was 1940, and World War II was on the horizon.

CHAPTER 2

THE BIRTH OF THE SAN FRANCISCO BAY AREA

While New York was experiencing its sudden escalation in population in the 1840s, California was still very much a frontier. Various Native American tribes were the first inhabitants of the region, the most prominent among them being the Ohlone. San Francisco's Mission Dolores, established in 1776, was a keystone of community life in those early days, and it still stands today, one of the oldest structures in the city. In fact, the area at that time was not much more than a wilderness with a few scattered haciendas, missions, and tiny settlements. Early Spanish explorers had thought that the territory was an island because of the Baja peninsula, and it apparently reminded them of a story about a mythical island inhabited by beautiful black Amazonian warriors as depicted in the novel *The Adventures of Esplandián*, written by a Spaniard, Garci Rodríguez de Montalvo, and published around 1510. Based on Greek mythology, the story tells of the queen of the women warriors, a statuesque beauty named Calafia, who ruled on an island off the coast of the East Indies called California. This is believed to have been the origin of the name given the territory. Interestingly, the island was depicted as a paradise, teeming with gold and other riches—a characteristic that turned out to be true of the region. Because explorers going back to Hernán Cortés referred to the peninsula as California, the territory was eventually labeled as such by mapmakers, and the name stuck.

In the late 1830s and 1840s, small settlements, mostly canvas tents and slab shanties, could be found along the shorelines of both sides of the great bay in the northern part of the territory. The western shoreline was called Yerba Buena, meaning "good herb," because of a fragrant mint plant that grew in abundance around the area. The Yerba Buena Cove settlement numbered about 200 people, pioneers struggling to survive and make a new life for themselves. Meanwhile, wagon trains carrying families of varying sizes were finding other places to settle in the East Bay, some near Mount Diablo, in what is now Contra Costa County. Still, these settlements were sparse.

In 1846, California was annexed by the United States as a territory, and on January 30, 1847, the *alcalde* (mayor) of Yerba Buena changed the settlement's name to San Francisco. Two years later everything changed. Gold fever spread like a prairie fire. The discovery of that mysterious and precious yellow metal at Sutter's Mill was, of course, a pivotal event in California's history and in particular its growth. The news brought fortune-seeking adventurers from all walks of life across the plains and over the great Sierra Nevada range to join encampments of prospectors scattered along its western foothills. Many also came from other parts of the world during the post-1849 years and eventually settled in the region.

That tiny San Francisco encampment, which had grown to about 800 people by the time gold was discovered, almost instantly became a community of 35,000. In 1850, because of its growing population, California was transformed from a territory to a state, and the city of San Francisco was a boomtown. Across the bay was the infant community of Oakland, which was incorporated in 1852. That city became a terminus for the First Transcontinental Railroad, which opened in May 1869, unifying the young nation as well as promoting a westward movement of population. From the Oakland terminus (at what was then called the Oakland Mole), ferries carried travelers across the bay to San Francisco, a 6-mile journey that might include a stopover at Goat Island in between. In the new city they disembarked and settled in the hills and along the infamous Barbary Coast. Ferries provided the quickest link between the two cities—a trip of between thirty and sixty minutes depending on tides and wind—with the other option being a trek around the bay in an overland stage or by horseback, a two-day ride. By and large, transbay travel was at best slow and problematic.

THE EMPEROR NORTON DECREE

On the sunny but brisk San Francisco morning of September 17, 1872, a portly bearded figure jauntily, but not without some difficulty, made his way along Market Street. He was dressed in his usual attire, a faded blue, bedraggled military uniform, complete with gold-plated epaulets. Most people he encountered on the street knew who he was and would offer a friendly nod; many dismissed him as an eccentric, a few thought he was insane, but overall he was considered harmless. On that day, his troubled gait had a sense of purpose, according to newspaper accounts of the period. His intention so early that morning was to visit the city's major newspapers: the *San Francisco Bulletin*, the *Chronicle*, and the *Examiner*, all evening papers. He carried with him an official decree that he had carefully concocted and which he desired to deliver before the day's newspaper deadlines. Even he probably did not realize the decree would have such historic significance.

As he made his way, his awkward step was helped by a cane he was never without. According to legend, he was accompanied by his two faithful dogs. Some folks at the time said he was known to imbibe at the local taverns along the Barbary Coast before noon. After all, the drinks were free for him, and so were the meals, as the businesses he frequented accepted worthless bonds with a face value of fifty cents that he had printed up himself. But on this particular day, he may have refrained from any drink, or at least tempered his intake so he could conduct his business with at least a modicum of soberness.

Joshua Abraham Norton—known by all as "Emperor Norton"—was among the first to suggest a tunnel be built under the bay to connect San Francisco and Oakland. He also promoted the idea of a suspension bridge, based on structures he'd seen growing up in South Africa.

The man was Joshua Abraham Norton, fifty-three years old at the time. He was better known as San Francisco's beloved Emperor Norton I, the self-proclaimed emperor of the United States and protector of Mexico. He had been born in England in 1819, spent his early years in Africa, and eventually wound up in San Francisco with a $40,000 inheritance, eager for adventure and enterprise. He soon parlayed his money into a larger fortune through real estate speculation, and as a young, wealthy real estate entrepreneur, Norton cut a dashing figure among his peers. But around 1853, he lost his fortune when he tried to corner the rice market in San Francisco after learning that China, facing a food shortage, had stopped the export of rice. With high hopes, he bought a shipload of rice from Peru. When other ships arrived, also carrying rice, the market plummeted. Norton spent the next few years in court trying to get out of his contract, but he lost everything. Declaring bankruptcy, he disappeared for a few years. Upon his return, he proclaimed himself emperor and was generally treated with deference as someone who had "gone 'round the bend."

The decree he carried to the newspapers on that September morning in essence ordered that the cities of Oakland and San Francisco join together to build either a suspension bridge across the bay or a tunnel under the bay. Here is the Emperor Norton decree verbatim:

> Whereas, we issued our decree, ordering the citizens of San Francisco and Oakland to appropriate funds for the survey of a suspension bridge from Oakland Point *via* Goat Island; also for a tunnel; and to ascertain which is the best project; and whereas, the said citizens have hitherto neglected to notice our said decree; and whereas, we are determined our authority shall be fully respected; now, therefore, we do hereby command the arrest, by the army, of both the Boards of City Fathers, if they persist in neglecting our decrees. Given under our royal hand and seal, at San Francisco, this 17th day of September, 1872.

One hundred years later, almost to the day, BART began operating test trains under the bay through the Transbay Tube between Oakland and San Francisco.

It was believed that Norton became acquainted with the concept of suspension bridges during his early years in Africa, though in fact they had first appeared in Tibet as early as 1433 and later were developed in England. Meanwhile, in 1873 Andrew Hallidie's first cable car line began operation in San Francisco from Kearny Street up the hill to Jones. That was a good system for many years, but cable cars and the San Francisco Municipal Railway (Muni) were, of course, limited to intra-city service only. Following World War I, the Bay Area saw significant growth and an increased need for improved public transit. Because transbay commuting between Oakland and San Francisco was growing, improvement to cross-bay travel was becoming an imperative.

TWO TRANSBAY TUBE PROPOSALS

Forty-eight years later, two proposals for a transbay tunnel made the news. The first proposal was heralded in an October 10, 1920, headline in the *San Francisco Chronicle* that read: SUBMARINE TUBE PROPOSED TO RELIEVE BAY TRAFFIC.

The proposal was to construct a tube under the bay to handle growing ferry traffic. It came from an eminent New York engineering firm, Eads & Beach. That firm's proposal called for building a giant cable, 14 feet in diameter, that would simply rest on the floor of the bay and be able to withstand strong underwater currents. Transit cars would be specially designed for such a tube and would run on greased ball bearings instead of wheels. Eads & Beach claimed it could be built in ten months. The proposal died.

Just ten days later, on October 20, another proposal made the front-page news, again in the *Chronicle.* General George Washington Goethals, who had been in charge of building the Panama Canal, came to San Francisco and laid out a plan for building a tube under the bay between Oakland and San Francisco. In his proposal, the tube would be like a giant conduit with two levels—the top level for trucks and cars, the bottom for trains. It would be built in a trench below the floor of the bay and travel from the San Francisco Ferry Building, passing south of Yerba Buena Island (formerly Goat Island) to Oakland. It would be constructed of concrete blocks that were shield-driven deep under the bay. Even with the prestige General Goethals brought with

San Francisco Chronicle

General Goethals, Panama Canal Builder, May Solve Transportation Problem by Transbay Tube Project

Comprehensive Plan for Vehicular Tunnel Across San Francisco Bay

OVERCOATS

CROWN SHIRTS

New LUMBER SPECIALS

JAMES H. HARDY, INC.

This front page of the *San Francisco Chronicle* from October 1920 shows a detailed proposal for a transbay tube, as put forth by General George Washington Goethals, who was fresh from overseeing the construction of the Panama Canal. Fifty years later, BART's tube alignment was almost identical to this original proposal.

his plan, it too fell by the wayside. Officials at the time simply could not imagine that such a venture was possible. Ferries continued to be the only mode of cross-bay transport.

THE HOOVER-YOUNG COMMISSION

In 1929, President Herbert Hoover, in partnership with California's governor, C. C. Young, ordered the creation of what became known as the Hoover-Young San Francisco Bay Bridge Commission. The commission's charge was to study the feasibility and potential location for a possible bridge spanning the bay. Previous studies had recommended against such a bridge, identifying the soft bay floor as an impediment to construction, and concluding that such a venture was not feasible. But Hoover and Young were not convinced. They were greatly concerned that the potential economic growth of the Bay Area would be extremely hampered without some direct west bay–east bay corridor. The commission hired its own engineers, who did a survey of the bay and concluded that, in fact, building a bridge was feasible, and they identified where it should be located. The report, completed and presented in 1930, resulted in Hoover providing federal funding to build the San Francisco–Oakland Bay Bridge. Construction began in 1933. When the Bay Bridge opened in 1936, it accommodated both autos and the Key System streetcars, which had previously connected only

Berkeley, Oakland, and Hayward. The following year, the Golden Gate Bridge opened, connecting San Francisco with Marin County and points north.

A 1947 ARMY-NAVY STUDY: THE GENESIS OF BART

In July 1941, the Seventy-Seventh Congress in its first session passed House Resolution 158 for the purpose of investigating and reporting on the need for and feasibility of constructing a bridge from Hunters Point in San Francisco to Bay Farm Island in Alameda, from the standpoint of national defense and/or the development of a peacetime economy. The resolution instructed the secretaries of the army and navy to submit their report to Congress. The initial report recommended against a bridge from Hunters Point, an important port, because it would have a negative impact on naval operations.

H.R. 158 was passed almost six months before the bombing of Pearl Harbor, though it was clear at the time that war was inevitable. Because of the strategic importance of the San Francisco Bay Area, some form of alternative cross-bay transportation to supplement the Oakland Bay Bridge was deemed necessary for possible troop movements. Put simply, in case of attack, there should be more than one transbay corridor. However, once the United States was officially at war, the final report was delayed.

The postwar years saw a great migration to California from across the nation. Tens of thousands of veterans who had traveled through the state during the war years returned with their families and settled. The nine-county San Francisco Bay Area saw an approximately 50 percent growth in population during this time, mostly in the suburban areas. With San Francisco and Oakland as the primary employment centers, the stage was once again set for a look at solving the growing transportation problem.

In early 1946, a study and report on an additional San Francisco Bay crossing was once again authorized, this time pursuant to H.R. 529, passed by the Seventy-Ninth Congress. The resulting Joint Army-Navy Board was made up of three ranking officers from the army and three from the navy. During the course of the board's work, several recommendations were reviewed, including an open causeway, an additional bridge, and a tube that would accommodate cars, trucks, and trains (similar to General Goethals's plan twenty-seven years earlier).

Another recommendation was to construct a twin tube or two separate tubes, two lanes going each direction, for vehicular traffic.

On January 25, 1947, after combing through previous studies and commissioning additional work, the Joint Army-Navy Board published its conclusions in a report titled "Engineering Study of Subaqueous Crossings." According to the report, it was clear that an "adequate system of rapid mass transit be a component of the overall general scheme to solve the Bay Area transportation problems over an extended period of years." Thus, the board's final recommendation was that a 6-mile subaqueous tube be constructed across the bay to carry trains that could hook up with the Key System in Oakland and with Muni service (the Municipal Railway) in San Francisco.

Moreover, the report recommended that, instead of using a diesel or steam-powered system, transbay trains be electrified to minimize potential ventilation issues. The board indicated that it was fully cognizant of the challenges associated with setting up an authority to carry out such a mission, as well as with the difficulty of resolving the many conflicts to be encountered with both private and public interests.

Another option considered was a "Southern Crossing," a bridge for motor vehicles built somewhere from Hunters Point or the Bayshore Highway across to Alameda. This idea became a controversial issue many years later when it materialized as a proposal to be put before the voters. The renowned architect Frank Lloyd Wright and engineer Jaroslav Josef Polívka collaborated on a design that they called the "Butterfly Bridge." With its great twin arches, it looked as though it had gracefully taken wing, ready to float gently through the air above the bay waters. Some thought the design was sheer poetry; others thought it was a loony concept. Though their conception received a wide range of media attention when it was unveiled, in the end it was not accepted. It eventually became moot as the voters rejected the Southern Crossing in 1972, apparently preferring instead to rely more on mass transit.

Throughout 1947 the Joint Army-Navy Board held a series of public hearings in San Francisco and Oakland with very little public response. The board also met informally with various officials and interested parties of both cities to acquaint them with its report. Again there was much skepticism concerning the feasibility of building under the bay. A few civic leaders were intrigued, however, and began to tout the report's importance to the region. The Bay Bridge, which shared its corridor with the Key System, was becoming intolerably congested. After all, these postwar years were like opening a grand cafeteria to a starving people. The purchase of commodities including gas and rubber tires no longer required ration stamps, and instead of tanks coming off the assembly lines it was new cars, which had not been available during the war years. As a result, an automobile culture was thriving in cities across America, particularly in Los Angeles and the San Francisco Bay Area.

Marvin E. Lewis, a dapper forty-seven-year-old San Francisco trial attorney and a member of the city's board of supervisors, took a special interest in the Joint Army-Navy Board's conclusion. He strongly believed that its basic recommendation to build a tube under the bay to carry trains should not be ignored. Lewis was determined to keep the concept alive, and he spearheaded a grassroots movement to put forward the idea of an alternative bay crossing and the possibility of some kind of regional transit network. He invested a great deal of time promoting the board's conclusion and organized an informal rapid transit committee. It included twenty-five business and civic leaders not only from San Francisco but also from neighboring counties. As in New York City in the 1800s, the members of the transit committee were concerned that the Bay Area region would eventually fall victim to its own success and reach a point of stagnation, or critical mass, in terms of future economic and population growth. They were determined to prevent that if they could.

THE FIRST ATTEMPT TO CREATE A TRANSIT DISTRICT

In 1949, at the urging of Lewis and his committee, the state legislature passed a bill establishing a rapid transit district. It was, however, doomed from the beginning. While the bill did identify rail as the preferred mode of transit, it was by and large a nebulous piece of legislation. It named several cities to be part of such a district, including Alameda, Albany, Berkeley, Emeryville, Hayward, Oakland, Piedmont, and San Leandro, plus Contra Costa as a county and the city and county of San Francisco. Each city and county would have to approve its involvement. It soon became clear that local officials did not want to stick their political necks out for some ephemeral idea; there were no takers, and the legislation basically never went beyond the conversation stage. The question for Lewis and others was what to do next.

CHAPTER 3

SEEKING A WAY

The problem as Marvin Lewis saw it was a lack of information. Nobody knew exactly what they were supposed to be approving. There was no plan, no cost/benefit analysis, no identified sources of funds. As a supplement to two-way auto traffic on the upper deck of the Bay Bridge, the Key System on the lower deck was thought adequate to meet the current transportation needs for East Bay workers commuting between Oakland and San Francisco. But that service was already on a downward slope and was ultimately headed for the chopping block. In San Mateo County, officials were complacent, since Southern Pacific ran a sporadic commute service up the peninsula from San Jose to 4th and Townsend in San Francisco.

Ever the tenacious champion of the Joint Army-Navy Board report, Lewis again approached the state legislature, requesting that it provide funds for a public awareness program to educate the region's residents and elected officials. Key state legislators, however, were adamant that state funds could not be used for such a purpose. For Lewis, though, the idea of a modern regional transit system was too important to let slide given the transformation of the region during the postwar years. Growing congestion, air pollution, freeway construction, and continued population growth were all part of the urban-suburban milieu. Also, one only had to look south to see how smog was permeating the Los Angeles basin (which was slowly becoming a giant parking lot) to understand where the Bay Area was headed. Freeways could be only part of the transportation mix.

Lewis knew there had to be another way to generate further interest in the Joint Army-Navy Board recommendation. Otherwise it would simply be forgotten and left to gather dust on a dark shelf somewhere. He was not going to give up. One way, as it turned out, was for the state to create a commission modeled on New York's Rapid Transit Act of 1891, which had been created to confirm the need for the New York

A Key Line train operates between San Francisco and Oakland on the second deck of the Bay Bridge, 1955.

subway system. The idea, then, was for a San Francisco Bay Area Transit Commission to coordinate a study of the region's transportation needs, both current and long-term. It was an acceptable mechanism for moving another step forward. In other words, the establishment of a transit district alone didn't go far enough.

THE LEGISLATURE ACTS

In 1951 the legislature in Sacramento passed an amendment to the 1949 bill, again drafted by Lewis, to create the San Francisco Bay Area Rapid Transit Commission. It was signed into law by Governor Earl Warren. The bill appropriated $50,000 for the commission to evaluate the need for a rapid transit district and then report back to the legislature. The new commission's work was intended to lead to the creation of a master plan for regional transit, although some feared the outcome of the work could differ greatly from what Lewis's unofficial committee was seeking. There were twenty-six members of the newly formed commission, representing the nine Bay Area counties. Most of the members were appointed by the governor and were certainly not beholden to the idea of a regional transit system.

With the official state-created commission now in place, Lewis's unofficial transit group dissolved. Lewis and other community business leaders, including San Francisco's venerable Cyril Magnin, Clair W. MacLeod from Piedmont, and John Beckett from Marin County, were among those appointed to serve on the commission. At the very least, these men, all of whom were advocates of a regional transit system, had a voice in the decision-making process, and as it turned out, the commission did end up on the same page as Lewis's unofficial transit committee.

The primary charge of the commission was to determine how the diversified economics of the region would potentially blend with its geographic features, and how a linear fixed-rail transit system would fit in.

The first thing the commission did in 1951 to help answer such questions was hire De Leuw, Cather & Company, an engineering firm. Its mission was to study the requirements of rail rapid transit from a technical perspective. In the late 1940s and early 1950s, very few regions or individual cities had master plans, as is common today. These plans, if they had existed, would naturally have answered relevant questions about the characteristics of the Bay Area, such as where housing, industry, and commercial development should be located, where recreation areas such as parks and open space should be placed, and how concerns for water availability and utility infrastructure should be addressed.

De Leuw, Cather asked the important questions: Where did the people of the region live? Where did they work? What were their travel patterns? Where was growth expected in the future? Because these questions needed to be answered in a comprehensive way, the consultant's work was mostly qualitative, in the sense that its findings could only pave the way for a more detailed study of the region. In 1952, De Leuw, Cather & Company submitted its preliminary study to the Rapid Transit Commission, recommending that the commission combine a regional land-use plan with a regional transportation plan, which would ensure that the plans were complementary. The estimated cost for further study and the development of such an ambitious undertaking was $750,000. A hard-fought deal was struck with the state to appropriate $400,000 if the cities of the region would cough up the remaining $350,000. It took a lot of doing, but the various constituent cites within the nine-county region did contribute their share based on population apportionment. The state legislature did not act until 1953 to appropriate its portion of the funds for the project. The goal then became to hire a firm to carry out a comprehensive land-use and transportation study. It was a tall order. Meanwhile, the writing was on the wall for the Key System.

THE KEY SYSTEM'S MANY DIMENSIONS

The BART story would not be complete without a brief review of its direct predecessor, the Key System. It first began operating on October

26, 1903, as the San Francisco, Oakland, and San Jose Railway (SFOSJR), founded by Francis Marion "Borax" Smith and a partner, Frank C. Havens. Its primary competitor at the time was the Inter Urban Rail Transit Company (IURT), which began service in the late 1800s and was still a steam operation. IURT was owned by Southern Pacific. Eventually, IURT converted to electricity and became the East Bay Interurban Electric Railway (IER). While it served many of the same areas that SFOSJR had, it eventually ceased operations and sold much of its equipment to SFOSJR long after that operation had been redubbed the Key System.

As part of its transit mix, the SFOSJR owned a fleet of ferries to provide transbay service for commuters to San Francisco. Among them was Borax Smith, who had built a fortune from his namesake cleaning product, Borax. (His company's logo, the 20 Mule Team wagon, was by then nationally famous.) After settling in Oakland in the late 1800s, he began to think of new enterprises, and he saw an opportunity in the transportation business, although his venture into mass transit had more to do with real estate development than simply wanting to help people move from place to place. Smith and his partner believed that rail transit could support development along its rights-of-way, a natural symbiotic relationship: create the destination and then transport people to it. Perhaps the experience of the transcontinental railroad, where whole towns sprang up along its owned right-of-way, spurred the idea. In other words, the transcontinental railroad was in the real estate business as much as it was in the transportation business.

The parent company of the new electric streetcar system, which had several investors, was in fact called Realty Syndicate. The company acquired large tracts of land in the East Bay and built two hotels, one of which was the famous Claremont, a towering classic white monument from a bygone era that still thrives today as a luxurious resort. As part of its business strategy, the company sold off plots of land for private development that could be served by its streetcars. As the years went by, the SFOSJR evolved into what became known as the Key System, so named because its track configuration and ferry piers resembled an old-fashioned skeleton key. It provided service from Berkeley, through Piedmont and Oakland to San Leandro, and eventually over the lower deck of the Bay Bridge. One example of how the rail service was integrated with the company's real estate development was the

E line. Its streetcars went directly to the Claremont Hotel, terminating between two tennis courts on the lower grounds that are still there today. Though Borax Smith was forced out of the company in 1911 by its investors, the system continued to thrive, particularly during World War II. After the war, the majority of its shares were bought up by a new company with a very different agenda.

A SCANDAL BREWS AS A PLOT UNFOLDS

While the effort was being made to move forward on the Joint Army-Navy Board's recommendation, the Key System was beginning to go through some dramatic changes. As early as 1947, service was being cut back by the system's new owner, Pacific City Lines, a subsidiary of National City Lines. During the war years, the Key System had seen its highest ridership since first operating, in part because no new automobiles coming off the assembly lines meant options for travel were limited and mass transit was king. After the war ended, however, the stated reason for reducing Key System service was sliding ridership, particularly on local lines. A contributing factor was deferred maintenance and a reduced reliability of service. At the same time, a fare increase may also have had some negative impact on ridership. It's not clear what the "elasticity of demand" was at the time, but in today's transit marketing mix, that is an important factor when determining periodic fare increases. The formula pits increased revenue against a calculated ridership decrease on a percentage basis. For example, if fares on a system are increased by, say, 5 percent, and ridership decreases by 1 or 2 percent, revenue more than likely wins hands down.

Meanwhile, although the Key System commute service to San Francisco was still holding its own, it too saw a dramatic decline over the years. Transbay ridership in 1946 was 22 million, dropping to 9.8 million by 1952. It would be another six years before the Key System's demise. The last train crossed the Bay Bridge in 1958, after which the system's infrastructure went by way of the wrecking crew. Although a major effort was made by AC Transit to keep the tracks for possible future use, in the end it was not successful. (In the next chapter we see why.) Meanwhile, about thirty of the two-unit cars from the fleet were sold to Buenos Aires, Argentina, for that city's federal rail system, and a few of the cars were saved and sent to the California Railway Museum (now the Western Railway Museum) in Rio Vista, California.

As it turned out, National City Lines (NCL) was actually a holding company for General Motors, the Firestone Tire Company, Phillips Petroleum, and Standard Oil of California. NCL was formed in 1936 after taking over a small bus company in Minnesota with the same name. The new company's express purpose was to acquire privately owned rail lines across the country and replace those lines with buses. In its first year alone, NCL bought thirteen streetcar systems. The following year, Pacific City Lines (PCL) was formed to buy rail transit systems in the West. By 1947, NCL and PCL combined had purchased more than one hundred electric streetcar lines in forty-five cities. In city after city, the rail systems were dismantled and replaced by buses.

In 1947, NCL and its subsidiary, PCL, were indicted by the federal district court in Los Angeles and convicted of conspiring to monopolize the sale of buses in those cities where they had purchased privately owned streetcar systems. The parent company was fined $5,000, and top executives were fined $1 each for their role in the scheme. Meanwhile, in 1948 local Key System trains in the East Bay, as in other cities, were replaced by buses. It was dubbed "the Great American Streetcar Scandal."

Still, the economics of owning and operating a local-service transit company were becoming untenable. More and more systems serving municipal or urban centers across the country were being taken over by public agencies before they closed down under private ownership. In 1958 the newly formed Alameda–Contra Costa Transit District (AC Transit) bought the Key System and began operating local and inter-county bus service, including service over the San Francisco–Oakland Bay Bridge to the East Bay Terminal (later the Transbay Terminal) in San Francisco.

THE SAN FRANCISCO BAY AREA RAPID TRANSIT COMMISSION

In 1953 the work was set to begin on the new BART system. By this time the postwar building boom was in full swing in the region's suburbs, with new communities springing up and creating what was referred to as urban sprawl. The work had a new sense of urgency, a feeling that time was running out in terms of potential right-of-way availability.

With the $750,000 funding supplied by the state and the various Bay Area cities, the transit commission advertised for consultant bids. Four proposals were submitted. On November 12, 1953, the transit commission awarded a contract to the New York–based engineering consortium Parsons, Brinckerhoff, Hall & MacDonald (PBHM). The firm's mission was to do a comprehensive study of the nine-county Bay Area from the standpoint of land use and fixed-rail rapid transit. The commission laid out four key questions: (1) Is a rapid transit system needed for the Bay Area? (2) If it is, what areas should it serve and what routes should it take? (3) What type of rapid transit should it be? (4) What will it cost, and will the cost be justified? One of the first tasks was to determine the current travel patterns in as definitive a way as possible. For this the joint venture conducted an origin-destination survey to quantify both commute and non-commute journeys taken each weekday, collecting information on destinations, lengths of trips, and key corridors used.

Two years later, on January 5, 1956, PBHM submitted its findings to the Bay Area Rapid Transit Commission. The report, based on a detailed study of the burgeoning Bay Area community, concluded that there was a pressing need for a balanced approach to meeting the region's transportation needs, both short-term and long-term. Moreover, the report recommended that a high-speed, grade-separated regional rapid transit system was critical as a complementary component of a highway network, stating also that it was economically justified. It was estimated in 1953 dollars that a rapid transit system serving all nine counties would cost somewhere in the neighborhood of $1.5 billion. It was also recommended that such a system should be built in three stages. The first stage would include an underwater tube between Oakland and San Francisco.

The first phase as outlined by the consultant's report included six counties. It called for building a line from San Francisco north to San Rafael in Marin County; south through San Mateo County to Palo Alto and on to Los Altos in Santa Clara County; and east to Concord in Contra Costa County, with Oakland serving as the East Bay hub. The vital link would be the tube built under bay waters. In 1953 dollars the estimated cost for an optimal first phase was $750 million. It would require a debt service of somewhere between $33 and $38 million a year for thirty years.

The financial plan report had been done by the Stanford Research Institute, whose reputation automatically lent credibility to the numbers. Federal funds were not available for such capital investment in those days, nor was the state providing capital funding. It was clear that future funding would have to come from Bay Area taxpayers. Thus the big question was the feasibility of local taxpayer support. When it came to taxing themselves, Bay Area residents historically tended to pull in their horns. As the report commented in its summary,

> Without rapid transit the region will ultimately pay many times its cost in additional hours of travel time, (lost productivity) in additional cost of trucking goods over highways congested by automobiles…, and in the premium costs of urban freeways and parking garages. We do not doubt that the Bay Area citizens can afford rapid transit; we question seriously whether they can afford *not* to have it. If the Bay Area is to be preserved as a fine place to live and work, a regional rapid transit system is essential to prevent total dependence on automobiles and freeways.

It should be noted that the engineering consultant's report recognized that plans were already under way for constructing a regional highway system.

The second phase of the recommended plan would construct the line from Fremont south to San Jose and circle back up to meet the line coming south from San Francisco to Palo Alto. Extensions to Antioch and Livermore in the East Bay and from San Rafael north to Novato were also identified as part of the second phase.

THE STATE INTERIM COMMITTEE HOLDS HEARINGS

The Bay Area Rapid Transit Commission submitted its final report to the state legislature on January 5, 1956. This prompted the appointment of a State Senate Interim Committee on San Francisco Bay Area Metropolitan Rapid Transit Problems. The interim committee then held public hearings in San Francisco to test the waters, so to speak, and to get a sense of the desirability and feasibility of regional rail transit. This may also have been a way for politicians to determine just how far out they wanted to stick their collective neck in making future decisions on the matter. As it turned out, the waters seemed pretty tepid. No significant opposition to the concept being touted by the PBHM report seemed to exist. One barometer was how the press heralded the report's recommendations: reporters mostly quoted local officials and prominent citizens who greeted the report with unqualified enthusiasm. Also, the results of a Bay Area survey conducted by the Stanford Research Institute showed 80 percent approval for rapid transit by respondents.

The interim committee, chaired by Senator John F. McCarthy of San Rafael, then published its own report, "Mass Rapid Transit," supporting the Bay Area Rapid Transit Commission's work and endorsing the PBHM recommendations. One later change was that, at the county's request, Santa Clara County was dropped from the proposed bill to establish the Bay Area Rapid Transit District. The bill, jointly sponsored by Senator McCarthy and the interim committee's vice chairman, Senator Arthur H. Breed Jr. of Oakland, went through several revisions. One involved how district directors would be selected, and another very key provision enabled the District to negotiate for unionization of its eventual employees, rather than making them come under civil service. This critical move was recommended by Clair W. MacLeod of Piedmont, who was a member of the Rapid Transit Commission. He argued that without the change, the proposed system was unlikely to get support from organized labor.

When it came to figuring out how to financially support this new district once it was created, that particular section of the bill caused a great deal of consternation, and the plan went through several more iterations.

"Everyone seems to be for rapid transit," MacLeod said, "but they run out the back door when you start talking about who's going to pay for it."

The outcome was that the District would have very limited taxing powers.

On September 8, 1957, a banner headline in the *Oakland Tribune* read: RAPID TRANSIT AGENCY GETS OFFICIAL STATUS WEDNESDAY. A three-column story, in advance of the bill being signed into law, set out what the next steps would be in establishing this brand-new agency.

The story's byline named a young urban-affairs writer, Bill Stokes, who was to become a very prominent player in BART's history.

On June 4, 1957, the California State Legislature actually approved the San Francisco Bay Area Rapid Transit District (BARTD) Act, which created a special district made up of five core counties: Alameda, Contra Costa, Marin, San Francisco, and San Mateo. The enabling legislation under the California Public Utilities Act recognized that some initial administrative funding would be necessary for the fledgling district. Part of the act gave the new entity the ability to levy a five-cent administrative tax on each $100 of assessed valuation of all tax-roll properties in the member counties, which was considered not much more than a stipend. This approach had been hammered out between Senator McCarthy and members of the Rapid Transit Commission.

On September 11, 1957, Governor Goodwin J. Knight signed the rapid transit bill into law. December 31, 1957, saw the San Francisco Bay Area Rapid Transit Commission fade into the sunset and the brand-spanking-new Rapid Transit District come to the forefront. Its charge: "Build and operate a regional rapid transit system." But even though the idea had reached this stage, its full execution was still no more than a gleam in the eyes of its longtime supporters. Although it had been created by the state, the new rapid transit district was in many ways born a political orphan, on the street and on its own. A multitude of hurdles and a lot of uncertainty lay ahead, but that first big step in the journey had been taken. Marvin Lewis must have been elated that his early efforts had finally gained traction.

A SIDELIGHT ON MARVIN

In addition to being considered a transportation pioneer for his efforts to bring about BART, Marvin Lewis was also known in his law practice as a pioneer in psychic injury. In a case related to public transportation, he made national news as the plaintiff's attorney in the high-profile and controversial "Cable Car Named Desire" case. In 1970, a young dancer from San Francisco's North Beach neighborhood claimed she had been jostled when a cable car she was riding hit an automobile, causing an injury that had apparently turned her into a nymphomaniac. The jury awarded her a reported $50,000, and newspapers across the country treated the story with a sense of disapprobation.

Lewis passed away in 1991 at the age of eighty-four. A plaque at BART's Embarcadero Station honors him with the label of "Determined Prophet."

CHAPTER 4

THE BARTD BOARD BEGINS ITS WORK

The newly formed board of the Bay Area Rapid Transit District (BARTD) held its first meeting on November 14, 1957, in San Francisco. Sixteen members represented the six first-phase counties. The all-male group was made up of businessmen and community leaders appointed by both the Mayor's Council from each county and the boards of supervisors, as outlined in the BARTD Act: four representatives each from San Francisco and Alameda Counties, three each from Contra Costa and San Mateo Counties, and two from Marin County. The representatives from each county were apportioned by population.

The first order of business was to name a president who would guide the board and help determine how to proceed. Clair W. MacLeod of Piedmont, who was president of the famous Skunk Line train in Northern California, was named by fellow directors as the board's first president. His work on the Rapid Transit Commission and the BARTD Act made him an excellent choice for dealing with the initial work that had to be done, namely taking the product of the commission to the next step. He was president for the first two years of the District's life.

In 1960 Adrien J. Falk was unanimously chosen for the job. He was a tall, lean man with an engaging and persuasive personality. As former chairman and chief executive officer of S&W Foods and chairman of the state chamber of commerce, he brought a lot of business acumen to the table and soon became the board's spearhead.

The question many had was whether this was truly a serious venture. George Silliman, a businessman who owned a gas station and later became a banker, represented the Fremont area in southern Alameda County on the new board, and although he strongly believed in the concept they were grappling with, he had the nagging sense that some on the board thought it was not much more than a charade.

In a discussion with me in the early 1970s, Silliman said there was a lot of skepticism in those early days. After all, BART was perhaps one of the most ambitious public works ventures in California history. Some thought that a grand regional rail rapid transit system would more than likely never see the light of day, that the idea would simply collapse from its own weight and go away. The initial financing, provided by the power as a special district to levy a five-cent tax for every $100 of assessed property valuation in the five counties, was just enough to set up a modest shop and hire engineering consultants to begin preliminary planning.

STOKES COMES ON BOARD

Like Marvin Lewis in the earlier days, Falk was a strong believer in the regional system's potential, and he was determined to move forward as aggressively as possible. In early 1958, while still serving as vice president of the BARTD board, he handpicked the young journalist from the *Oakland Tribune* who had been writing about regional transit to be the District's first employee. Billy Richard (Bill or B. R.) Stokes, who in the years ahead would become a lightning rod for the District and a controversial figure in his own right, was thirty-four at the time of his hiring. He had been an urban-affairs writer for the *Oakland Tribune* since the late 1940s, after mustering out of the navy, where he was an officer on a destroyer. During the 1950s he was a passionate champion of the Bay Area Rapid Transit Commission's recommendations, often writing feature stories advocating the need for a new regional transit network. Harre Demoro, a well-respected transit writer, described Stokes as a hard-driving newspaperman with a slight Oklahoma drawl (he grew up in Shawnee, Oklahoma). His new job title with the fledgling District was Director of Public Information. Falk had great faith in Stokes as the person who could best inform the public about the first phase of the plan the Bay Area Transit Commission and state had incorporated into the BARTD legislation. Anyone looking at the plan would gulp at what a massive undertaking it would be. But, more importantly, would the public buy it?

Stokes's work would be based on how PBHM's transit and land-use plan had materialized. During the 1950s, those commuting daily by automobile, usually one person per car, did not need to be told that key corridors were congested; they lived it every day. But empirical data was needed—hard numbers to crunch that would tell a story. It was important to know actual overall traffic volume and what the volume was at critical points, particularly for travel in and out of the two urban cores, Oakland and San Francisco.

PBHM DEVELOPS A PLAN

During the course of their work, PBHM engineers in 1954 carefully identified twenty-three specific areas that they considered bottleneck areas, or potential bottlenecks, to measure on heavily used corridors. These test lines, as they were referred to, were strategically located throughout the nine counties that make up the Bay Area. Another goal of this methodology was to determine the capacity of existing highways during peak periods. The results showed that capacity on corridors serving the outlying areas in the north, south, and east had not yet been exceeded, but these were not as yet high-density areas. Good land-use planning by incorporated cities and counties would have to be integrated with transportation planning in anticipation of future growth. In fact, PBHM planners regarded the coordination of existing surface transit, both local and interurban, with a new system as a critical component of the overall plan.

"The success of a rapid transit system will greatly depend on establishing relationships with already established carriers such as AC Transit, a regional bus system which had taken over the Key System routes, and San Francisco Muni," the planners said. Both of these local systems, as well as other local systems, would play an important role as feeder or connecting lines for local destinations. In the outlying areas, private automobiles would more than likely be driven to stations where parking would be made available. However, it was estimated that for every parking space at a suburban station there would be ten or more passengers competing for it.

Meanwhile, the most severe congestion thus far identified by the "test lines" in 1954 was, of course, found on the routes between

Oakland and San Francisco on the Bay Bridge. Stop-and-go traffic between Marin County and San Francisco across the Golden Gate Bridge was also recorded, as was heavy northbound congestion on the peninsula's Bayshore Freeway along Highway 101. Southern Pacific commuter trains from San Jose offered some relief but did not go deep enough into San Francisco's commerce center and thus could attract only a small portion of the market.

Although PBHM understood the importance of estimating demand for a rail rapid transit system in the years ahead, the planners were under no illusion that auto commuters would suddenly switch to mass transit once a fixed-rail system was in place. The fact that commuters were wedded to their automobiles argued for a regional freeway system, a network of arteries that would accommodate demand. But highways also had a greater social, environmental, and financial impact; once freeways reached capacity, they could not simply expand to accommodate growth, as a train system might do by adding cars in a much narrower corridor.

The original first-phase plan had recommended building 123 miles of routes and fifty-one stations in six counties. Santa Clara County ultimately dropped out of the first-phase plan because of several considerable concerns, the largest of which was that the first phase called for only two stations in Santa Clara, both ending at Palo Alto. The supervisors had a problem with the idea of their taxpayers throughout the county spending several years paying for services that wouldn't directly benefit them. They were promised more stations once the second phase kicked in, but not everyone was convinced that would ever happen. Also, because Santa Clara at the time was predominantly an agricultural county with few commuters, the county's Taxpayers Association strongly opposed being included in the District. The irony of the county's decision to pull out of the District became clear in the 1970s and 1980s, when a burgeoning Silicon Valley, with its hundreds of thousands of new employees, saw Interstate 880, the road connecting Alameda and Santa Clara Counties, become one of the most congested corridors in the state.

The modified five-county first-phase rapid transit plan now called for the construction of approximately 118 miles of grade-separated double track, served by forty-nine stations. It would run from Santa Venetia, just north of San Rafael in central Marin County, south across a lower deck of the Golden Gate Bridge through San Francisco, and continue south along the peninsula to Palo Alto in San Mateo County on the west side of the bay. In the East Bay, the line would run from Richmond in western Contra Costa County to Fremont in southern Alameda County, and out to Concord in eastern Contra Costa County. Oakland would be the East Bay hub of the system. The key link, as recommended by the 1947 Joint Army-Navy Board report, would be a transbay tube between Oakland and San Francisco. PBHM's estimated price tag, again for a five-county system in 1953 dollars, was $716.5 million. Broken down, the costs were allocated as follows: track and structures, including a transbay tube, $353.3 million; stations, $74.8 million; yards and shops, $20 million; electrification, $71.6 million; signaling and dispatching, $30.2 million; right-of-way acquisition, $51.3 million; construction management fees and contingencies, $55.1 million; and other contingencies, including insurance costs, $60.2 million. These numbers become important in the historical context of BART's actual cost because of how drastically they changed in just a few short years.

While PBHM's final report included such detail, in fact it was not meant to be the definitive blueprint for what a regional rail system should look like, nor were the corridors suggested supposed to be unchangeable. In general terms, it was an overview of what was possible, feasible, and certainly needed to serve the nine-county region. It also went so far as to suggest potential different modes of rail transit available, such as a monorail, which would offer a super-modern look, or the more conventional double-track system. Without question, though, a modern system would have to be computer operated if it were to compete with the automobile.

When submitting its final recommendation to the Rapid Transit Commission, PBHM optimistically estimated that, if construction of the first phase of the rapid transit system began in 1957, it could be completed by 1962. Such a timetable was, of course, unrealistic, particularly since it would first have to be approved by the voters in the District's member counties.

AC TRANSIT HAS AN OPINION

At the same time that the new BART District was taking shape, AC Transit, the newly created interurban bus service (which had purchased the Key System) had an issue. Against the desire of the State Division of Highways and Toll Bridge Authority, AC Transit wanted to continue to operate train service across the Bay Bridge to the East Bay Terminal (later the Transbay Terminal) in San Francisco. The agency hired De Leuw, Cather & Company to study whether or not the tracks across the lower deck of the Bay Bridge should be maintained in the face of impending demolition. De Leuw, Cather came back with a recommendation that the tracks be kept and that some form of rail service continue. However, the BARTD board, which now had jurisdiction over transbay rail service, moved to ensure that the tracks would be dismantled and thus blocked any attempt to keep them. This aligned well with the state's plans to turn the lower deck into a section of the freeway system.

STOKES AT WORK

After moving into his office on the sixth floor of the Flood Building in San Francisco, Stokes immediately set to work on his two primary objectives, or at least those he hoped to accomplish in the near term. The first was to gain respectability for the concept—in other words, to move the idea from a planner's dream into the real world and create a public mindset that believed rail rapid transit was a serious and feasible venture. The naysayers were already legion in their denunciation of the idea of a vast regional rail system. They argued that it would be costly and disruptive to build. Some of the harsher critics were saying the whole thing was nothing more than a pie-in-the-sky fantasy concocted by a bunch of will-o'-the-wisp planners and had no basis in reality. Some of the strongest opposition was coming from the American Automobile Association (AAA); the Southern Pacific Railroad, which was operating the commute service to San Francisco from the peninsula; and several papers in eastern Contra Costa County. (AAA would eventually change its policy and support rapid transit.) How much impact these organizations would have was as yet unknown. Several self-styled citizens groups that adamantly opposed the plan were also meeting secretly in private homes and at local halls.

Stokes's first objective was integrated with his second objective, which was to find a general manager with certain credentials. Stokes worked closely with Falk in searching for potential candidates.

"We were like Batman and Robin," Stokes recalled of those early days. "Falk had a keen understanding of what was needed. We worked well as a team."

The person they finally selected was a conservative Republican named John M. Pierce, president of the Winter Oil and Gas Association.

"We hoped that Pierce's name and his Republican affiliation would bring important credibility to the District," Stokes said.

Other powers granted the BARTD board by the state were the ability to issue general obligation bonds, with approval by the voters, to pay for the basic construction of the system, and the power to levy a tax on property to pay the interest and principal on such general obligation bonds until they were retired. Additionally, the District could issue revenue bonds to help pay for equipment, which would be repaid from the fare box. The PBHM analysts were certain that once trains began operating they would generate sufficient revenue to pay the system's operating costs. Given the economics of public transit during the postwar years, this was a very optimistic view.

A major task now facing the BARTD board was to finalize plans for the design and construction of the first phase of the system. The original cost estimates would clearly have to be revised, given that they were based on a timetable of construction between 1958 and 1962 that was no longer realistic. Also, the original estimates did not include the cost for transit cars, fees paid to underwriters for the purchase of bonds, and basic start-up money. The BARTD board brought on Parsons Brinckerhoff again, along with the Tudor Engineering Company and the Bechtel Corporation. Together they formed Parsons Brinckerhoff–Tudor–Bechtel (PBTB). The joint venture immediately began to refine the work that had already been done by PBHM into a final five-county plan. It also began a seismic study of the San Francisco Bay Area, including the bay floor, in preparation for the design of the Transbay Tube.

While the engineering and final planning work was going on, a parallel effort now had to be made to educate the voters of the member counties about the benefits of a high-speed-rail rapid transit system. It would be touted as a critical component of a balanced transportation network and essential to the future well-being of the region. The population of the Bay Area had more than doubled between 1940 and 1960, and a decentralization of growth was making longer commutes into the major urban centers more problematic without any additional choices. In addition, interurban travel within the central counties by all forms of transportation was estimated to increase by 51 percent between 1960 and 1975. Freeways and bridges alone would not meet the growing need.

Another heralded aspect of a regional rail system was that, if approved by the voters, the system would also serve as an important planning tool, particularly for the outlying areas where growth was imminent. Train stations could attract cluster development around their peripheries or even be integral with development, thus creating a built-in ridership as well as preserving open space. Environmental issues were just beginning to come to the forefront as planners looked south to observe with alarm the sprawl in the Los Angeles Basin. Air quality was another potential benefit of such a system.

THE SELLING OF BARTD

It was determined by the BARTD board that the project should go on the ballot during the general election to be held on November 6, 1962. This schedule would give the consulting engineers enough time to finalize a comprehensive plan. They basically had a little more than two years to sell a specific proposal to the public. The question was, would the voters tax themselves to pay off a debt of $716.5 million, which was the most current price tag for basic construction? Again, this figure did not include the cost of building the tube, which would be paid for with bonds backed by bridge toll funds, nor did the construction cost include transit cars, estimated at an additional $90 million. The Stanford Research Institute had indicated in its early cost estimates that bonds backed by fare-box revenue might be one way to pay for transit cars. This approach, however, would prove unfeasible, given that fare-box revenue would not fully cover operating costs.

Bill Stokes, who was elevated to assistant general manager in 1961, was charged with developing a comprehensive information campaign, a tricky business at best. The campaign would present what a modern rail rapid transit system might look like, where it would go, and generally how it would serve potential riders. However, the campaign could not cross the line into actually advocating for the transit system, since it was against the law to spend taxpayer dollars on promoting a publicly financed project. In other words, the information could not in any way advocate for a yes vote for the project, which went on the 1962 ballot as a general obligation bond referendum. But of course such advocacy was implicit in the information campaign.

Stokes began taking on additional staff for what proved to be a herculean effort. He hired Phillip Ormsbee, managing editor of the *Contra Costa Sun* (a member of the *Contra Costa Times* chain), and a San Francisco public relations professional named George MacDonald. Meanwhile, the statutory officers of the District now included not only the general manager but also a controller, a secretary, and a general counsel who was under contract from the esteemed San Francisco law firm of Pillsbury, Madison & Sutro. BARTD had yet to bring on a full-time general counsel.

As the nascent District began to take some shape, Stokes and his tiny staff set to work on a public relations strategy and specific plan to educate the voters in the five counties about the concept of a high-speed regional rail transit system.

"We determined that one of the best ways to give the public a sense of what they might eventually be voting for was to put together visuals which would show a very space-age-looking transit system in the context of specific locales using actual photos," Stokes said.

> As an example, we had an artist do a series of renderings showing sleek trains operating under ground, on aerial structures and at grade. Then we'd overlay or integrate the renderings in those areas photographed where the plan called for tracks to be laid, such as under Shattuck Avenue in Berkeley, or under Market Street in San Francisco. The photos would show cutaways that offered a strong visual component to the overall information campaign. Other renderings gave examples of clean, well-lighted, and very modern-looking stations, with marble concourses and in some cases the interior of stations with sweeping arches, and gleaming fare-gates, and ticket machines. These composite photo-renderings were then turned into a slide show as well as made available to the local press as glossies.

Left: This illustration showing future space-age BART trains under a San Francisco street was created as part of the public information campaign leading up to the 1962 bond referendum.

Below: This illustration from 1962 showed what a future aerial line might look like.

Stokes said that between 1960 and 1962 he gave more than three hundred speeches and slide presentations to local gatherings, such as meetings of the Lions and Rotary Clubs, the Bay Area Council, the Commonwealth Club, and a variety of community groups around the five counties. "Most of the presentations were done in the evening, which made for long days," he said.

While Stokes and his staff were working aggressively to inform the public about the proposed project, private concerns interested in seeing a successful vote at the ballot box were also gathering steam. A committee chaired by a Bank of America executive Carl F. Wente was raising money from the business community to pay for a parallel campaign calling for a yes vote for a regional rail transit network.

This private group, made up of San Francisco business leaders, hired a renowned public relations expert, Henry Alexander, to put together a strong advocacy campaign to supplement Stokes's information program. One of the first things Alexander did was instigate getting BART on the ballot as Measure A. Another group, formed by the Zellerbach people, was also raising money to support the measure. As long as private money was paying the bills, it was perfectly legal to promote a yes vote on Measure A, and these groups did so with gusto. The campaign included newspaper ads, radio spots, and billboards, all calling for voter approval of the five-county plan.

TROUBLE AHEAD

In September 1961, after a series of public hearings and a comprehensive draft plan published by PBTB was circulated among officials in the five counties, rumblings about possible defections began to surface. Later that fall, the first major threat to the five-county unit emerged when the Golden Gate Bridge, under the Redwood Empire Association Authority, refused to allow trains on a second deck. In a duel of engineering studies, two affirmed that a second deck of the bridge could handle trains, while two others paid for by the bridge authority concluded that trains would put too much stress on the support cables. Using the second deck to connect the proposed train system with Marin County had always been contemplated as part of the first-phase plan for BART, but the bridge authorities refused to budge on the issue. End of story. The only other option was to build another tube from San Francisco to Sausalito at an enormous extra cost, which would have to be borne by Marin County taxpayers. With virtually no industrial tax base to help support such a venture, plus opposition from environmentalists saying that BARTD trains would bring growth and crime to this staid bedroom community, the prospect for Marin looked grim. Some, however, thought the growth issue was a red herring. For the time being, the planners were giving more thought to this new wrinkle.

Then came another blow to the plan. In December 1961, San Mateo County withdrew from the District. County supervisors cited the fact that the peninsula commute service operated by Southern Pacific was already in place, and they did not want to burden homeowners with any additional property taxes. In fact, it came out later that the county board of supervisors had been lobbied heavily to drop out by a prominent and well-respected real estate developer on the peninsula, David D. Bohannon. Coupled with the aforementioned concerns, San Mateo supervisors were just too uneasy about putting BARTD on the ballot. With San Mateo out, the tax base to pay for the first phase was considerably weakened.

Looking north to Marin County again, the BARTD directors were concerned that Marin, given the circumstances, could very well vote against the project and possibly sink the entire enterprise. Reluctantly, the BARTD board voted to request that Marin County supervisors withdraw their county from the District. There was debate on the issue by the supervisors, but in the spring of 1962 they voted the county out, noting that they were doing it involuntarily. Prior to the November 1962 election, Marin made overtures to be let back into the transit district, but they were rejected by the BARTD board, who again feared that Marin would drag down the entire project.

CHAPTER 5

THE COMPOSITE REPORT

Now down to three counties—Alameda, Contra Costa, and San Francisco—the PBTB planners and engineers had to scramble to revise the earlier five-county plan. The new plan was assembled into a comprehensive document showing routes, stations, renderings of what the system might look like, a breakdown of costs, and even a recommended fare schedule. In early May of 1962, PBTB consultants published the document, the Composite Report, a copy of which was sent by BARTD to each of the supervisors in the three counties. The price tag for the basic construction of the physical system was now $792 million: $790,493,000 for construction, $1,057,000 for bond insurance, and $450,000 to reimburse the state for its original loan in 1953 to the Rapid Transit Commission. At this point PBTB's basic work was done.

As called for in the enabling legislation, construction of the BART system was to be funded by general obligation bonds, guaranteed to be paid from property taxes if the voters approved. Such bonds were to be sold between 1963 and 1970 and amortized over thirty years. The District's taxing authority could not exceed 15 percent of the assessed value of real properties in the District. Again, the basic cost no longer included construction of the Transbay Tube or the purchase of train cars. The BARTD board soon set about finding a way to pay for these components.

THE ISSUE OF THE TUBE

A little-known sidebar to the Transbay Tube issue had occurred earlier in the game. On November 26, 1958, Adrien J. Falk, then a board director from San Francisco, urged that BARTD support a recommendation that the state build the tube to the transit system's specifications and then lease it back to the transit district. The tube would then be owned by the state. At that time, the City of San Francisco's official position was to support a Southern Crossing as a second transbay corridor, and Mayor George Christopher was strongly in favor of that plan. The estimated price tag for the tube was now $84 million, plus $31 million for approach-ways. While discussions about financing the tube were going on, BARTD's general manager, John M. Pierce, suggested that a proposal for the entire project go to the voters in 1960. This, of course, did not happen, and for good reason—the District did not yet have all of its ducks in a row. The proposal would surely have gone down in defeat had that course been pursued.

On Thursday, February 5, 1959, state senator John F. McCarthy of San Rafael, a strong proponent of regional rapid transit, introduced a bill that would allow tolls on state bridges to be used to back bonds to pay for the Transbay Tube if taxpayers approved the project. On May 5, Senator Randolph Collier of Yreka, who chaired the Senate Transportation Committee, vigorously opposed the bill and temporarily bottled it up in committee. He was supported by one other senator on the committee, Richard J. Dolwig of Redwood City. Dolwig preferred a Southern Crossing. Collier said, "Building such a tube would be a step backwards. Nobody would use it. All you could do is cut it up and sell it for post holes." Luckily the postponement of moving the bill along didn't last too long. Collier ordered more hearings on the matter, and finally a deal was struck that would require that the voters approve at least a $500 million bond issue. The full legislature passed the bill before the end of the year.

LOCAL SUPPORT BEGINS TO BUILD

Meanwhile, on January 14, Edgar F. Kaiser of Oakland announced that he was forming the Citizens Committee, which would vigorously support a public information program in support of the rapid transit plan. The public relations firm of Whitaker and Baxter was retained to work with the committee. In San Francisco, the Bay Area Council and members of the business community were also building public support for the plan.

BARTD HANGS BY A THREAD IN THE HANDS OF ONE MAN

Alameda and San Francisco supervisors approved the plan presented in the Composite Report on May 24, 1962, the same day the U.S. space program made history by launching Scott Carpenter into orbit. The five-member Contra Costa board of supervisors was a major question mark. Although the board had delayed its vote, four of the supervisors had already gone on record, with two supporting putting the project on the ballot and two against. The swing vote lay with Joe Silva, a supervisor who represented the Brentwood area in eastern Contra Costa County. The stakes were high, and everyone, on both sides of the issue, was feeling enormous pressure. If Contra Costa County's supervisors did not put the issue on the ballot, the game was pretty much over. A two-county system simply was not feasible from a financial point of view, and it could be years before another attempt was made to push the revised Phase One plan through, and at a much greater cost. The dream of a regional rail rapid transit system might remain no more than a gleam in the eyes of its proponents.

Silva had been on the board for six years and had voted on several weighty issues during his tenure. He was no stranger to controversial matters facing the board, but this was big. He had carefully studied the Composite Report that laid out the proposed three-county system; he wanted to be sure what he was voting on. Almost all of the newspapers covering the area he represented were opposed to the project; on the other side, in favor of regional rail transit, was Dean Lesher's powerful *Contra Costa Times*, which covered the central and more densely populated portion of the county. Meanwhile, Silva was receiving numerous calls daily from constituents and friends urging him to vote no on putting BARTD on the ballot. Some of the calls were threatening. His colleagues on the board were also leaning on him from both sides. Joe Silva, however, was not about to be bullied.

Silva had been a farmer for most of his adult life, tilling the land in his corner of the county where many Portuguese families had settled since the late 1800s. Standing around six feet tall, with a swarthy complexion, he had an open, oval face distinguished by a trim gray moustache. His friendly demeanor masked an inner strength and stubbornness that was the hallmark of how he played the political game, usually with his cards close to his chest. He had an office in the Martinez courthouse, where fellow farmers often dropped by to chat with

Contra Costa County supervisor Joseph Silva was a key player in the fight to put BART on the ballot.

their old friend. According to Silva, in a discussion with me in 1973, the conversation usually got around to a favorite topic: the proposed rapid transit plan. The argument against it centered on the fact that, while the plan served the more densely populated areas in the central and western parts of the county, it offered nothing in the way of direct service for people in the outlying areas who would still have to pay a share of the cost. Under the BARTD Act, the counties were considered as units, which offered no relief for those unlikely to use the service directly. Almost all of the visitors who came to see him from his area were opposed to the plan. Silva listened to the arguments and usually responded by saying he had not yet made up his mind but that he appreciated hearing their concerns.

THE COFFEE SHOP MEETING

On a Monday morning in July 1962, Silva reluctantly agreed to meet with San Francisco mayor George Christopher and BARTD board president Adrien Falk to hear them out. At two that afternoon, the Contra Costa board of supervisors had scheduled a special meeting to take up the issue of whether to put the proposed rapid transit system on the ballot for the upcoming November 6 general election. It was the only item on the agenda, and a great deal of debate was expected before it would be put to a vote. A few days earlier, California governor Edmund G. (Pat) Brown had telephoned Joe Silva and urged him to vote in favor of putting transit on the ballot. "I think the way the highways are going now, we will run out of money and use of land. We have to have some kind of transit alternative," the governor said, according to Silva's recollection.

Still, Silva refused to make any commitment as to how he might vote. When George Christopher called him on Sunday, the day before the scheduled vote, to set up a Monday morning meeting, he hoped Silva would come over to San Francisco. But Silva had refused to meet in the city. Christopher recalled years later that Silva had said he did not want anyone accusing him of going to some fancy breakfast with the city boys. Silva told Christopher that if he wanted to meet, it would be on his turf, and he suggested an unnamed place in Martinez. He would meet Christopher and Falk at five in the morning and gave no more than the address. Christopher was somewhat taken aback by the early hour, but he agreed.

At first only he and Falk were going to meet with Silva. According to Christopher, he was worried about "this guy Silva" and ruefully thought they needed reinforcement. At eight o'clock Sunday night, he called Oakland mayor John Houlihan.

Houlihan recalled the telephone conversation in which Christopher thought it would be good if he, Houlihan, would join forces with Falk and him at the meeting with Silva: "I asked Christopher what this guy Silva wanted. 'He must want something,' I said. 'I mean, he's been stalling for some time now.'"

Christopher had no idea what Silva wanted but strongly believed that they should at least go meet with him and try to convince him to vote yes to put the project on the ballot. Houlihan told Christopher he thought it was a waste of time and complained about the early hour. "Silva is a no vote in my book," Houlihan said. "Primarily because of the area he represents. Those farmers out there in Brentwood would probably knock him off if he voted for BARTD."

In the end, Houlihan reluctantly agreed to join in on the meeting. He was sure Silva just wanted to see the two mayors out there groveling for his vote. "I decided that, despite my misgivings, it was too important not to give it a try," he said.

At five o'clock the next morning, San Francisco mayor George Christopher, accompanied by BARTD board president Adrien Falk, arrived—in the mayor's official black limousine—at the address Silva had given them. Oakland mayor John Houlihan arrived separately at about the same time. The address was on Alhambra Avenue, just outside the town's center. The visitors were nonplussed when they saw the meeting place: a down-home combination truck stop/doughnut shop. "I thought we were going to meet at some hotel," Christopher recalled many years later, with some amusement. "There wasn't a single table in the place. All the place had were one long counter and a row of stools. I asked Joe, who greeted us, how could we meet? And Silva just looked at me as if it was a silly question and said we'll meet at the counter." The four men grabbed stools, ordered some coffee, and were soon discussing the idea of a regional rapid transit system and how crucial it was for Silva to vote in favor it. According to Christopher, a reporter and photographer were also milling about the place. It turned out they were from the *Antioch Daily Ledger*. Silva had notified the paper about the impending meeting right after Christopher had confirmed getting together. However the conversation went, Silva wanted the public to be aware of it. He did not want to be accused of having private backroom meetings. Falk, Christopher, and Houlihan, who was beginning to think it was some kind of set-up, each talked in turn to Silva, who sat on a stool sandwiched in between Christopher and Houlihan. Falk stood behind them.

"We all hammered away at him for a good hour or so, but he wouldn't make a commitment one way or the other," Christopher recalled. It soon became clear that Joe Silva was leaning toward voting against the proposed transit plan, and Houlihan thought then that their mission was a failure and the whole thing was going down the tubes even before it had been given life. He was disgusted. According to Christopher, Houlihan leaned over and whispered to him: "Tell Silva to go to hell, George, and let's get out of here." But the San Francisco mayor and Falk did not want to give up just yet.

"I decided to give it one more try, using as persuasive a sales pitch as I could come up with," Christopher said. "I told him, I said, 'Look, Joe, this rapid transit thing has got to happen, and I believe it will happen, if not now, then someday. I know it's going to cost a lot of money. It's a big deal. So what I'm saying is, vote to put the project bonds on the ballot and let the voters decide. If they vote no, okay, that's their decision. I think the voters will approve the plan, and you'll have a great transit system. You'll be known as the man who made it possible.'"

Silva just nodded, acknowledging Christopher's speech.

Upon leaving the coffee shop in Martinez, Christopher, Falk, and Houlihan still had no idea how Silva was going to vote. Houlihan reiterated his skepticism.

THE CRITICAL VOTE

Later that afternoon, the Contra Costa board of supervisors took up the question of whether or not to put BARTD on the ballot for the upcoming election on November 6. The two no votes were cast first, and then the two yes votes. After a long pause, Joe Silva voted aye.

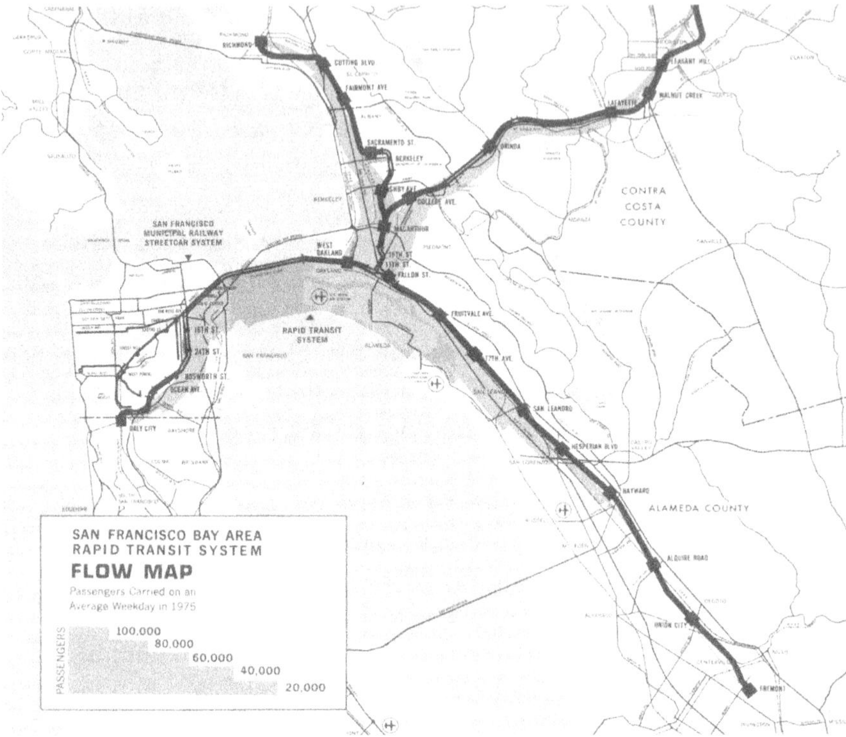

This 1962 map from the Composite Report shows the construction schedule for the BART system.

Thus, a vote of 3 to 2 meant the plan would be put on the county ballot. It was a jubilant moment for supporters of the rapid transit plan, and a very disappointing one for its detractors. At least now the voters in the three counties would get the chance to have their say about whether to tax themselves to pay for the first-phase plan.

While Silva was considered something of a hero by advocates of regional rail rapid transit, many of his friends and neighbors in the eastern part of the county were angry and felt betrayed. At one point some time later, he was hung in effigy in Brentwood. Those who recalled the meeting with Christopher, Houlihan, and Falk at the coffee shop—which had been reported in the *Antioch Daily Ledger*—accused him of having made some kind of deal. In a way, Silva's determination to be as transparent as possible in his political dealings, particularly with regard to how he would eventually vote, came back to haunt him. Most people in his area had never expected the proposed transit project to get the required votes from the board of supervisors, and certainly most of his constituents assumed Silva would vote no. After all, he was one of them.

Elsewhere, institutional opposition had come from the Pittsburg and Brentwood chambers of commerce and city councils, which were adamantly opposed. The Antioch city council and the Central Labor Council of Contra Costa County were also opposed. On the other side, strong support came from the central area of the county, which also had the most population density. The city councils of Concord, Pleasant Hill, and Walnut Creek; the Contra Costa Taxpayers Association; and the Contra Costa County Building and Construction Trades Council all supported the plan. Silva at one point or another had heard from all of them, mostly just saying they hoped he was going to vote "the right way."

On August 7, 1962, the Contra Costa board of supervisors unanimously passed Resolution 1136, which affirmed its intention and called for the consolidation of the "bond election" with the State of California's general election to be held on November 6, 1962. The abridged language on the ballot would be as follows: "Shall San Francisco Bay Area Rapid Transit District incur a bonded indebtedness in the principal amount of $792,000,000 for the object and purpose of acquiring, constructing and operating a rapid transit system…?"

LOWERING THE TWO-THIRDS REQUIREMENT

The year before the scheduled vote, BARTD's assistant general manager, B. R. Stokes, and Frank Chambers, a political consultant who was close to Governor Pat Brown, went to Sacramento to implore the legislature to lower the required vote for approval of the referendum from 66.66 percent of the vote to 60 percent. A study of voting patterns between 1948 and 1958 suggested a truth about the chances of getting voter approval for the referendum: during those years, sixty bond issues had been put forth, but only twenty-eight of them (about 47 percent) passed under the two-thirds vote requirement. Clearly, the chances of success for BARTD were slim to none if the two-thirds requirement stood. This prediction was in spite of the fact that a poll conducted by the Stanford Research Institute (SRI) in 1957 indicated that more than 80 percent of the electorate in the original six counties approved of a regional rapid transit plan. Hired by the Rapid Transit Commission to conduct the poll, SRI had sent out questionnaires to randomly selected homes in each of the counties. The numbers were there, but Stokes and Chambers knew the motivations of voters often shifted when their pocketbooks came into the equation.

Opinion polls later conducted by Penfield Associates, however, showed that a vote for rapid transit actually had a 95 percent chance of success if the required percentage needed for approval was lowered to 60 percent. Under the state constitution (article XI, section 18), special districts that required special votes were normally subject to only a majority vote. This fact was used as a wedge to argue the case. With encouragement from business leaders who supported the project, J. Eugene McAteer, a state senator from San Francisco, authored a rider attached to another bill to lower the requirement to 60 percent. Intense lobbying would have to be conducted in Sacramento to get enough legislative support, and the effort would be politically tricky because legislators generally did not like to go out on a limb on such issues.

Pat Brown said later in an interview that Adrian Falk had also talked to him about supporting such a bill. "I told him there was no question but that I would support and sign the bill if it gets to my desk," Brown said. But that was a big if. Stokes said he and Chambers talked to everyone who would give them a moment in the halls and offices of the capitol. Unsurprisingly, the proposed rider was strongly opposed by Randolph Collier, the powerful chairman of the California Senate Transportation Committee, who was also considered the father of the state's freeway system. Ultimately, on June 6, 1961, the legislature passed a bill lowering the required percentage. The bill was signed by Governor Brown. As it turned out, it was a brilliant move.

THE 1962 GENERAL OBLIGATION BOND REFERENDUM

The BARTD referendum went on the November 6, 1962, ballot with the best possible placement. Its designation as Measure A meant that it was at the top of the ballot for local measures. From a psychological point of view, its placement gave a greater sense of importance to the choice than if it had been buried somewhere in the heap of other measures and propositions. Also, it was the first local measure the voters saw. Getting that position on the ballot constituted another masterstroke, which Stokes credited to San Francisco public relations man Henry Alexander.

When the ballots were counted, the proposed rapid transit project by BARTD had squeaked through with a winning margin of 8,705 votes, or 61.215 percent when averaged over the returns from the three counties. Slim as it was, that margin put the endeavor in the yes column. The total vote count for Measure A in the three counties in the District was 716,331, with 277,827 no votes and 438,504 yes votes. Breaking it down on a county-by-county basis, the highest approval count was San Francisco, with 66.888 percent voting yes; then Alameda County, with 60.039 percent; and finally Contra Costa County, with 54.479 percent. The Contra Costa vote, and the election in general, would soon become a major issue for litigation.

B. R. Stokes, the staff, and the board were overjoyed that the proposed transit project could now go forward. The essential piece of financing, $792 million, was now assured. The vote also meant that the state Toll Bridge Authority would now have to make good on the commitment to fund the Transbay Tube with revenue bonds backed by bridge tolls. The victory was even more outstanding because the smart money had always betted against the project being approved by the voters.

Much of the praise was given to Adrien Falk for his business sense and strong personal connections to the business community, which helped finance the several "Yes on Measure A" campaigns. But the lion's share of the credit went to B. R. Stokes for spearheading a skillful, even brilliant, public relations effort that managed to get the job done despite being legally unable to advocate for a yes vote.

AN INTRIGUING CONSPIRACY STORY: THE PACIFIC RIM STRATEGY

Years later, the *San Francisco Bay Guardian*, a weekly independent tabloid, published a story by Burton H. Wolfe titled "Bechtel's Baby." While the story did not receive a lot of play in the mainstream media, it centered on the intriguing premise of a conspiracy theory. According to Wolfe, all strings were being pulled by Stephen D. Bechtel Sr.; he was the secret mastermind behind the plot to build BART, as he and a group of coconspirators had met sometime in the early 1950s and hatched the master plan for the region, at whose center would be a new rapid transit system.

When the story appeared on February 14, 1973, Bechtel was seventy-two years old. The Bechtel Corporation had been founded by his father, Warren A. Bechtel, in 1898, primarily as an engineering firm, and, in combination with several partners over time, the fledgling company made a name for itself, including as the designer and builder of the great Hoover Dam in 1931. Over the years, Stephen Sr. greatly expanded the company into an engineering and construction management giant, building major projects all over the world. Some of those projects included shipyards, Liberty and Victory ships during World War II, oil refineries in Saudi Arabia and Kuwait, and various rail lines. He was the company's chairman from 1933 to 1960 and was once named by *Time* magazine as one of the hundred most influential people of the twentieth century. He remained active with the company well into the 1980s.

By this time the Bechtel Corporation, headquartered in San Francisco, was one of the largest and most successful engineering and construction companies in the world; Wolfe in his article referred to it as "the most colossal engineering dynasty in history." Stephen Bechtel Sr., who by all accounts was a charming and outgoing person, was generally viewed from afar by journalists who simply could not get access to him or to the inner workings of the company. The family-owned corporation rigorously maintained its privacy.

As Wolfe's story goes, a strategy to maintain and enhance property values and promote business growth in San Francisco was supposedly hatched during the post–World War II years. Allegedly leading the charge was Stephen Bechtel Sr., along with other top business leaders on both sides of the bay. According to the story, the objective of the plot was to make San Francisco the gateway to emerging markets around the Pacific Rim, including China and Southeast Asia. The idea was loosely referred to as "The Pacific Rim Strategy."

In order to realize this objective, the city had to become a magnet for corporations and top business and technical talent from other parts of the country and the world. Since land, particularly in the downtown area, was scarce, development was constrained, and the only way to go was up. New high-rise office buildings would have to be built to replace many of the Financial District's venerable structures. Additional living spaces would also have to be built.

This process was termed, by Wolfe and the *Bay Guardian*, "the Manhattanization of San Francisco," or simply the "Manhattan-BART scheme." According to the story, a necessary tangential element of this grand blueprint was an efficient mode of transportation. In other words, an interurban rail rapid transit system would be needed in order to transport personnel from the growing suburbs to the growing high-employment centers of Oakland and San Francisco. All of this alleged scheming, of course, eventually led to the BART project and some big-money contracts for all of the elements that make up the system today.

While the writer more than likely intended the story to be viewed in a negative light and as an exposé of behind-the-scenes corporate finagling, it could also be interpreted as a testament to the American genius for progress and business acumen. In any case, the premise of the story is questionable, especially when one follows BART's evolution from the beginning. Early planners had one set of goals: to relieve growing congestion and foster sound land-use planning. Marvin Lewis, one of the early prime movers, who also chaired the Bay Area Council's Transit Committee, always maintained that offering alternative transportation with a view to relieving congestion was his primary goal.

In the final analysis, it might also be fair to say that the San Francisco business community strongly supported the proposed rapid transit concept. One motive may well have been to better equip the city center for urban renewal and to better position it as a center for West Coast commerce seeking Pacific Rim opportunities. But providing a good mix of transportation and business naturally go hand in hand.

One thing is certain: what happened along the Market Street corridor when BART did arrive was, without question, an explosive transformation of the San Francisco skyline. At a party one evening in the early 1970s, I ran into Bruce Brugmann, the founder and publisher of the *Bay Guardian*. We had a drink and discussed the impact BART was having on the city. "Just look at all the new buildings," Brugmann said. "It truly is becoming the West Coast Manhattan."

"Is that a bad thing?" I asked.

He looked away and then grinned.

"Yes," he said. "The corpuscles have gone awry!"

CHAPTER 6

WHAT THE VOTERS VOTED ON

The Composite Report was primarily a selling tool, not a definitive plan for building the proposed system; it might best be viewed as the link between what PBMH produced and the actual final detailed design. The report did lay out the rough basic routes and made some specific recommendations, but the next step in this evolutionary process would involve detailed planning and engineering, with thousands of hours of work ahead.

BARTD would be building and operating the first all-new rail rapid transit system in this country in almost sixty years. While there had been upgrades to older systems during the previous twenty years or so—such as the Lindenwold line running between New Jersey and Philadelphia, and the Shaker Heights line in Cleveland, Ohio—there had been nothing totally new since the completion of the Philadelphia transit system (now called the South Eastern Pennsylvania Transit Authority [SEPTA]) in 1907. The new San Francisco Bay Area system would also be the largest locally financed public works project in the country's history. PBTB estimated that it would take eight years to complete the basic construction, which meant that, in the best of all possible worlds, it could open its first line in 1969.

As stated earlier, the voter-approved bond issue for $792 million was for the system structure, excepting the Transbay Tube and rolling stock. At the time, the cost estimate for the tube was $133 million, hopefully to be paid for from bonds backed by bridge tolls. According to the report, the total number of cars needed would be 450, at an estimated cost of $71.2 million, to be paid for from revenue bonds. According to a public-opinion poll taken before the November 6 vote, it all looked good. The public had a preponderance of optimism, even enthusiasm, about the proposed regional rail system as presented. B. R. Stokes and his tiny staff had done a brilliant job. But of course, a world of difference lies between the vision of such a project and the reality of its actual construction.

Long before the anticipated election, the BARTD board and its supporters had to overcome a major stumbling block in the struggle to put all the necessary pieces in place. The proposed project clashed with the state's highway interests over the additional financing needed for constructing the Transbay Tube. The most logical source of funds, as recommended by the Stanford Research Institute and later outlined in the Composite Report, was the selling of bonds backed by tolls from the three East Bay bridges: the San Francisco–Oakland Bay Bridge, the San Mateo–Hayward Bridge, and the Dumbarton Bridge. Again, state senator Randolph Collier led the charge against the use of bridge tolls for a transit system, on the basis that the bridges were part of the highway/freeway network. BARTD struggled to get in place this critical piece of the overall financing before putting the project before the voters. Once again, the state legislature came down on the side of the transit district, and in 1959 it voted to approve the use of the bridge tolls. Funds from the bridges would not be available until after July 1, 1964, because of prior capital-improvement costs, yet despite the delay in available funding for constructing the tube, preliminary design work could proceed.

As presented to the voters, the final plan had shrunk from its original first-phase plan calling for a 123-mile system across five counties. The new plan now called for a three-county, 75-mile project, with 71.5 miles of BART tracks and 3.5 miles of San Francisco Muni rail. The Muni line, on a separate level, would share the subway corridor under Market Street with BART trains. That line would be built to Muni specifications for a modern streetcar fleet to be ordered sometime in the future. Meanwhile, the BART system would be a modern high-speed rail system with fully automated trains traveling up to 70 miles per hour (45 miles on average, including station stops) on grade-separated lines of double track, with thirty-three stations. (The system, which was referred to as BARTD in the early days, became

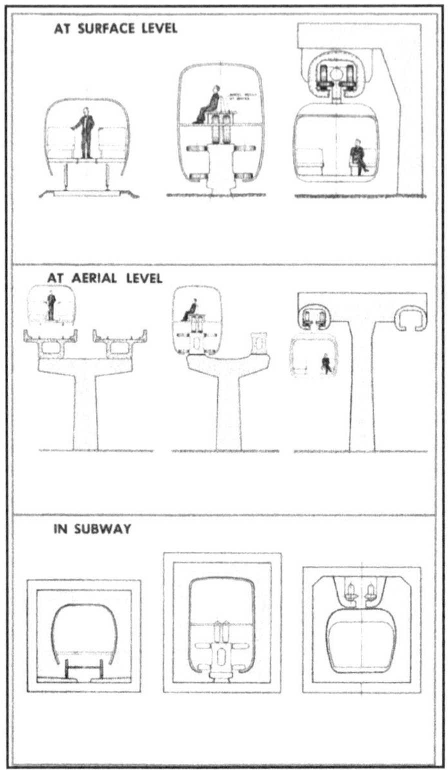

Before BART decided on a track with two steel rails, engineers considered a variety of monorail options, as pictured here. Studies ultimately determined that a monorail design would not meet the switching needs required by the system's complicated track configurations.

known more popularly as BART when the system's logo was adopted in 1970.)

Before reaching its final decision on what to propose, PBTB had explored the concept of a suspended monorail, which called for the transit cars to hang from a single rail. However, problems of swaying and switching made this mode impractical. A dual-track monorail, which offered more promise, was also dismissed as potentially too costly, because tunnels and aerial structures would have to be much higher to accommodate the hanging cars. Some critics down the road believed that the monorail would have been a better way to go. After all, it worked at Disneyland. Another possibility considered was the use of rubber tires on a steel-track guideway, similar to the French-built Montreal system or the Paris Metro, but the hilly Bay Area topography would cause as much as a 4 percent grade in some areas, and rubber tires would not provide enough traction. Also, that system was known to be very noisy. In the end, PBTB decided on steel wheels on steel track, with the gauge set at a recommended 5 feet, 6 inches instead of the worldwide standard gauge of 4 feet, 8.5 inches. The nonstandard gauge—chosen because the lighter cars that ran on the narrower track would be more stable in Bay Area winds—received harsh criticism, primarily because BART trains could not share traditional railroad tracks.

Parking at all suburban stations would also be provided, comprising about 20,000 spaces system-wide, primarily at the suburban locations.

Using the city of Oakland as the East Bay hub of the system, the four lines stretched out like a slightly askew *X*: 11 miles to Richmond in western Contra Costa County to the north, 26 miles south to Fremont in Alameda County, 19 miles to Concord in eastern Contra Costa County, and 15.5 miles across the bay through San Francisco, ending at Daly City. The plan generally called for one-third of the structure to be at grade, one-third aerial, and one-third subway, including the Transbay Tube. BARTD saw the project as an opportunity to advance state-of-the-art technology, which could be a catalyst for a renaissance of rail mass transit in America.

A MAJOR DECISION FACING THE BOARD

At this point, PBTB's work was essentially completed. Now it was time for the BARTD board to make a critical decision about its options. The first option was to staff up by bringing designers, engineers, construction managers, and work crews on board to plan and build the system. The issue with this method was that once the job was completed the construction personnel would not be needed for the day-to-day operations, which would require a totally different workforce, meaning layoffs would be considerable. After some debate, the board decided instead to hire an outside firm to build and deliver a completed project, or a "turnkey" system.

On November 29, 1962, just three weeks after the election, the BARTD board approved a $47.2 million contract for the final engineering of the project, based on a percentage of estimated costs rather than a fixed fee. The contract was awarded to the consortium joint venture PBTB, as recommended by the board's own Engineering Committee. Other engineering firms that were interested in the work protested the letting of this contract, claiming it was simply a giveaway or a sweetheart deal. They went to court and tried to bring a restraining order keeping BARTD and PBTB from going forward with the project, claiming that there was no competition and that the arrangement created an inverse incentive to find economies as work progressed. In other words, the claim was that PBTB would greatly benefit from increasing costs, with no incentive to achieve savings. A Contra Costa judge ruled against the engineers. They did not pursue the matter further.

THE FIRST OF SEVERAL COSTLY DELAYS

Soon after that first attempt to stop the work, a second group of four individuals, including an elected official and a former elected official, was more successful. They brought a taxpayers' suit against BARTD and PBTB. The lawsuit, filed in the state superior court in Martinez, charged that the November 6 general obligation bond referendum was invalid because the public had not been given the true facts about the project, and because public funds had been improperly used to sway the voters to vote yes on Measure A. The suit also challenged the contract just approved by the BARTD board to retain PBTB as the consulting engineers and questioned the formula for how fees were established, claiming that the fees were excessive. Another part of the suit challenged the salaries of staff, particularly that of assistant general manager B. R. Stokes, the architect of the pre-election information program. The suit claimed that the "information campaign" was designed to deceive and mislead the public about the project. The plaintiffs wanted whatever salary Stokes had received to be returned to the taxpayers. "This became something of an amusement around the office," Stokes said. "Staff put up a large tin cup with my name over it for donations, in case the suit was successful."

The District's chief engineer, Kenneth M. Hoover, who advised the BARTD board on engineering matters, was also named in the suit. It charged that his advice to the board constituted practicing engineering without a license, because he was not licensed in the state of California. Hoover had earlier worked as an engineering consultant to the New York engineering firm of Quade & Douglas, one of the PBTB partners. Walter Douglas of Quade & Douglas had, in fact, recommended Hoover for the BARTD job. The staff and the board felt that someone with an engineering background should be on hand to help evaluate the work and offer expertise in any related decisions that had to be made.

Finally, the suit brought by the four men sought an immediate halt to all work involving the transit project. One anecdote from Stokes was that the suit may have received financial support from a prominent developer in Cleveland, Ohio. While the story of a mysterious person behind this lawsuit could not be substantiated at this writing, it offers an odd twist to the story. The motivation for such support, if true, remains cause for wonder.

THE TRIAL

It was determined that a nonjury trial would be held in the court of Judge Martin E. Rothenberg. All work was put on hold until a final judgment was made by the court. The four plaintiffs who joined forces to bring the taxpayers' suit were Dewayne E. Boblitt, Junior G. Gertsch, Stanley E. Nunn, and Robert L. Osborne. At the time, Boblitt was serving as mayor on the El Cerrito city council, and he also owned two doughnut shops, one in El Cerrito and one in Berkeley. Even before joining in the lawsuit, he had publicly voiced his concern about the proposed routing of an aerial structure through his city, and during his court appearance, he claimed on the stand that an elevated track, thirty feet above the ground, would have a detrimental psychological effect on El Cerrito residents, dividing the community. He wanted the line to be placed closer to the freeway, west of the proposed route.

Boblitt was also the plaintiff who charged that the District had put out information with the "intent to mislead and deceive the voting public," and that Stokes had improperly advocated for a yes vote using taxpayer money. He testified in court that his initial opposition was on the basis of the routing, but he then expanded his concern to the overall plan itself, saying, "I feel it does not serve the number of people it should for the amount of money involved." He also charged that BART officials had made no effort to meet with AC Transit officials to make use of existing facilities. "Alternatives to the plan were not considered," he said. "When any objections came up they bulldogged their way over them."

Junior Gertsch lived in San Francisco and owned a self-service laundry. His primary criticism was of the contract with PBTB for the final engineering. Like the three firms who had earlier tried to get the restraining order, he was also critical of the "cost plus" fee deal. He claimed that the BARTD directors had not built in adequate controls of expenditures to be incurred under the contract. In court he stated, "There will be no effective way of preventing unjust enrichment at the expense of every taxpayer within the District."

The attorney representing the District asked Gertsch, who was on the stand, to explain. "Can you tell me what you mean by that allegation?"

"My attorney is more familiar with it than I am," Gertsch said, at which point his attorney told him to just say he didn't know. He then admitted that he did not know what he meant by his allegation.

"Did you ever review the contract?" asked the attorney for the District.

"No," answered Gertsch. "I have read about it in the newspapers."

Next, the attorney for the District asked the plaintiff if he knew anything about the engineers who had been awarded the contract for the final design of the transit project, that is, about any previous work they had done. Again Gertsch answered no. The BARTD attorney then asked, "Do you have any criticism of these engineers?" Answer: "No." The attorney then asked Gertsch what the nature of his disagreement was.

Gertsch replied, "The routes."

"Pardon me?" the attorney for BARTD said.

"The routes," Gertsch repeated.

"The routes?" the attorney said.

"Yes, the routes," Gertsch said again.

The attorney for the plaintiffs was taken aback when BARTD's attorney turned to him and requested that he be able to look at his files on the case.

"Over my dead body," the plaintiff's attorney shot back after BARTD's attorney repeated the request.

"Well, if I am going to find some basis here for the charges, and I don't get them from the plaintiffs, I thought maybe we could see what you have."

Robert Osborne, one of the four plaintiffs, lived in Oakland and was the owner of the Malabar Manufacturing Company located in San Leandro. He had formerly been a member of the Oakland city council. He stated that he also felt the voters in the three counties had been deceived and misled. He said he based his belief on conversations he had had with "hundreds of people." He went on to say in his testimony that the basic nature of the proposed system had never been made clear to the voters. "Well," he said, "I think primarily—and this is my main objection to this—is that the people never realized that this was a rail transportation system."

The attorney for the engineering firm asked him about the Composite Report of May 1962, the document that spelled out what the system was and what the costs were expected to be.

"Have you ever seen it?" the attorney asked.

"No," Osborne answered.

"Did you make any effort to see it?"

"No," replied Osborne.

Osborne said he also objected to the "open-ended" $47.2 million contract between BARTD and the engineers. The attorney for the District then asked, "Do you have any information yourself from which you criticized the engineers[...]?"

"No, sir," Osborne said.

In the end, Osborne admitted that he had very little information on which he based his complaint and assumed that his attorney had more knowledge of the project and the engineers.

Later in the proceedings, John M. Pierce, the District's general manager, was questioned about the function of the District's chief engineer, Kenneth M. Hoover. Hoover was a trained electrical engineer and had a wide range of experience with commuter rail systems in the East. He had been hired by the District in January 1959, serving as the only engineer on staff. Pierce testified that Hoover's lack of a license to practice engineering in California was not a critical factor. "He did not make key recommendations," he said. "Engineering recommendations concerning the system were made by our consulting engineers."

Adrien J. Falk, president of the BARTD board, was also called to the stand. He concurred with Pierce's testimony, saying that Hoover was hired as a transit expert and could act as a knowledgeable liaison person between BARTD and its hired engineers.

When Hoover himself was called to the stand, he was asked if, aside from his recommendation to the BARTD board concerning the contract with PBTB, he had ever been presented with alternative "reports of engineers."

"No," Hoover answered, "not counting newspaper reports quoting curbstone engineers, or some crackpot writing with complaints."

When questioned about the propriety of the District's contract with PBTB, he stated, "My opinion of these fees, after careful study, is that they were right and proper within the field of custom for this type of work."

Falk went even further, stating that he was not as concerned about the profit the engineers might make from the contract as the overall reasonableness of their charges and the methods of charges. He also emphatically defended the District board's award of the contract to the same engineers who had done the preliminary engineering and cost estimating without consulting or soliciting bids from other engineers. In 1959, the District had talked to forty or fifty engineering firms before contracting with PBTB for the preliminary work. Many of the people involved had already worked on the early studies, going back five years. "In view of their knowledge and long association with the proposed project, we believed the simplest and least costly approach would be to go ahead with them instead of inviting in new people who might want to come in with another set of ideas," he said. Falk was adamant that the terms of the contract had to be acceptable to the District and fair to the taxpayers who would be paying the bill.

In answer to whether or not the District board gave sufficient consideration to alternative proposals, the District's general counsel, Wallace L. Kaapcke, took the stand. He testified that, at numerous meetings, the BARTD board entertained suggestions for changes in routing and station locations, which frequently came from communities and municipalities to be served. Engineers then were often asked to go back to the drawing board and explore the feasibility of the proposed changes.

Attorneys for the plaintiffs grilled Ralph A. Tudor, president of Tudor Engineering, a member of the PBTB joint venture. "We supervise construction; but we do not do any construction," he said. He explained that compensation under the contract was basic cost, plus a fixed fee, plus an overhead factor of 1.25 times that of actual cost. Tudor said the terms of the contract were well within the guidelines suggested by the American Society of Civil Engineers.

Later, John Roche Kiely, senior vice president of the Bechtel Corporation, was also called to testify. While he admitted that Bechtel's experience was not specifically in mass transit, the company did have a great deal of experience in the construction of railroads.

THE COURT'S DECISION

On June 10, 1963, Judge Rothenberg handed down his decision in favor of BARTD on all counts. In his published opinion on the charge of deliberately withholding information from the public as alleged by the plaintiffs, Rothenberg found: "The District openly discussed criticism and suggestions that were presented to it concerning the proposed system and did not repress or withhold opposition to the plan." Further, he found: "The public information program of the District, including publications, press releases, and speeches, was designed to and it did present the facts concerning the District and its activities and the proposed plan so that all interested persons could be informed, and none of the public information activities was deceptive or misleading."

The judge went on to say that Stokes did not engage in any deceptive or misleading activities, and he conducted the program honestly and fairly informed the interested parties. He noted that, as part of the information program, the District itself arranged for the presentation of opposing viewpoints at debates and forums.

Addressing the issue of chief engineer Kenneth Hoover, the judge found that his work did not constitute practicing without a license in the state of California. Further, Rothenberg found no breach in the fiduciary relationship between BARTD and the engineers.

Rothenberg swept on to his conclusion: "The District's special bond election of November 6, 1962, was valid in all respects, and it duly and lawfully authorized the issuance of general obligation bonds."

Thus the halt to work was lifted. Once again the District and PBTB were ready to jump out of the starting gate. The bad news, according to a paper presented by Richard J. Shephard, the District secretary, was that the six-month delay had cost between $12 and $15 million—the first of several negative impacts on the District's limited funding.

CHAPTER 7

BEGINNING ON A TURBULENT ROAD

Some minimal effort did, in fact, take place during the general moratorium while the trial was in progress. Six PBTB engineers were allowed to work during that period with the court's knowledge. However, PBTB was paying its engineers on faith alone. Mostly they did pencil-on-paper work prerequisite to the draft of the final design. Where the moratorium hurt the most was in land acquisition, staff costs, and inflation. For example, the research and development program had included the purchase of the first piece of right-of-way, which was initially planned to have been acquired immediately following the election.

Between early 1963 and mid-1964 the planned research and development program cost had escalated 27 percent. Except for the right-of-way to be used for experiments that would be incorporated into the system, this program was not part of the budget as outlined in the Composite Report. The right-of-way was a 4.5-mile stretch between Concord and Walnut Creek on the old Sacramento Northern Railway right-of-way along the Diablo route. That line had been an electric interurban railway that provided passenger service between Oakland and Chico, northwest of Sacramento. The service had been abandoned in 1941, but the right-of-way was still owned by Union Pacific, which had taken it over from Western Pacific. It was slated to be the site of a test track for BART that would be critical to the overall advancement of technology to be employed by the new system. A grant from the Department of Housing and Urban Development (HUD) for $4.8 million helped to pay for the test program.

Meanwhile, developers, speculating that parcels along other proposed transit routes were going to increase in market value, began gobbling them up where possible.

In November 1963, Bill Stokes was named BARTD's general manager when John Pierce left the job to become the District's director of finance for the next few years, a post he was well suited for, having been director of finance for the State of California. Bill Stokes soon became referred to as B. R. Stokes on District press releases and, before long, by the media. Making Stokes, a non-engineer, general manager was a bold move on the part of the BARTD board. Many questioned whether Stokes could hold PBTB's feet to the fire when serious questions concerning engineering or design work arose, since at the time only one engineer was on the staff to monitor the work and plans as they were submitted for approval. But board president Adrien Falk, who engineered the appointment, had great faith in the young Stokes, and Falk and Stokes basically ran the District together, according to board member George Silliman. Again, Batman and Robin.

Armed with vision, drive, and a high-powered personality (according to another of the early directors), Stokes would guide the project through the construction years with broad powers that he used to the fullest advantage to get things done. His charisma included knowing

B. R. "Bill" Stokes was BART's first employee. He was hired in 1958 as the information officer, and six years later he was general manager of the system.

and remembering the first names of everyone on the young District's growing staff of around twenty-seven, as well as other important players he would have to deal with down the line.

Turbulence and controversy, however, were there to greet the project every step of the way. The initial goal, set prior to the 1962 vote, was to inaugurate revenue service as early as 1967, a plan that had clearly become an impossibility after so many delays. Stokes emphasized that this new transit system, whose full-scale plan was still on the drawing board, had to be spectacular in its look and performance if it were to compete with the automobile. It had to be enticing, almost entering the realm of science fiction. A major key would be the District's efforts, through the engineering consultants, to make breakthroughs in signaling, propulsion, and automation, thus advancing the state of the art to benefit not only the BARTD system but also future systems.

"We were living in an automobile culture, and in order for a transit system to attract drivers out of their cars it must be sleek, comfortable, convenient, and cheap," Stokes recalled. "This new system had to be a very marketable product."

Stokes wanted the trains to be fully automated and, if possible, to operate without drivers. In fact, that was the original plan. Automation would take the potential for human error out of the operational equation and would give the system an edge in terms of achieving minimal overhead. The new system would also benefit from what had been learned and developed during the creation of eastern systems. William Parsons, who had founded Parsons Brinckerhoff in the late 1800s, had employed several innovations of the period, including electricity, when designing the New York City subway. BARTD's plan was to push the envelope and be on the cutting edge of advanced technology.

Also in 1963, Jerome Waldie, at the time a member of the state assembly representing eastern Contra Costa County, sponsored a bill to exempt his constituents from having to pay for BARTD through their property taxes. After all, according to popular reasoning, they would be paying for something that would not directly serve them. Joe Silva, on the other hand, believed that eastern Contra Costa residents *would* be served, since pressure on major traffic arteries in the eastern part of the county would see some relief when the new system was up and running. "They would have an indirect benefit," he said.

While Waldie's bill did not pass, it had the effect of forcing the BARTD board in that same year to pass Resolution 245, which in effect was a promise to place a priority on building future extensions to Pittsburg and Antioch in eastern Contra Costa County, and to Dublin/Pleasanton and Livermore in eastern Alameda County. Many years in the future, this issue would become a subject of bitter controversy among board members and east versus west, so to speak.

THE CRABGRASS FRONTIER

Now it was time to negotiate permits and right-of-way agreements with the communities making up the District: the suburban cities within Alameda and Contra Costa Counties, and Daly City in San Mateo County. These suburbs were sometimes referred to as "crabgrass frontiers" because of their burgeoning populations in the postwar years. While the court had cleared BARTD and PBTB of all the charges in the recent trial, residual criticism of BARTD's contract with PBTB lingered. The primary issue suggested by the lawsuit was that the District's board had relinquished a great deal of its power to the joint venture of PBTB, and as the project moved forward, it seemed the tail was indeed wagging the dog. PBTB was, in fact, authorized to deal with local communities on various critical issues, and also to negotiate with full autonomy with subcontractors. In effect, the line between BARTD and PBTB became blurred. The new joint venture of Parsons Brinckerhoff Quade & Douglas had taken the lead in managing the early work, after which Bechtel became the primary overseer of the project's construction.

One of the problems, partly due to funding constraints, was the perception that the engineers had an inflexible attitude when dealing with local suburban communities. Yet a key goal of the project was for the design of each station to reflect each community's aesthetics and be as unobtrusive as possible, to meld with the environment. Negotiating agreements with local jurisdictions became a very bumpy road, costing time and money because of delays. The process had no precedent, and it had not been incorporated into the Composite Report as a potential factor when costs and construction time frames for each segment had been estimated. The engineers assumed that basic lines and stations identified in the report's preliminary plan were fully accepted by the communities and that getting agreements would be routine. Nothing,

NOW UNDER CONSTRUCTION
RAPID TRANSIT FOR THE BAY AREA

A CONGESTION FREE 75-MILE NETWORK OF
SUBWAYS AERIAL LINES SURFACE LINES
COMPRISING THE WORLD'S FASTEST, SAFEST AND MOST MODERN URBAN TRANSPORTATION SYSTEM

SPECIFICALLY DESIGNED TO SOLVE THE BAY AREA'S AUTOMOBILE CONGESTION PROBLEM—AND TO PROVIDE RESIDENTS WITH A NEW AND EFFICIENT FORM OF INTER-COMMUNITY TRANSIT SERVICE

This 1962 Composite Report satellite view of Bay Area topography shows how the line would overlay the region.

of course, was further from the truth. The various communities had suddenly woken up to the reality of the massive undertaking that would occur in their respective backyards. Numerous public hearings were held in the local communities as specific designs of system components became available. These included, among the more critical issues, station locations and designs, color schemes, landscaping, track routing, and noise abatement.

No one ever believed that overlaying a 75-mile system onto the topography of the Bay Area was going to be a piece of cake. But conflicts between the engineers and the local incorporated cities often intensified to the level of accusations and shouting matches in city council chambers and town hall gatherings. The acrimony was, of course, good fodder for the press. In a way, this process was the beginning of a new activist movement fighting for a participatory process in which many voices could be heard. People did not want to be passive when they realized what impacts a rapid transit system being built in their backyard might have. Local jurisdictions, suddenly confronted with the reality of bulldozers and steam shovels, were looking for quid pro quos. What could BARTD contribute to the betterment of a community in return for signed agreements adjudicating its presence? One engineer, who shall remain nameless, said the process was often one of out-and-out extortion. Just as often, the builders showed strong resistance.

While the BARTD staff was sensitive to community concerns, the consulting engineers were often pushing decisions without regard for cooperative community relations. In order to tackle a monster like the BARTD project, some thought, you had to be almost ruthless, with a single-minded approach. "If you acceded to every demand for alternatives, it would not only increase the cost but probably never get done," said Erland Tillman, one of the BARTD chief engineers from the early days. Still, several modifications, particularly to station designs, were agreed to by the consulting engineers and the District. Meanwhile, beginning in November 1963 with the lifting of the court's moratorium, the District began to acquire land in four counties. A total of 1,100 parcels would be purchased, including plots in San Mateo County for the Daly City Station. Much of the acreage was preexisting railroad rights-of-way.

ARCHITECTURAL FIRMS HIRED

Sixteen architectural firms were employed to design the planned thirty-three BART stations and four Muni stations. Three of the thirty-three stations planned were designed to serve the Market Street corridor at Montgomery Street, Powell Street, and the Civic Center. But soon a thirty-fourth station, at the Embarcadero—which had never been part of the original plan as outlined in the Composite Report—became a must for the city and the city's redevelopment agency. The germ of this idea began during San Francisco mayor John Shelley's term, and it eventually was promoted by Shelley's successor, Joseph Alioto. Identifying funding for such an addition would be a challenge, of course. Private concerns led by businessman Terrance Hill were beginning to tin-cup the business community and the city for seed money. Eventually the city put up a share of money to leverage a federal grant for the rest. The sticker price would be $38 million.

The Embarcadero Station would be the fourth station to serve the Market Street corridor. It would be close to the foot of Market Street, where Davis and Drumm Streets intersect, an area that was pretty much dead until the advent of BART. A primary reason for the push to get a station to serve this area was the concurrent development of the Golden Gateway Redevelopment Project on land that had been the home of San Francisco's venerable produce market and warehouses and an assortment of low-end businesses, including a shabby residential hotel. The redevelopment would include a complex of high-rise residential units, town houses, 45,000 square feet of commercial space, and a tennis club. The redevelopment area was located on the Embarcadero a short walk north from the foot of Market Street, and easy access to the new mass transit rail system was considered a must. The closest station in the original plan was at Montgomery Street, several blocks up Market, a position that was inadequate to handle the projected vibrant traffic flow to be generated by the new development. This once-dying part of town would become not only a major employment center but also a busy tourist hub, equal in commerce and traffic to the bustling Financial District a few blocks up.

FIRST CONSTRUCTION: THE TEST TRACK

Before construction could begin in the various communities, exactly 166 separate agreements had to be negotiated with various political jurisdictions, including special districts, railroad companies, and the Division of Highways. Each agreement had both a design and a financial impact on the original final plan. For example, the first agreement, for the construction of the 4.5-mile track between Concord and Walnut Creek, which came to be known as the Diablo Test Track, was not in the Composite Report. The agreement with Concord, Walnut Creek, and the county required the District to build two additional underpasses and a pedestrian overcrossing, also not included in the original plan, as well as extending a street for 1.25 miles that initially was supposed to be only two blocks long. Additionally, the agreement called for the replacement of a substandard road and a drainage ditch with a 72-foot-long storm pipe. All of these changes, of course, had cost factors that further eroded the construction budget. These situations became the rule rather than the exception as the project progressed. The lesson seemed to be that such agreements should have been resolved before costing out the final plan.

GROUND-BREAKING

On the gray, drizzly morning of June 19, 1964, President Lyndon B. Johnson stepped out of a helicopter in a field on the outskirts of Concord and happily presided over the very first ground-breaking for the new transit system. This festive occasion kicked off not only the construction of the 4.5-mile Diablo Test Track but the whole 75-mile project as well. The test track would eventually be incorporated into the Concord line. A large crowd of local dignitaries, BARTD staff and board members, local residents, and members of the secret service were in attendance. Joining President Johnson on the stand were Governor Edmund G. (Pat) Brown and BARTD board president Adrien Falk. BARTD general manager B. R. Stokes was also on hand to accompany the VIP guests. Following his introduction by Falk, President Johnson commended the "victory for vision" that BART represented. He went on to explain the important role mass transit must make in a modern world; total dependence on the automobile was no longer viable. When he finished, he was invited to push the plunger that set off a small charge of dynamite, signaling the start of a new era in rail rapid transit.

President Lyndon Johnson presides over the ground-breaking for the United States' first all-new rail transit system in more than sixty years. It was the beginning of a new chapter in the evolution of public transit.

Back in Washington, Johnson initiated the Urban Mass Transportation Act (UMTA) of 1964, a watershed bill for America's mass transit industry. Before this act was passed, no specific government department existed to assist transit operators with capital for projects that met federal guidelines. Since most transit systems in the early days were privately owned or operated, money for infrastructure from the government was not an option. Like the highway trust fund, UMTA, under the Department of Transportation, would be the mechanism for issuing most federal grants for mass transit projects across the nation. Some grants also came from the Department of Housing and Urban Development. As UMTA made its way though Congress, a Public Transit Employee Protection section was added as amendment 13(c). Under this amendment, transit operators and municipalities were required to be signatories to 13(c) in order to be eligible for federal money. The agreement protected union employees who worked for one agency but might be negatively impacted by a new agency or an expanding agency. An affected employee would have the right to transfer over to the new or expanding agency. This provision applied not only to union workers, such as drivers and agents at public agencies, but also to personnel from private operators, such as Peerless Stages and Greyhound. Years later, amendment 13(c) would have significant impacts on BARTD.

WORK BEGINS

Following the ground-breaking, the actual construction of the test track took about a year and was completed in April 1965. A linear slab of concrete along a completely refurbished bed replaced the old Sacramento Northern tracks. Bridges, grade crossings, and the overhead electrical system had been removed several years earlier, when passenger service stopped on the Sacramento Short, as it was called. Lightweight models were tested in a wind tunnel to determine that the final plan should call for a wider-gauge track: 5 feet, 6 inches instead of the standard 4 feet, 8.5 inches. The wide gauge would offer more stability for the lightweight transit cars being contemplated. The plan recommended that the cars have stainless steel or extruded aluminum bodies that would be much lighter than traditional transit cars and offer a higher efficiency in terms of electrical power consumption. Because of the often gusty northwesterly winds experienced in the Bay Area, stability for the lightweight trains was an issue.

The Diablo Test Track served as a laboratory for research and development. The goal was to advance the state of the art of key aspects of this all-new system. Every component was to be tested and measured, starting with traditional wooden ties as a benchmark for experimenting with concrete ties on a gravel bed. BARTD tested laying track directly on a concrete slab cushioned by hard rubber pads at close intervals. The pads promoted a smooth ride and helped reduce noise.

A major part of the research program was the lab cars. Three specially designed lab cars—A, B, and C—were built by the St. Louis Car Division of General Steel Industries.

Engineers began by testing potential power sources, such as three-phase alternating current at over 4,000 volts from a third rail. Eventually, 1,000-volt direct current, also from a third rail, was chosen.

A new kind of automatic train control would be a key component to the success of the new system. In order to find the best approach to meet performance standards and written specifications, four companies were invited to demonstrate their equipment and engineering

B. R. Stokes (lower left) and BART board members bolt down a section of the 4.5-mile Diablo Test Track in Contra Costa County in 1965. Board president Adrien Falk is standing in the center.

approaches. The companies were the Westinghouse Electric Corporation, General Electric, the General Railway Signal Company, and the Westinghouse Air Brake Company. Following more than one thousand hours of testing, all four companies in fact met BARTD's requirement. A fifth company, Philco, a subsidiary of the Ford Motor Company, provided special instrumentation that was used to measure the performance of each company's effort. All four companies eventually bid on the train-control contract, and Westinghouse Electric Corporation won with a low bid of $26 million.

Other items to be tested were the trucks that would support the transit cars—each with a 150-horsepower engine on each axle—and the propulsion system. After another rigorous testing, a "chopper" system proved to be the best bet. Because the voltage was "chopped" at incredibly high frequencies, it would provide smooth acceleration and deceleration.

Terry Sanders, a Westinghouse engineer and liaison with PBTB and BARTD, managed some of the early testing of the chopper propulsion system. "This was a project we had been working on for some time and believed it would be perfect for meeting BARTD's requirements," Sanders said. "In fact it was one of the major selling points Westinghouse had in being awarded the BARTD contract, in addition to coming in with the lowest bid. But early testing did not go well."

Sanders told the story of how he and a small crew were testing the chopper propulsion system prototype on a piece of unused track of the new Sea Beach line to Coney Island in Brooklyn. He and his crew worked out of the Coney Island shops of the New York Transit Authority and had the use of four transit vehicles borrowed from the transit line. "The actual propulsion testing was only conducted on one of the cars," he said. "During one of the tests, using two-car consists, we lost track of where the other two cars were. We came around a blind curve in the track, going about 30 miles an hour, and suddenly there they were, parked right in front of us. Someone yelled, 'Hit the deck, we're going to crash.' In the next instant we slammed into two parked transit cars, causing a great deal of damage. Luckily, no one was injured. But one of the cars we hit had been outfitted with the prototype propulsion system. We were certain we were all in big trouble. But, strangely enough, it was never investigated by the authorities.

Somehow the cars were repaired in the dead of night and no one was the wiser."

As for Sanders and his crew, they hightailed it back to Pittsburgh, Pennsylvania, to continue work on the new system. They redesigned it to get ready for further demonstrations on the BART test track out in California. In addition to producing smooth acceleration and deceleration, the chopper system also reclaimed about 15 percent of the electrical power through regenerative braking, feeding the power back into the third rail—another significant selling point.

CHAPTER 8

THE 1960S: VARIOUS ISSUES PLAGUE THE WORK

Without question, building this new transit system from the ground up raised more than a few concerns. Many critics—local, national, and academic—considered it an overly ambitious scheme. Some engineering experts voiced the opinion that this new system should use more of the old tried and true, that any machinery using more than 10 percent new technology was courting disaster. But the old tried and true, particularly in signaling systems, required more human involvement, and one of the goals of the project was to minimize the potential for human error where train operation and protection were concerned.

If this new transit system were going to be marketed as a premier space-age rail network, it would have to represent a quantum leap in the development of new technology. The BARTD board and staff, through their consulting engineers, were determined to advance the state of the art on several fronts. It was a bold policy. The eyes of the nation and other parts of the world were on this endeavor, and if it were successful, the BART system could be the template for a new era in modern mass transportation. For that reason, the test track project received a grant of $4.88 million from the federal Housing and Home Finance Agency (which later became the Department of Housing and Urban Development). The grant had been approved on the basis that significant information would come out of the test program that could be applied to future transportation systems.

The year 1964 marked not only the start of construction on the BART system, beginning with the Diablo Test Track, but also the launching of a new age of activism. If the 1950s had been the decade of innocence and the Man in the Gray Flannel Suit, by comparison the 1960s were like an erupting volcano as a new generation took hold and demanded a new social order on many fronts. The world was captivated by the civil rights movement in the deep South, the free speech movement radiating from the Berkeley campus of the University of California, the anti–Vietnam War demonstrations hitting the streets across the nation, and new health and environmental concerns, such as those described in Rachel Carson's *Silent Spring.* All shared center stage.

The new activism seeped into a wide spectrum of public policy debates and endeavors, including the building of the rapid transit system. Members of the public wanted more and more involvement in local decision making about BART's design and construction. This citizen input became a double-edged sword. On the one hand, much of the public input was positive in its contribution toward achieving an optimal end product. But changes to the original plan also added to the bottom-line cost. On top of that, the dollar was losing muscle as inflation began to creep higher than anticipated during the latter half of the 1960s. It jumped from the historical pattern of around 2.5 to 3 percent per annum to 5 and then 7 percent, eating away at each dollar's value. Legislative analyst A. Alan Post issued a report in September 1967 stating that, in the aggregate, inflation during the mid-1960s totaled about 25 percent.

Still, the BARTD board, to its credit, took the position that wherever possible it should accommodate local demands on route alignment and station location in individual communities. In preparing final engineering plans, which were based on the concepts outlined in the Composite Report, the board's policy was for the District and the joint-venture engineers (PBTB) to work closely with the cities, counties, and unincorporated communities that would be impacted by the new lines. As stated earlier, this policy often ended up in contentious gatherings during which plenty of acrimony filled the meeting halls before some final compromise was achieved. Joint-venture engineers, representing the project for BARTD, argued that some of the demands were unreasonable or would be detrimental to the project, while the affected communities negotiated for not only route alignments and station locations but also extra amenities such as pedestrian walkways or special landscaping, none of which were included in the original plan or accounted for in cost estimates. One result of all of this was an earlier-than-anticipated drawdown of available funds. However, as a practical matter, construction could not begin until formal agreements were signed off on by each community, a situation that gave them a certain amount of leverage in forcing BARTD to satisfy their demands. In Oakland, Mayor John Houlihan demanded that BARTD build its headquarters in Oakland in return for the city's agreement to allow tunneling and/or cut-and-cover construction where practical along the city's streets. BARTD agreed and purchased two square-block parcels bounded by Madison Street, Oak Street, and 7th and 9th Streets.

Agreements also had to be negotiated and signed with numerous other entities. Of the 166 agreements required, 34 were with railroads, 11 with the State Division of Highways, 96 with cities, 10 with counties, and 15 with special districts.

Overall the community input resulted in significant changes to the original plan for the 75-mile project, including the location of the critical Oakland Wye, the East Bay crossroads of the system. (A *wye* is a triangular junction of rail tracks.) Rerouting also took place along 15 miles, and sixteen of the thirty-three stations were to be relocated. (The thirty-fourth station was barely on the drawing board.) While these changes were necessary steps to obtaining the final agreements with the various communities, they carried substantial associated costs outside the budget.

"There is no question but that the changes demanded by the local communities contributed to the cost increases, along with inflation," B. R. Stokes said in a speech given in San Francisco in 1967. But he was not lamenting the changes to the original plan brought about by the local communities. "I believe it's a greatly improved project because of the changes," he said.

Using 1960 budget dollars as a cost basis, total additional expenditures beyond the Composite Report estimate, including increased engineering costs, were approximately $86 million. Other items that affected the increased cost included the design of the automated fare-collection system, which originally had been identified as a cash system only. It also required engineering and design work not contemplated before; the Composite Report had assumed that whichever company won the bid to manufacture the fare equipment would be responsible for developing its design and specifications. Another significant added expense was the retention of sixteen architectural firms to provide aesthetic designs and a modern look for station finishes and the system in general. The price tag was growing at every turn.

RAPID RAIL TRANSIT PERFECTLY TIMED

In hindsight, it becomes clear that, for various reasons, the development of the BARTD system could not have come to fruition any earlier or later than it did. Any earlier and broad support may not have been there. Any later and land availability along the established corridors the new lines planned to follow—including in the freeway medians—would have diminished. And inevitably the cost of such an ambitious project would have skyrocketed with inflation, making it a great deal more difficult to gain public approval.

Another plus in terms of the timing was the emerging issue of air quality. Management of air pollution was becoming one of the dominant social issues of the period, and it had moved to the forefront of public consciousness in the Bay Area. Tons of hydrocarbons were being dumped into the air each day as traffic congestion continued to worsen, particularly in places such as Los Angeles, where residents were regularly exposed to blankets of dense smog.

While industries took some of the blame, the primary focus was on the single-occupant automobile spewing carbon monoxide. Environmentalists were looking to BART to save the day. One question often asked by transit experts and critics was, would this new regional rail rapid transit system actually take existing cars off the streets and freeways? Or would it simply accommodate more growth in the suburbs as well as steal riders from already established bus systems? Only time would tell, but transit officials maintained that, once in place, mass rail transit would be a viable alternative mode of transport. Many survey respondents said they would leave their automobiles and at least try the new system, a result that suggested BART would enjoy a healthy patronage.

THE SAN FRANCISCO FREEWAY REVOLT

On May 17, 1964, just a month prior to the start of construction on the test track, San Francisco witnessed an angry freeway revolt. More than 200,000 people gathered in Golden Gate Park that day for a rally to protest any further work on the Embarcadero Freeway. The double-decker viaduct came off the Bay Bridge and ran along the Embarcadero, cutting off views of the bay and the venerable landmark Ferry Building. It had opened in 1959 but had not yet been completed; it ended with an exit ramp onto Broadway across from Pier 3. A project of the California Division of Highways, it was one branch of a series of arteries planned within the city to connect the peninsula to the south with the Golden Gate Bridge and Highway 101 to the north. The plan called for the Embarcadero segment to end at Doyle Drive, with access to the Golden Gate Bridge. To many, it looked like a brownish-gray behemoth, an eyesore of the first order. City Hall agreed that it was not in keeping with the aesthetics that San Francisco had always prided itself on, and in the end, the Embarcadero Freeway never went any farther than the stump that extended just beyond the Broadway exit. Twenty-five years later the Loma Prieta earthquake caused enough damage that the structure was deemed unsafe and Caltrans was forced to tear it down. The state wanted to rebuild it, but the city had other plans. Also, the city had adopted a "transit first" policy in 1973 that would guide future decisions involving city egress and ingress as well as intra-city traffic circulation.

In 1948, as the notion of a regional rail transit system first began to grow, San Francisco residents and elected officials protested the state's proposed Trafficways Plan. Like the postwar plan for Los Angeles, it called for a series of freeways cutting through the city in every direction. The protest called the proposed structures ugly and intrusive. Moreover, the planned freeway system would only attract more automobiles into the city from the growing suburbs. As the idea for a regional rail system took shape during the 1950s and early 1960s, it was viewed as a possible savior for the forty-seven-square-mile city, which was suffering from automobile congestion, particularly in its city center. Would BART be a panacea for solving all of the social ills of the city and the region? Some thought so. BART officials were always careful to state that the new system would help to balance the transportation challenges of the region and would most definitely contribute to air quality and energy efficiency. One thing was certain: the Freeway Revolt gave impetus to the advent of regional rail transit.

FIRST SUBWAY CONSTRUCTION BIDS

The PBTB joint venture had recruited the finest engineering talent available to work on the project, including both American engineers and engineers brought in from other parts of the world, all bringing special skills that could be applied to this giant public works project. PBTB's plan was to divide the system construction into manageable segments for the letting of contracts. The segments involved various types of construction: cut-and-cover, aerial, tunnel, at-grade, and the subaqueous tube.

Toward the end of 1965, the first contract was advertised for Phase One of the entire construction of the Oakland subway. (Phase One dealt only with the construction of very basic steel and concrete structures. Phase Two contracts were designed for more specific jobs, including detailed finish work in stations, the laying of track along raw structures, electrification, and so on.) The Oakland Phase One contract comprised the shells of three stations—the Lake Merritt Station at Oak Street and the 12th Street–Oakland City Center and 19th Street Stations, which would both be built under Broadway—plus the line of the approach-way between 24th Street and Broadway just north of downtown. The subway under Broadway, Oakland's main thoroughfare, comprised three tunnels, one at the bottom level and two at midlevel. What came to be known as the Oakland Wye was also part of the subway contract. The Wye involved a critical track configuration that would allow trains to switch at that juncture from east-west lines to north-south lines.

Earlier Phase One contracts had been either below or pretty much on target in terms of meeting the engineers' estimates, even though added costs, driven by community input, delays, and inflation, had affected the budget or not been budgeted at all. The result of this Phase One bid, however, presented BARTD with a major new crisis. District staff and PBTB project managers were alarmed not only because of this bid itself but because it could portend the outcome of future bids. And they were right to be worried.

BLACK FRIDAY: A SHOCKER

On Friday, December 3, 1965, only two bids for construction of the Oakland subway were received by the District. "And they were not pretty," as one staffer commented years later. Competition between major contractors at that time had been diminished because of the high demand of work associated with other projects and with the Vietnam War. The Composite Report in 1962 had estimated $26 million for this particular segment, but including inflation in the projected cost during final engineering brought the revised estimate to $49 million. The low bid from the Perini Corporation was for $61.5 million—an increase of 28 percent over the revised estimate and 135 percent over the original estimate. The high bid was for $70 million.

Both bids were rejected. PBTB scrambled to repackage the work into six smaller contracts, which in turn delayed construction on the Oakland subway section by several months. Breaking the project into six smaller segments allowed smaller firms, which had not been able to bid on the much larger segment as first advertised, the opportunity to bid. The bids for the six segments were opened in January 1966. Combined, they brought the total cost down to $47 million—$2 million under the revised estimate—which brought a sigh of relief to the BARTD board and staff.

Meanwhile, the City of Oakland demanded that a fourth station be added to the Oakland subway work to serve Jack London Square, which was being redeveloped. The city, together with the Port of Oakland, felt a rapid transit station at the foot of Broadway would enhance the marketability of the Square, which would be filled with shops, restaurants, and a hotel. After calculating the cost, and upon recommendations from the staff, the BARTD board turned down the request, noting that there simply wasn't enough money. Moreover, a station in that location would increase travel time between the East Bay and San Francisco.

FINANCIAL CRISIS LOOMS

As 1966 wore on, it became clear that the $792 million generated from the sale of bonds approved by the voters four years earlier would not be enough to complete the basic 75-mile project. At the time, 60 miles of the system were already under construction. While approximately $200 million in bonds had yet to be sold, the money from the sale was already committed. PBTB engineers were scrambling to reevaluate system construction costs against original estimates, and by the summer of 1966, the engineers had done a complete revision of cost estimates for building the system. The news was bad: cost overruns due to inflation and additions to the original scope of the project would result in a significant funding shortfall. Another $150 million would be needed to complete the system. By the end of 1966, yet another $50 million was added on to bring the total cost of construction, exclusive of the Transbay Tube, to $992 million. The Transbay Tube and approach-ways, which had originally been estimated to cost $133 million, were now estimated to come in at $180 million, bringing the total project cost to approximately $1.2 billion. The assumption was still that future revenue bonds could be used to purchase rolling stock. Even then, however, this new financial picture placed the BARTD board firmly on the horns of a dilemma.

Unless the District could find $150 million somewhere, it would be forced to truncate the system size and not build more than the 60 route miles already under construction. And this was only Phase One work. This new blow to the project generated a great deal of debate on the BARTD board. A 60-mile nonfunctioning system was not what had been promised to the voters. It would also negatively impact potential revenues, meaning the District could not sell revenue bonds to purchase transit cars. Imagine 60 miles of infrastructure just sitting there, without tracks or finished stations, collecting dust and bird droppings. Close observers believed a truncated project as described would be one of the country's all-time boondoggles, as public works projects went. Keeping in mind all the arguments, on September 8, 1966, the board, in a bold move, adopted a policy on long-range financing that said it would not accept anything less than the 75-mile system promised, and that everything possible should be done to secure the needed additional funding. B. R. Stokes was adamant that this was the only position for the board to take. He was optimistic that somehow they would come through this. "This will not be just another transit system," Stokes said. "Someday BART will become part of the fabric of life in the Bay Area for generations to come, and there is simply no way we are not going to give the people what they voted for."

Some early skeptics were worried that the lab car was a prototype of the train car, which obviously did not look very modern.

Meanwhile, an austerity approach was ordered to achieve savings where possible, without lowering the bar on standards. Aggressive cost-control measures were adopted. It was determined that unless more funding was secured, the project would reach the drop-dead point—at which work would have to stop—toward the end of 1968 or in early 1969. Meanwhile, work continued as if this looming abyss did not exist.

Several alternative sources of additional funding were explored. One possibility was to seek another bond issue, which would once again have to be approved by the voters. Could the three counties composing the District absorb the $150 million required? That would mean going back to the state legislature and requesting that the 15 percent cap be raised to 20 percent. But analysis showed that even if that approach was successful, it would generate less than half the amount needed, around $68 million. Federal funding and direct state funding were sought. Things looked dark.

The good news was that while a relentless lobbying effort was going on in Sacramento to come up with the money to save the system, the BARTD project was hailed for having an outstanding safety record. By 1968, 55 percent of the construction of the basic system, exclusive of the Transbay Tube, was complete. Work was continuing on all fronts of the transit system throughout the counties of Alameda, Contra Costa, and San Francisco, plus Daly City in San Mateo County. (The Daly

City Station would be the southern end of the San Francisco line.) Employment peaked at 7,000, with a payroll of $4 million per month. For maintaining a stellar, almost miraculous, safety record, especially given the size of the project, the District was honored on a national level. On a practical level, the District actually received rebates from its insurance carriers in the face of generally exploding insurance costs. No fatalities occurred during the years of the system's construction, in which 50 million man-hours were expended—a remarkable achievement.

Eventually a debate began in Sacramento about the possibility of making sure BARTD would complete the system. Legislators took into account the report on the transit district's financial woes from legislative analyst A. Alan Post and his office's analysis of the cause of the financial shortfall now facing the project. John F. Foran, who was then chair of the Assembly Transportation Committee, began pushing for a resolution in 1967. Three years later, the legislature, after much

In 1969, Governor Ronald Reagan signs the bill that provides the needed financing to complete construction of the system. Left to right are BART general counsel Wallace Kaapcke, BART board member William Reedy, general manager B. R. Stokes, board members Arnold Anderson and Harry Lange, government relations advisor Frank Chambers, and board president James Doherty.

wrangling, passed a bill to rescue the project. The bill gave BARTD the authority to raise $150 million through the sale of bonds guaranteed by a one-half-cent sales tax to be levied in the three counties making up the District. In a special ceremony in Sacramento, Governor Ronald Reagan signed the bill with some smiling BARTD directors and general manager B. R. Stokes looking on. The District would be able to complete construction of the system as originally planned, and other important components of the system could now move forward.

In 1967 the District received bids for 250 transit cars. The contract had been advertised only after which point BARTD could anticipate receiving the needed funding to complete the construction. The timetable for building the cars had to be meshed with the time frame for beginning operations, so BARTD had to hold off on pursuing transit car funding until the state legislature was ready to move forward. Because it took three years for the legislature to act, the bids were not opened until 1969, which of course meant inflation had once again taken its toll on the cost per unit. The initial estimate was for 250 cars at an average price of $153,000 each. By the time the winning bid was accepted, the price had gone up to $236,000 per car. (Today the price tag per car is about $2.2 million. Also, there are no longer any U.S. manufacturers of rail cars.)

Meanwhile, a fight that had been brewing for some time would come to a head in the late 1960s.

CHAPTER 9

REBELLION IN BERKELEY

In 1960 the city council of Berkeley passed a resolution calling for the BART line within the city to be all subway. PBTB, partially acceding to community pressure, redesigned the downtown segment, which originally had been planned as an elevated line slicing through the entire city from one end to the other along street medians. The new plan called for a short section of subway for about three quarters of a mile in the city center. Tracks would dip down at Shattuck Avenue and Derby, run under Shattuck to University, and curve west one block to Milvia Street, with a single subway station at Center and Shattuck. The rest of the aerial structure first envisioned would now extend from the southern Berkeley border to the downtown subway strip along Shattuck Avenue and reemerge to follow Hearst from Milvia Street, west to Sacramento Street, and then north toward Albany, El Cerrito, and Richmond. The Ashby Station at the southern end and the North Berkeley Station on Sacramento would also be elevated. All told, this plan still represented about 3 miles of elevated, or "aerial," line within the city boundaries. (BARTD had made a conscious public-relations determination not to use the word "elevated" when referring to track structures high above ground, but instead always referred to them as "aerial" lines or structures. One source said it was an attempt to distance the BART image from the old el systems in the East. After all, this was going to be a sleek, modern transportation system and the language should reflect that.)

The revision was incorporated into the Composite Report after several public hearings, and though some concern was voiced, no real dissension was shown regarding the planned elevated portions of the line. When the published Composite Report was distributed in the spring of 1962 to the seventeen incorporated cities and the supervisors of the three counties that the lines would be going through, there was virtually no pushback. PBTB engineers saw this lack of response as a clear path to final engineering and design. But nothing could have been further from the truth, as various communities suddenly woke up to the reality of what this "behemoth intrusion" would mean going through their backyards.

A NEW VOICE

In 1963 one man in Berkeley made it known that he was very unhappy with the plan as outlined in the Composite Report. His name was Wallace Johnson, the newly elected mayor of the city. (Johnson is to date the last Republican mayor to have been elected in Berkeley. At the time, the city council, now known for its predominantly liberal progressive politics, was mostly made up of conservative Republicans. When Johnson ran for reelection in 1967 his opponents would be Jerry Rubin, a leader of the Yippies; Peter Camejo, considered a Trotskyite; and Fred Huntley of the John Birch Society.)

A graduate of the California Institute of Technology with an engineering background, Johnson took a close look at the rapid transit plan for Berkeley and determined that putting just the central area under Shattuck Avenue underground was not good enough for his city. Johnson publicly denounced the planned aerial structures in the engineers' renderings as a potential eyesore, calling them "aesthetically unattractive." More important, he feared that the elevated tracks leading into and out of the city and the two elevated stations would divide the city psychologically along racial lines. The future route would run parallel to Grove Street (now Martin Luther King Jr. Way), an unofficial dividing line between predominantly white neighborhoods to the east and black neighborhoods to the west. Johnson also believed the elevated line would negatively impact businesses along the route. Under his leadership, public opinion coalesced behind the challenge to the BARTD plan.

Johnson began by appealing to the BARTD board and its consulting engineers to redesign the line through Berkeley as a subway from end to end, with all three stations underground. His appeal, which soon turned into a strong demand, fell on deaf ears. While the transit district board's policy was to work closely with local communities and make requested changes where possible, Berkeley's request was thought to be over the top. PBTB and the BARTD board, with recommendations by the staff, took the position that this would be a major and expensive change after the basic plan outlined in the Composite Report had seemingly been approved.

"There is not enough money," was the District's straightforward message back to Berkeley. "What the voters voted on is essentially what you get."

Berkeley, of course, was not exactly thrilled with the District's response. It was clear the agency and its consultant engineers were now locked into the plan as presented in the Composite Report. Johnson called this "a myopic viewpoint" of the BARTD organization. Thus began a protracted battle between Berkeley on one side and BARTD and the joint-venture engineers on the other that would last more than three years before a resolution was reached. Wally Johnson later wrote that the project was well into the gestation stage by that time, which meant that the train had almost left the station, metaphorically. The drama of how that resolution between the entities finally came about is a story unto itself.

As the battle moved into second gear in July 1963, the city officially requested that the BARTD staff and engineers submit the cost differences between aerial versus subway construction. City officials and staff wanted to see for themselves exactly what the transit district was talking about. How expensive would it be? Everything was put on hold, including final design work and land acquisition. Engineers went back to the drawing board, slide rules in hand, to come up with some calculations.

Berkeley had something in mind, though. With Wally Johnson leading the charge, a special committee was created to deal with the subway issue. It devised an alternative scheme to put the transit line underground through the entire city. Johnson and the committee's proposed plan called for the sale of tax allocation bonds. A portion of the proceeds, $6.2 million, would go toward making up the difference in cost between construction of a subway and construction of an aerial line. The committee hired its own engineering consultants. They, along with three council members, went to Toronto and Montreal (which were in the midst of building their own subways) to obtain some numbers firsthand. Based on information they got from transit officials in those cities, and since they did not yet have numbers from BARTD, the $6.2 million figure seemed reasonable. Another element of the plan called for the city to purchase the right-of-way using federal urban-renewal money. If the city were successful in obtaining such grants, it would then sell air rights to the properties. Berkeley planners believed that the properties' values would increase along the subway route, particularly in and around the stations. And tax increment funds would be generated to pay for putting the tracks underground.

On March 10, 1964, PBTB engineers representing the project on behalf of BARTD presented some figures they had worked up for cost differences. The cost submitted for subway construction was $10 million per mile for cut-and-cover construction, while the cost for an elevated structure was $2.5 million per mile, which was covered by the bond-issue money. Given the mileage involved, this meant that an estimated incremental cost of $21 million would be added for constructing a total subway line, plus $2.5 million each for the two stations, Ashby and North Berkeley. The Berkeley people were stunned. What's more, they didn't believe the figures. Their consultants had told them the cost per mile should be half of the BARTD figures, or about $5 million per mile.

Johnson demanded that the engineers attend a special meeting set for April 7, 1964, and bring with them all of the technical data used to support the estimate of $10 million per mile. The engineers arrived with briefcases bulging with reams of paper containing calculations. But when Johnson asked the project's chief engineer and estimator to give a breakdown of how he had arrived at his figures, the response was negative. Johnson later described the engineer's expression: "The chief estimator's eyes narrowed," he wrote. The engineer then said, in a characteristically terse style and raspy voice, "I don't think we have to explain to anyone how we arrived at our estimates." Seemingly insulted, he made it clear he didn't think he needed to provide backup data. Further, he pointed out that he was a professional engineer with many years of experience in estimating. His reputation was apparently that of a tough, top-notch engineer and a straight shooter. That April 7 meeting did not go much further. The encounter left an indelible impression on Johnson and some of his fellow city council members. Several meetings followed in which BARTD and the city remained steadfast in their respective positions concerning cost.

Johnson revved up the anti–aerial line campaign—which hovered very close to being an anti-BARTD campaign, though that was not its stated intention. At one point he personally paid to have scaffolding erected along sections of the route at both ends of the city where elevated structures were to be built. The scaffolding was roughly thirty feet high to approximate the height of the planned aerial structure, and its strong visual argument gained media and public attention as the conflict raged on. The Berkeley Citizens Committee, created to collect donations for a public information program to supplement the anti–aerial line campaign, managed to attract $14,000 in private donations, which paid for large signs that were strategically posted around the city, saying BURY THE BART TRACKS. The anti-aerial Citizens Committee paid for radio spots on local station KPFA. BARTD was getting anything but good press at this point.

Meanwhile, Johnson studied the San Francisco Bay Area Rapid Transit District Act as passed by the state legislature in 1957, looking for clues about how he might "get the elephant's attention." The enabling legislation was seventy-seven pages long. According to his later writings, Johnson found what he was looking for on page 25 of the act, in Chapter 6, article 5, section 29039. Paraphrasing, the section says that a municipality having territory located within the District may request a hearing before the District's board concerning any proposal for fixing the location of facilities by the District. In this case, thought Johnson, "fixing the location" could mean moving it from elevated to underground. What could be plainer! Adopting this interpretation, the City of Berkeley requested that a full-blown hearing take place on May 14, 1964. The BARTD board agreed to the request and set the hearing in the District's San Francisco meeting room at 814 Mission Street, a building that the BARTD organization shared with the PBTB joint venture.

Twenty separate sessions followed until, at a final hearing on August 14, Berkeley and the District were at an impasse over the numbers. The BARTD project engineers were now estimating that the cost to put the tracks underground, border to border, was in the range of $24 million to $30 million. Berkeley's estimate was $11 million. The sessions mostly involved dueling calculations and speeches by the attorneys for each side. Berkeley's numbers, which were less than half of the District's, were still based on information from the

Canadian systems in Toronto and Montreal, which were building subways at a cost of $5 million per mile. The acrimony greatly intensified over the course of the hearings, giving the media lots of grist for the mill, mostly unfavorable to BARTD. Local editorials were generally supportive of Berkeley's position and painted BARTD as being unaccountable, and the issue was now receiving national as well as local press. "This was sort of a David-against-Goliath thing," one reporter said to me a few years after the fact when discussing what had happened during the battle.

Berkeley's attorney thanked the District directors for the opportunity to hold a "public airing of the mysteries [with] which we contend the engineers for the Transit District have attempted to surround the building of this system." He went on to say that a great deal had been learned about the rules governing heavy construction of rapid transit subway lines and that there was really no mystery about it. The attorney for the city further stated that his goal in representing the city had simply been to find the truth, to find the facts that would then determine whether or not it was economically feasible for the citizens of Berkeley to pay the additional cost of an all-subway system within its borders. While he felt the attitude of the BARTD staff and its consulting engineers was that Berkeley was an interloper in this matter, Berkeley was, in fact, "a constituent part of the District" and had "the same stake as everyone else." The city's attorney went on to accuse the engineers of not wanting to be confused by facts: since their minds had been made up, they simply weren't interested in adjusting their figures, he said.

The attorney for BARTD noted that over the course of the hearings there had been thousands of pages of testimony, "scores of exhibits and many tedious days spent considering this matter." He described the arguments as an absurdly simple matter. "Never have so many listened so long to so little," he said. He reiterated that the Composite Report had been approved by the electorate and that it did not contemplate a subway throughout the city as part of the plan. The city was being labeled as a "Johnny-come-lately" in suddenly deciding on a dramatic change to the plan after the electorate had approved it. Therefore the District had no obligation, legal or moral, to construct an all-subway system through Berkeley. However, a resolution passed by the city on May 5, 1964, had authorized the city to spend $6.5 million to purchase the right-of-way through the city, which was the estimated cost budgeted by the District for the property. The attorney for BARTD noted that "even if we were to construe that this was a commitment on the part of Berkeley to pick up the tab for those property acquisitions' costs, then the District could commit no more than an equal amount—$6.5 million of its own money—toward an all-subway line." The implication being, of course, that it would not be enough, given the District's stated costs. He went on to say that the right-of-way resolution was not a true commitment on the part of Berkeley and accused the city of juggling figures to reach the lower costs for subway construction it had put forth during the hearings. The transit district's attorney closed by saying that it was clear the citizens of Berkeley would not and could not commit to paying the actual costs of putting the system underground—that is, the cost according to the BARTD engineers. Further, the rest of the Bay Area taxpayers could not be expected to subsidize Berkeley to the tune of millions of dollars.

Having the last word in the final hearing, the attorney representing Berkeley called on the BARTD board not to be "slaves to the engineers and staff and make its decision based on its good judgment." He said that in fact the city had made a case that clearly established that "we will be able to finance this proposal." Further, the costs would be within a range that the city would be able to provide.

On September 11, 1964, the BARTD board decided unanimously to reject Berkeley's attempts to get the District to construct a subway all the way through the city. While the District agreed that underground tracks would be preferable, there was simply no money for it. At issue now was the threat of any continued delay in moving forward. Every day added cost. The BARTD board gave Berkeley an ultimatum: come up with the difference in funding a subway versus the planned aerial line or step back, because construction would begin. The city was given thirty days.

However, the door was left open for continued negotiations behind the scenes. Talks went on for several weeks, primarily between Johnson and BARTD president Adrien Falk. On October 22, the two men announced an agreement that called for BARTD to advertise for two sets of bids. One bid would be for construction of the aerial line in four parts of the city as planned. The other would be for subway extensions from the north and south ends of the central part of the city. This agreement would both settle the argument over the difference between the numbers once and for all by offering actual costs and also allow time for Berkeley to arrange for the needed financing. Both the city and BARTD agreed to abide by the results.

The District's engineers estimated $25 million based on very preliminary bids received. Wally Johnson managed to get his council's approval to create a separate district within the BART District for the purpose of holding a special election to put a bond issue on the ballot. They created Special District No. 1. Voters within the city boundaries would have to approve the sale of $20.4 million in tax-exempt bonds. The difference in cost, if the District's estimate was correct, would come from an already approved federal HUD grant.

Amazingly, on October 4, 1966, Berkeley voters approved the measure with an 80 percent majority. In May 1968 the final bids came in for the difference between what had been budgeted for an elevated line and the construction of a subway. The low bid was $12.4 million, about $2.4 more than the city had originally

Controversy over BART's planned aerial line through Berkeley ends with the city residents voting to tax themselves to put the line underground. Board president Adrien Falk and general manager Stokes were often referred to as Batman and Robin.

estimated. But it was close enough to offer some vindication. One of the deals the city made with BARTD during right-of-way acquisition was an exchange of land along the Hearst strip in return for air rights over the Ashby Station property. Again, Wally Johnson was the architect of the deal; he believed the air rights would be very valuable to the city some time in the future. In an ironic twist in this part of the BART story, Wally Johnson was appointed to the transit district's board of directors in 1966.

A NEW WRINKLE FROM BERKELEY

A new chapter of disagreement between BARTD and the city of Berkeley soon began. The Ashby Station, in agreement with the city and the council, was still planned to be constructed partially above ground, as was the station in North Berkeley, while the tracks would be underground. In the meantime, around December 1967, a Berkeley city councilman by the name of Ronald V. Dellums demanded that the Ashby Station be built underground as part of BARTD's agreement with the city. The proposed design of the station called for a 700-foot-long, 5-foot-high surface skylight. The idea was to provide natural light for the underground station, even though it would create a barrier above ground. When BARTD refused to change the design, Dellums, leading a citizens' revolt, took the matter to court, arguing that the people of Berkeley were paying for an entirely underground system. The matter went before Alameda County superior court judge Robert Bostick, who ordered a halt to any further work on that station until a decision had been rendered. Almost at the same time as the receipt of the bids, the court in May 1968 found in favor of the plaintiff and ordered the station to be built underground. The BARTD engineers estimated that it would cost another $2.5 million to build the redesigned station, a cost that would be absorbed by the bond money generated from Special District No. 1. Dellums went on to represent Berkeley and Oakland in Congress for twenty-seven years.

Many years later, around mid-1978, the Ashby Station would be at the center of another controversy involving a weekend flea market. The flea market, run by Community Services United (CSU), needed a new home for its vendors and made a deal with BART real estate to lease the station parking lot until the system's weekend service began. The system's board approved the lease agreement, with the caveat that the market would have to find a permanent home elsewhere when the station opened for Saturday and Sunday service. However, when the time came to vacate, the Berkeley Flea Market management contended that a staff member had indicated that they could probably stay there indefinitely. The staff member denied this, indicating there had been a misunderstanding; it turned into a "he said–she said" situation. BART attorneys argued that only the board could approve an extended lease with CSU. The issue garnered a great deal of media attention and it, too, went to court. Newly elected municipal judge Julie Conger found in favor of CSU and ordered that the flea market could stay. The market continues to thrive today, with more than 150 vendors organized in rows at the northern end of the parking lot. Music from various musicians floats through the colorful scene providing a festive atmosphere. The flea market has become a very popular destination, not only for locals but also for people from all over the Bay Area. And, of course, many get there on BART.

CHAPTER 10

THE RIPPLE EFFECT FROM BERKELEY

The rumblings in Berkeley, the epicenter of discord over the District's original intent, were well observed by officials and citizens across the planned BARTD spectrum; the protracted conflict between BARTD and the city had a wide and lasting ripple effect. Negotiating agreements with all of the stakeholders—various cities, the three counties, and the Division of Highways—was often an exercise in frustration for the planners and engineers, and it always added time and cost to the project. The affected communities were probably no less frustrated as they sought reasonable compromise solutions for their issues.

"We have relocated fifteen of the thirty-three planned BARTD stations," B. R. Stokes said in a 1967 speech before the Commonwealth Club of San Francisco. He noted that the $792 million bond issue had built in 10 percent for contingencies and factored in 20 percent for inflation. "These are extraordinary times," Stokes said. "By the end of last year, 1966, skyrocketing inflation had already eaten up our inflation cushion." Still, most, including Stokes, would agree that, in the long run, the changes resulting from noncomplacent local officials and citizens offered optimal improvements over the original plan outlined in the Composite Report. Sixteen architectural firms from around the three-county District were employed to design the stations and make changes to conform to local community standards and aesthetics.

One inverse example of change was the controversy over the City of Richmond's reluctance to let BARTD relocate the station and route in that city. The original plan in the Composite Report had called for

Workers lay track on the Berkeley/Oakland line during the late 1960s.

locating the station at 6th and Macdonald, west of downtown. The BARTD engineers later changed their minds and decided the station should be sited at 16th and Nevin, east of downtown along the Southern Pacific route, a better position should the line be extended in the future. One document claimed that the change of location was actually at the city's request, but further investigation showed otherwise. The BARTD request caused divisiveness between city officials, with the city council split almost evenly over the issue. BARTD reached an agreement with the city in May 1967, and the Richmond Station was relocated to 16th and Nevin. The plan then called for the line to extend into a critical maintenance and storage yard that would serve the Richmond line. But a major consequence of the relocation negotiation was that it delayed construction of the storage yard, which was to be used for testing in conjunction with the line. Abandoning this plan in turn delayed design and construction of the southern Alameda line.

Meanwhile, the Richmond line through Berkeley was altered to emerge from underground north of the Sacramento Station (now the North Berkeley Station). From this point on it was to be an aerial structure through Albany and El Cerrito all the way to Richmond.

It was believed that the Richmond line would share the Southern Pacific right-of-way on the west side of the Atchison, Topeka and Santa Fe. (Amtrak and the Capitol Corridor trains now use those tracks.) Since the tracks run right alongside where the Richmond

Station was now going to be located, a cross-platform transfer connection was added to the design. The Composite Report and final engineering record identified two stations along the way, one located in Albany and the other in El Cerrito, the latter to be the El Cerrito del Norte Station. Later the City of Albany expressed concern about the route alignment and the station location, which city officials believed would negatively affect the city's already skimpy tax base. The station and parking would require a large piece of land that would come off the city tax rolls. Further negotiations led to an agreement between the parties that the route alignment would remain the same but the station would be relocated farther north, to become the El Cerrito Plaza Station.

TWO KEY CONSULTANTS SUDDENLY QUIT

In September 1966, a festering conflict finally erupted when two prominent landscape architects and urban design consultants, Lawrence Halprin and Donn Emmons, abruptly quit the project. Both men, both highly esteemed in their fields, took strong issue with what they described as the overbearing management of the PBTB engineers. The two consultants claimed interference continually constrained their efforts to enhance station and system design, the job they were brought on to do. The conflict was heralded by the press as a new major controversy that once again focused on the question of who was running the show; the media in general was highly critical of the relationship between the District and the consulting engineers. As a result, the buffer zone that had limited access of contractors to the BARTD staff and general manager B. R. Stokes was softened considerably. Subcontractors in certain instances would now have direct access to Stokes and, when appropriate, to the board as a court of last resort.

One effect of the lawsuit that challenged the validity of the 1962 election that approved the BART project was that it threw off the timing for some segments of the project that corresponded with other work. A significant instance concerned the Grove-Shafter Freeway project. On July 20, 1960, the California State Legislature had approved a plan for BARTD to construct its Oakland-Berkeley line in the planned freeway median. While the moratorium on the transit project's work was in force, the California Division of Highways was busy moving ahead designing the complex freeway interchange without BARTD. Once the rail project had the go-ahead, BARTD had to negotiate with the Division of Highways. Luckily the window of opportunity was still open, but in the end, the Grove-Shafter project had to be redesigned at the transit district's expense. It was one of the most critical route alignments, in which the MacArthur Station, the East Bay's primary transfer hub, would be located. The station, situated between 40th and MacArthur and between Telegraph and Grove (now Martin Luther King Jr. Way) is now one of the most utilized stations on the system. Meanwhile, the MacArthur Freeway median for a southern rail route was now too far along to include the transit system. Instead the line would use the Southern Pacific right-of-way parallel to Interstate 880, the Nimitz Freeway.

CONSTRUCTION MOVES AHEAD

By this time, 1967, Phase One construction was moving well ahead in Oakland on a revised schedule. The method of cut-and-cover construction was employed along Broadway through downtown, and in addition to the subway line, great subterranean vaults at 12th Street and 19th Street were dug out for three levels: a concourse and two track levels. As with all of the system's stations, the platforms were 700 feet in length to accommodate ten-car trains.

A third platform and tunnel was also included in the construction of the two downtown Oakland stations. Due to lack of funds, the third tunnel was left as an unfinished concrete tube and closed off until the mid-1980s, when an omnibus federal grant for $500 million made it possible to finish the tunnel, which provided a critical enhancement to the overall system operation, primarily in terms of flexibility.

Under that same federal grant, BART built a maintenance facility and storage yard in Daly City, which also added to the system's operating flexibility. Opposition to the construction of this yard came from Contra Costa BART director Nello Bianco, who believed it was the "camel's nose under the tent." In other words, he suspected the Daly City project was in reality a sneaky prelude to building an extension to San Francisco International Airport. Throughout his tenure on the board, Bianco was a strong advocate for BART to meet its commitment to building East Bay extensions before considering a line to the San Francisco airport. What was particularly galling for Contra Costa officials and Dean Lesher's *Contra Costa Times* was that an airport extension would also benefit San Mateo County, which had not put a dime into building the system. BART directors from San Francisco were, of course, very much in favor of an extension to serve the airport. A political solution would eventually have to be found, but it would be several years before the actual extensions could become a reality.

BART'S NEW HEADQUARTERS BUILDING

A third Oakland subway station, Lake Merritt, located at 8th and Oak Streets, was dug out for two levels. It was part of a complex that would include an underground control center, reminiscent of Houston's NASA Space Center, for the 71.5-mile BART portion of the 75-mile project. BART's new headquarters would rise five stories above the station at 800 Madison Street. However, the staff would not move from its San Francisco location at 814 Mission Street until January 1972, when it was ready for occupancy. Adjacent to the station's concourse would be a belowground open-air plaza complete with a large fountain and pond.

System-wide, Phase Two contracts were let to various contractors for the finish work in each of the raw boxes that would house the stations and subways. The work included the laying of tracks;

BART's central control room looks like something out of a science-fiction film. Here, train controllers monitor the movement of all trains on the system and stay in contact with train operators. Other functions include control of public address announcements, the visual checking of station platforms, the electrification of the 1000-volt DC third rail, and emergency response.

electrification; installing escalators, arrays of fare gates, fare vending machines, booths for station agents, and marble or ceramic bricks in some stations; and completing assorted other checklist items. The original plan and funding estimates did not include curb cuts, the installation of elevators at all stations, and other features designed to accommodate the disabled.

ACCESS FOR THE DISABLED

To date no public transit system in the nation's history, and perhaps around the globe, had ever provided full access for the disabled. The issue had always remained just below the surface of social consciousness, for not just public transit agencies but also public and private buildings, most of which were largely inaccessible for the disabled without special assistance.

One man in the San Francisco Bay Area was determined to bring the issue into the open as he became aware of this new modern mass transportation system. He knew, after some investigation, that the design of the system did not include full access for the disabled. The issue had simply not been considered. He believed that it was still early enough in the evolution of the BART project to include a design fix, but he also knew that getting the powers that be on board for such a change was not going to be easy.

His name was Harold L. Willson, and he envisioned a lofty goal: a time when architectural barriers would be a thing of the past and wheelchair-bound people and nonambulatory seniors would be able to access the world without special help, when they could live their lives in an independent fashion and be on a par with society in general. Willson possessed not only a hardened determination but also an engaging charm; he could be incredibly persuasive. His road to that point, however, had not been an easy one.

Willson was born on May 13, 1926, in Oak Hill, West Virginia. In early 1946, when he was almost twenty, he began working in the West Virginia coal mines. Two short years later, Willson was the victim of a mine disaster, an explosion and partial cave-in that left him paralyzed from the waist down. John L. Lewis, at the time the head of the Coal Miners Union, took a special interest in Willson's plight and arranged for his long-term treatment with the help of Edgar Kaiser, head of Kaiser Industries. Following his initial hospital care, Willson was transported to the Kaiser Foundation Rehabilitation Center in Vallejo, California, where he received physical therapy and learned to use a wheelchair. Eventually he got a job with the Bank of America while at the same time putting himself through business school at Golden Gate College (now Golden Gate University). Later he went to work as an accountant with the Kaiser Foundation Medical Care Program.

In the early1960s Willson began a campaign to create awareness that BARTD should consider providing access for the disabled. He became the chairman of the Architectural Barriers Committee of the Easter Seal Society for Crippled Children and Adults of Alameda and Contra Costa Counties. Willson wrote letters, met with staff, and resolutely pushed the transit district to be among the first to be 100 percent accessible. "You could be a pioneer in being the first major public transportation system to be accessible to the handicapped," Willson told the staff and the board as early as 1963. He said that if the District adopted the plan as it was, it would exclude 4 percent of the population in its service area.

At first he was met with strong resistance. Given the funding issues the project was already facing, the idea of adding elevators seemed simply impossible; the answer was always "no money." Still, the BARTD board accepted Willson as a volunteer consultant on the issue of how to serve people with mobility problems.

A TENACIOUS WILLSON REFUSES TO GIVE UP

Willson formed a multipronged strategy. First and foremost he felt that endorsements of support from high-profile organizations that were devoted to the welfare of the disabled and elderly were paramount. He met with officials from numerous such organizations to enlist the needed support. Once endorsements were obtained, a letter-writing campaign was the next step. Letters in support of removing architectural barriers from the new transit system were sent to BART directors, staff, consulting engineers, and the state legislature. The essence of the letters was that disabled people, representing a specific segment of society, should not continue to be shut out. While the goal was to take the fight directly to BARTD and the state without involving the media, the campaign nevertheless attracted press coverage.

Willson also sought support from mainstream society. He gave numerous talks, mostly in the evenings on his own time, to service

Harold Willson, a pioneer of access to public facilities for the disabled community, called for the removal of architectural barriers that would hinder the ability to use BART. His efforts during the system's construction led to elevators in all stations, and ultimately became a national movement.

organizations, churches, and professional groups around the Bay Area. His primary goal was to get the BARTD board to adopt a policy to make it possible to add elevators from street level to platform level in the future if funds were not provided in the near term.

In 1965, Willson saw his first major success. The BARTD board adopted a construction policy that opened the door for future accessibility for the disabled and directed that engineering and construction cost estimates be worked up for the design change for all stations to include elevators. Three years later, on February 29, 1968, the board adopted a policy to communicate to all concerned that the engineers had estimated that the additional cost to provide elevators in all stations would be $5 to $7 million, a figure later revised to $10 million. Further, the board said that the state legislature was to be notified that the transit district would be willing to include elevators if funding were made available. Willson had achieved a significant step in the right direction, although securing needed funding was still a daunting challenge.

The coalition of organizations led by Willson and the Architectural Barriers Committee of the Easter Seal Society then focused its efforts on persuading the state legislature. The legislature finally came through with Assembly Bill No. 7, chapter 261, which was signed into law by Governor Ronald Reagan on June 6, 1968. The bill was sweeping in its intent, to wit: "It is the purpose of this chapter to ensure that buildings and facilities, constructed in the state by use of state, county or municipal funds, or funds of any political subdivision of the state, adhere to the American Standards Association specifications A 117.1-1961 for making buildings and facilities accessible to, and useable by, the physically handicapped." Shortly after that the state authorized $10 million to be granted to BARTD to include facilities for the disabled, including telephones in elevators, toilets designed to accommodate persons in wheelchairs, special service gates to the stations, special handrails, and closed-circuit television where needed.

While Harold Willson was actively pursuing the lifting of barriers to the disabled, others took up the cause as well. During the mid-1960s a Committee for the Rights of the Disabled, working with the organization East Oakland Parish, was also active in trying to get BARTD to install elevators. Their slogan was "BART, give us the shaft," according to Barbara Walsh Yoder, one of the organizers of the group. She said they passed out leaflets and went door to door, primarily in East Oakland neighborhoods, to inform residents and promote the concept of access for the disabled on the new transit system. According to one source, some proponents for the disabled lay down in front of bulldozers to make their point.

U.S. SENATE COMMITTEE HOLDS A HEARING IN WASHINGTON

On October 20, 1971, Harold Willson and Wilmot R. McCutchen, an engineer and chief of design for BARTD, testified before a special U.S. Senate Committee on Aging. The purpose of the hearing was to explore "A Barrier Free Environment for the Elderly and the Handicapped." Senator Frank Church, a Democrat from Idaho, chaired the committee and presided over the hearing. Willson, as the first witness, gave a glowing review of what had been accomplished at BART and credited the transit district with overwhelming support and cooperation. "I believe the staff and the board of directors are very proud of the fact that the BART system is the first, not only in advancing technology, but first to be 100 percent accessible to the disabled and people with severe mobility problems." McCutchen acknowledged that facilities for the disabled had not been in the original plan and had not been a part of the District's concern before Mr. Willson's many presentations. The state provided the additional funding needed to install elevators in BART's thirty-four stations (including the added Embarcadero Station) and the four Muni stations that were part of the overall 75-mile project. Following the BART template, the new Washington Metropolitan Area Transit Authority (WMATA) and the Metropolitan Atlanta Rapid Transit Authority (MARTA), the first new systems to be developed after BART, made their systems accessible for the disabled. When Senator Church asked McCutchen how much federal contributions to the project had been compared with the total cost, he answered $166 million versus $1.6 billion overall, or about 10 percent. New systems coming along, however, would be getting up to 75 percent federal assistance under the Urban Mass Transportation Act, thus reducing the pressure on local taxpayers. "I guess BART was too early," McCutchen said.

In the final analysis, the Senate committee hearing was an important precursor to raising public consciousness of the issue of disabled access. In the years that followed, a disabled rights movement emerged across the country. Militant groups targeted the American Public Transit Association, which represented both bus and rail systems throughout North America. Their protests led to federal legislation: the Americans with Disabilities Act (ADA), signed into law on July 26, 1990.

THE LONG-TERM IMPACT OF MOVING THE OAKLAND WYE

Once BARTD had reached an agreement with Oakland mayor John Houlihan and the city over the location of the critical underground wye track configuration, it was nuts-and-bolts work. But getting the agreement BARTD wanted was not going to happen. The underground wye in Oakland was where three lines converged: the Richmond–Fremont line, the Concord–Daly City line, and the Fremont–San Francisco line. The original location of one leg of the wye was to be under 8th Street, but construction there would have required razing the very popular Simon's Hardware Store, which at the time was the premier hardware store in the city. According to owner Aaron Simon, the store was grossing anywhere from $9 to $10 million a year in sales. Because the original planned location offered a wider track radius, BART was willing to pay to relocate the store, and although Simon was agreeable to a change in location, Mayor

Houlihan did not want to see the store moved and insisted that the line be relocated instead. Since Houlihan was generally an important supporter of the transit project, the BARTD board did not want to proceed against his wishes. The new alignment spared the hardware store but did create a tighter turning radius, meaning that to negotiate the sharpness of the curves, the trains would have to travel at much lower speeds than originally planned: no more than 25 miles an hour through the juncture. Another result in the years ahead would be the screaming sound of wheel flanges scraping the rail as trains rounded the curve.

Ironically, a few short years later Simon's Hardware Store declared bankruptcy. In 1966 Mayor Houlihan, by then a member of the BARTD board, abruptly resigned his office. He was charged with and convicted of embezzlement involving an estate he was handling as a lawyer; he went to prison for two years. After making restitution, he was later pardoned by Governor Reagan.

The next phase involved the most challenging aspects of the project's construction.

CHAPTER 11

THE TUNNEL AND THE TUBE

THE BERKELEY HILLS TUNNEL

In November 1964, excavation began on the Berkeley Hills Tunnel, which would carry trains in and out of the burgeoning suburban communities of the East Bay's Contra Costa County. The tunnel would consist of a double bore, with each bore 18 to 22 feet in diameter with approximately 50 feet of separation between the bores. Pedestrian and maintenance tunnels would connect the bores every 1,000 feet.

Shea-Kaiser-Macco was the joint-venture contractor. The hill, consisting mostly of hard rock, presented the construction crews with an arduous task, which some said would be the toughest job of the project, second maybe to the building of the Transbay Tube. With each bore 3.2 miles in length, making 6.4 miles of total tunneling, the challenge seemed to many onlookers to be almost insurmountable. Nevertheless, the crews were going to get it done. When completed, the Berkeley Hills Tunnel would be the fourth-longest vehicular tunnel in the world. Adding to the challenge, the tunnel would cross the Hayward Fault, and geologists said the tunnel workers would have to deal with almost twenty different kinds of "tipsy-turvy strata," each requiring a different method for penetration.

Despite the resistance from the hill's formations and general make-up—as if the very earth did not want to give way to the invading machinery and dynamite—progress was steady. The crews digging from each side had a pool going as to which one would break through first. At 4 A.M. on February 24, 1967, the west-side crew broke through. At 10 A.M. BART held a ceremony to commemorate the event. Board members, staff, guests, and the press were invited to ride into one of the tunnel bores to mark this symbol of progress. Almost seven more years would pass before a passenger train would swish through the Berkeley Hills Tunnel between Oakland and Berkeley and Contra Costa County.

BUILDING THE TRANSBAY TUBE

The most intriguing and incredibly challenging component of the BARTD project was, of course, its world-famous Transbay Tube. Though it constituted the very heart and most important segment of the system, it would also be the most treacherous of the project's endeavors. Although tubes had been constructed in other parts of the world, none compared to the ambitious scope of the one that Parsons Brinckerhoff–Tudor–Bechtel was about to build for BARTD.

Six years of design and preparation preceded the undertaking. That work had been done by the engineering team made up of Parsons Brinckerhoff Quade & Douglas, the New York firm that formed part of the PBTB partnership. The team was led by renowned engineer Walter Douglas, who had a long history with the project going back to the 1950s. The tube would stretch 3.6 miles, the longest and at points the deepest vehicular tube in the world, and one of the most ambitious such projects in history. Completion of the tube was under a very demanding two-and-a-half-year schedule.

A little-known fact about the Transbay Tube was that its placement across the San Francisco Bay had to be formally approved by the federal government. Even though it had been recommended by the Joint Army-Navy Board report in 1947, its construction was not a foregone conclusion, though no one expected there to be any problem. Congress had to pass a bill authorizing it because it would cross navigational waters that came under the jurisdiction of the navy and the coast guard and thus was of national interest. On February 20, 1960, that permission was officially granted when President Dwight D. Eisenhower signed the bill allowing construction of the proposed tube to go forward.

Even before federal approval, planning had begun on this most challenging of all of the project's elements. PBTB had begun looking at the seismic issues that might be involved in the tube's design. Stretching from the Oakland Mole, curving south of Yerba Buena Island, and ending at the San Francisco Ferry Building, the tube would be the key link of the rapid transit system. Without the tube and the ability to build it, it is doubtful BART would have ever come into existence.

When the Oakland and San Francisco approach-ways were added, it would be 6 miles in length total. Interestingly, the alignment and profile of the tube followed the same route and alignment of General George Goethals's proposed plan back on October 17, 1920. One wonders if it would have actually been possible back then to build such a tube as Goethals had proposed.

In 1959, PBTB hired Converse Consultants, experts in seismic analysis, who performed examinations of soil data, geologic surveys, and the history of temblors in the area. While the planned route of the tube did not cross any active faults, engineers wanted to build certain design features into its structure that would make it resilient to any ancillary activity. From 1960 to 1966 several geophones were placed in the bay to record vibration differences between overlying alluvial deposits and rock formations and possible earthquake vibrations. Mild tremors that took place during that period provided important data that was then fed into the design process. A key feature to come out of the almost six years of study called for placing the tube in a deep trench on a soft alluvial mud bed with a layer of gravel to cushion it against any residual shock waves from the San Andreas or Hayward Faults. With this in mind, PBTB engineers in 1964 set about preparing the full-scale design of the tube by creating a scale model of certain sections. Another important design feature to add to the tube's resilience during any temblors was the inclusion of flexible joints at each end of the tube to allow it to move several inches vertically and horizontally.

In December 1965, the first bids for the tube came in, again higher than estimated by the Composite Report, even accounting for normal inflation. The bid price for Phase One came in at $90 million, a 51 percent increase from the $59 million estimated. The final engineer's estimate, however, was $82 million, somewhat closer to the actual bid. Other costs included $90 million for ventilation caissons at each end, 2 miles of aerial structures as part of the West Oakland approach, and a quarter of a mile of subway approach from the Embarcadero in San Francisco, plus final finish work and electrification. The overall price tag for all elements of the tube and approaches came out to $180 million. (In 2002 the Metropolitan Transportation Commission estimated that a new tube would cost from $7.1 to $10.3 billion.) Since this part of the rapid transit project was being funded by bridge toll–backed bonds, the cost did not add to the transit district's financial woes. In April 1966, the initial $90 million contract was awarded to Trans-Bay Constructors, a joint venture made up of Peter Kiewit Sons, Raymond International, Tidewater Construction, and Healy-Tibbitts Construction. Together, these companies brought a great deal of experience in underwater excavation and construction, although on nothing as vast and complex as the Transbay Tube.

The tube project would be done in several operational phases. In mid-1966, Phase One of the tube construction began with a ceremonial first scoop of the bay floor. This was not your typical ground-breaking, with shovels in the dirt and the cutting of a ribbon to mark the event. The dripping spoil was brought up by the giant steel jaws of a clamshell dredge, hanging from and manipulated by heavy cables from a tall crane anchored to a barge. Invited guests, dignitaries, and BARTD officials looked on and cheered from the decks of a nearby chartered ferry boat as the dredge broke water. That was the beginning of an incredible journey that would take the next three years to complete, only six months beyond the optimal schedule.

Digging out the trench took just about a year to finish, and precision was a formidable challenge, in part because the line had to have two horizontal and six vertical changes in direction. One aspect of digging the trench was, at the time, like something out of a science fiction story. Surveyors used seven laser beams, placed at fixed points on each side of the bay, to guide the dredging barges along the adopted alignment. The laser beams were left on night and day and could be seen from as far away as 5 miles. Fog was the enemy of this method of alignment, but luckily it had minimal effect on the timetable. Using the laser beams as plumb lines for the trench and tube alignment was a significant innovation. They had never been used in that manner before, and they helped to achieve pinpoint accuracy. A sextant was also used to measure the distance between the laser and a blinker set on the eastern shore. The whole setup used 125 watts of power.

During the course of the work the dredge took out roughly 5.7 million cubic yards of mud and silt from the bottom of the bay. The spoils for the most part were taken out to sea and dumped beyond the Farallon Islands. Specifications called for the trench to have a 60-foot-wide floor, with sloping walls that cut from 30 to 90 feet deep into the bottom of the bay. The depth of the trench's floor ranged from 75 feet near the shorelines to 135 feet at its deepest point.

Once the basic digging of the trench was completed, it was time for Phase Two. This work consisted of placing a 2-foot layer of "3-inch minus gravel" bedding from one end of the trench to the other on the soft mud bottom. Just this portion of the work alone was no mean feat. An ingenious specially screened barge was designed specifically for a transbay contractor to do the job. It was 240 feet in length, 85 feet wide, and rose more than 40 feet on large pontoons. Gravel was poured into three separate hoppers and then shot below the water through a series of pipes. A traveling bridge moved this massive machinery the length of the barge to evenly distribute the gravel in the trench. Another specially designed device, called a box screed, leveled the gravel.

THE TUBE ITSELF IS BUILT AND PLACED

Meanwhile, work had also begun on Phase Three of the tube project: manufacturing the shells of the tube itself. Fifty-seven prefabricated individual sections would be built, and each section was numbered to mark its designated place in the cross-bay alignment, which totaled 19,113 feet. Specifications called for each section to be on average about 330 feet in length, or longer than a football field, and 48 feet wide and 24 feet high, with a double bore, each bore being 17 feet in diameter. The sections were also designed to have an 8-foot-wide maintenance gallery, or corridor, running between the bores. It would run the entire 3.6 miles when all of the sections were in place. Doors would be installed every 330 feet for access to the gallery from each bore for workers and emergency personnel, and for passengers, if evacuation ever became necessary. A second story to the gallery would house conduit and utility equipment and serve as an air duct. A cross section of the tube might remind one of a double-barreled shotgun or a pair of long, giant binoculars. The tube shell sections were being constructed at the Bethlehem shipyard in South San Francisco, similar to how ships were built on shipways during World War II.

Each section was carefully constructed with the utmost precision, demanding the tightest of tolerances. Three-eighths-inch-thick steel plating was used for the shell's skin and was reinforced with steel T-beams set 6 feet apart on the interior of the shell. Evenly placed box-like steel bins were constructed on top. Next, the shell was laced with

Crowds gather to give the first section of the Transbay Tube a sendoff from the Bethlehem shipyard off Hunters Point in San Francisco. It was symbolic of one of history's greatest engineering feats and the beginning of building what was at the time the longest subaqueous tube in the world.

steel reinforcing bars throughout in preparation for the pouring of the concrete walls and the floor for the track bed. However, the concrete was not added until the steel shell section was launched. Once in the water, it was towed to a barge, where 4,200 cubic yards of concrete were poured to cover about 70,000 square feet for each tube section. When completed, the concrete formed 2.3-foot-thick interior walls and the track bed. The section's displacement was 10,000 tons, leaving it just enough buoyancy to stay afloat.

Before being placed, each tube section was sealed at both ends with watertight bulkheads in preparation for the next step. The first section had to be outfitted with a complex flexible joint, specially designed to absorb seismic activity. For this operation, the tube was floated up the delta to the Kaiser Steel plant in Napa, where the flexible joint was installed, and then towed back down to the bay.

In February 1967 the first section was placed between the pontoons of a specially built mammoth catamaran and floated out to a designated position on the east side of the bay at the old Oakland Mole, not far from the estuary. Five hundred tons of ballast were then poured into the bins on top and carefully distributed to keep the weight evenly dispersed. Cables and divers guided the tube section as it was lowered into place, where it would connect with a specially designed ventilation building. By the spring of 1968, twenty-six sections had been towed out and sunk into place, making the tube stretch about 2 miles. From the first section, the tube was built west from the east side of the bay. The work of laying the tube began on the Oakland side because across the bay a giant caisson was being built that would serve as a vent structure or portal to the San Francisco side.

Each section of the Transbay Tube was floated out into water and then lowered into a trench that had been dredged across the floor of the bay.

THE CAISSON

The caisson was conceived and built especially for the project by several consultant firms under the direction of Walter Douglas and Jack Everson of Parsons Brinckerhoff. Like the design of the tube, it was considered an unprecedented engineering marvel. No one had ever built anything quite like it before. Some viewed it as the fifty-eighth section of the tube, albeit a very different one, and one that would play an extremely vital role in the functioning of the whole. Constructed of steel and concrete, the caisson was 68 feet wide, 122 feet long, and 108 feet high—about as tall as a ten-story building. It was designed to withstand lateral earth and water pressure in the range of 90,000 pounds per linear foot at its deepest point. Divided into three sections, the caisson provided track bedding on the lower level, electrical power supply equipment and giant transformers in the middle section, and, on the upper level, blowers and air shafts to vent the powerful forces of air that would be pushed by trains acting like pistons through a cylinder at 70 miles per hour.

Like the tube shells, the caisson was constructed on a shipway and then launched. Once it was in the water, concrete was added to the reinforced steel walls, and an elevator and a stairwell were installed for maintenance access. The caisson was then floated out to a designated spot about 400 feet off San Francisco's Ferry Building. Originally it had been thought that the Ferry Building, or a portion of it, might have to be demolished to make way for the vent structure to be built onshore, but the city was adamantly opposed to this suggestion. Thus the idea for the caisson as a substitute was born. The caisson was positioned to solve the problem of transition from the actual tube to the subway approach tunnel being constructed in San Francisco. The transition track running through the lower portion of the caisson, about 80 feet deep, would also have switchgear for operational flexibility. Another critical function of the caisson, which would come to be known in the new system's lexicon as simply "the vent structure," was to provide ventilation for the tube and the connecting tunnel. It contained huge fans, 9 feet in diameter, to clear the air in the tube in case of emergency.

When the caisson was placed, one writer for an engineering magazine in 1968 described it as a little like an iceberg. While you could see the tip that rose a bit over 8 feet above the bay surface, most of it was invisible as it lay submerged under the dark waters, anchored to a specially built gravel-and-concrete platform on the bottom placed about 100 feet below mean sea level in the excavated trench below the bay floor. Once the first tube section was attached, the bulkhead was removed, which allowed for access to the interior through the double-bore caisson. A similar ventilation structure was built on the East Bay shore where the old Oakland Mole once operated.

PLACING THE TUBE SECTIONS

Once that first section had been towed out and sunk into place on the Oakland side, the tube came together at the rate of two sections per month. So precise were the design specifications that tolerances were no more than half an inch as each section was lowered. This was a very delicate operation. Engineers devised a special guidance system and carefully monitored each tube section to ensure that it was lowered at the proper angle to correspond to the different depths of the trench. As they had done in dredging the trench, engineers also used the innovation of a laser as an optical plumb line, in conjunction with a special survey tower that was temporarily placed on top of each tube section.

When a section was in place, four hydraulic railroad car couplers capable of exerting 50 tons of pressure pulled the sections tightly together. The sections were sealed with neoprene gaskets inside the rim of each section. Excess water collected between sections was pumped out to create a watertight vacuum. Next, divers went down in zero visibility and welded the seam of each section. The divers could only be down for four hours at a time and then had to come up for decompression in one of two decompression tanks located on the placement barge.

Once the sections were sealed, the bulkheads were removed, allowing workers to move on to the next section. Gravel and stone were then packed into the sides at the bottom to lock the tube sections in place. Section seams were also welded on the inside and then filled with concrete to create a smooth transition between the sections. Once the first section had been attached to the caisson on the San Francisco side, work proceeded from both sides of the bay and it became a race to see which crew would break through first by removing the last bulkhead. On April 3, 1969, tube section number 23, the last of the fifty-seven sections, was lowered into position just east of Yerba Buena Island to complete the Transbay Tube.

The excited crew members, believing they had been the first to break through the final tube section, got a big surprise when the last bulkhead was removed. There on the other side were two tube workers, Don Hughes and Shad Wilson, sitting at a table covered with a checkered cloth, as if in a restaurant, toasting their achievement with champagne.

When the last bulkhead was removed to complete the joining of the Transbay Tube from opposite sides of the bay, workers from the San Francisco side were surprised to see Don Hughes and Shad Wilson enjoying a bottle of champagne. "What kept you guys?" Shad said, according to lore.

CATHODIC PROTECTION SYSTEM: THE KEY TO TUBE LONGEVITY

Steel in saltwater is subject to electrolysis, which in effect causes ionization, or corrosion of the metal. To keep this from happening to the tube and any of the steel-skinned structures, such as the caisson vent structure and subway sections in areas with high water tables, a cathodic protection system was installed. The cathodic system consists of arrays of positively charged anodes placed more than 250 feet off each side of the tube and connected to the exterior by protected cables. The arrays create a reverse-ionization process in which the negatively charged tube attracts ions instead of shedding them. The arrays must be replaced every few years. Over several years, calcareous deposits coat the tube and eventually diminish the cathodic protection requirements.

A COOL HIKE UNDER THE BAY

A few months after the tube's completion, in August, the public was invited to take a walk through a portion of the tube to see this engineering marvel firsthand.

Thousands of adventurous souls lined up along the railroad tracks that had once led to the Oakland Mole on the east side of the bay and along San Francisco's waterfront to be among the first for this historic event: to walk, run, or ride a bike under the bay. Some felt as though they were entering a great cavern under the world. The sound of people's voices, conveying awe, echoed along the tube's great curved walls. And on a warm summer day, it was the coolest place in town.

HOLLYWOOD COMES TO BART

Before the tracks were laid in the tube, film director George Lucas decided that the BART Transbay Tube would be the perfect location for the final scene of his first movie, *THX 1138*, which had actually started as a short dissertation film for the University of Southern California's cinema department. He had his star, Robert Duvall, crawl along the rebar, which was in the shape of handles protruding from the concrete floor, but the angle at which the scene was filmed made it look as though he were climbing up a long tunnel to sunlight at the end. Lucas also shot some scenes at the system's Lake Merritt control center.

At about the same time (1970), the tube was also the site for a scene in the film *They Call Me Mr. Tibbs!,* starring Sidney Poitier as San Francisco homicide detective Virgil Tibbs. The scene called for Poitier's character to run through the tube. Years later, *Predator 2,* starring Danny Glover, was also shot in the tube, although it was supposed to be a Los Angeles subway.

It took about four more years to fully complete the installation of the tube's support equipment, such as train controls, electrification, and so on. The first test train streaked through the tube on automatic train control on August 10, 1973.

CHAPTER 12

SAN FRANCISCO SUBWAY CONSTRUCTION PRESENTS NEW CHALLENGES

On the bright, sunny morning of Monday, July 24, 1967, 125 or more children, out of school for the summer, lined up along San Francisco's Market Street near Powell, poised with shovels in hand waiting for the signal. The children chatted among themselves with laughter and a general feeling of gaiety. They had a sense that something very important was about to happen, that history was about to be made in this "Baghdad by the Bay," as iconic columnist Herb Caen referred to San Francisco. Along the curb of the street a path of hard surface composed of concrete and asphalt had been removed to expose the dirt underneath. Press photographers and television cameras were at the ready. On cue, the children began to dig, pushing their shovels into the soft earth for the official ground-breaking of BART's Market Street subway. Following the ceremonial ground-breaking, the children were bused out to Contra Costa County and taken for a ride in a lab car on the Diablo Test Track.

This was another example of the public relations genius BARTD had come to be known for. The children symbolized the future, just as the transit project itself was striving to personify space-age ground transportation for current and future generations. BARTD referred to the event as a "dig-in," presumably a takeoff on the jargon of the time. Market Street would be one of the most important segments of the 8.3 miles of the San Francisco BART portion of the 75-mile project. "Unquestionably, BART will become the central force in the wave of beautification, reconstruction, and new construction, some of which is already under way," said Jack Barron, who managed the Transit Task Force created to coordinate the system construction with all city departments. Every aspect had to be negotiated.

Of course, not everyone was happy that morning. Many of the shopkeepers who owned businesses along that corridor balked, and understandably so. Some of the small businesses had been located there for more than fifty years. The owners knew that the coming of the BART trains was going to mean big short- and long-term changes for Market Street in terms of its new look and its economics. Some referred to the change as the "Manhattanization" of downtown San Francisco, a term meant as a criticism. There were always those who did not want to see change of any kind.

In the short term, the chaos of construction was going to be extremely disruptive, impeding general traffic flow in the vicinity of the Market Street corridor, and many business owners feared that customers would not want to fight the chaos and big machines that would come with the work. The street would more than likely be torn up for years, and they feared their shops would not be easily accessible. They were right. Many of the small businesses did close up shop, never to return. On the bright side, some of the major buildings, such as the Wells Fargo building and the Emporium-Capwell Department Store, planned to construct special entrances to the BART stations. At the Powell Street Station, a pedestrian tunnel was supposedly hollowed out that went all the way down to Mission Street. According to lore, this tunnel was intended to provide an underground walkway to the future Yerba Buena Gardens, but it was sealed up and never used.

The city saw the end of some of the anachronistic small shops as no great loss. Over the years a sleazy, honky-tonk element had mushroomed along Market Street, particularly at the lower end near the Embarcadero. Otherwise, the once-bustling east end of Market had been considered all but dead in recent years. Like the 1906 earthquake and fire that led to the demise of the old Barbary Coast, the coming of BART was considered a new turning point in San Francisco's evolution. The city was anxious to revitalize Market Street, and, in fact, construction had already begun on high-rise developments along or close to the new BART line.

An addition to the Golden Gateway Redevelopment Project (mentioned in Chapter 7) was the ambitious four-block Embarcadero Center. Beginning a half block from BART and running west at a slight angle parallel to Market Street, the Embarcadero Center was to include four high-rise office buildings comprising about 3 million square feet of office space, and three levels for restaurants and shops. Part of the development would be the new Alesa Building at One Maritime Plaza and the 840-room Hyatt Regency hotel, located a few steps from the entrance of the eventual Embarcadero Station. The city, which agreed on the need for the added station, determined that the tax increments from anticipated higher property values would help fund Phase One of the unplanned Embarcadero Station through the sale of bonds. City supervisors allocated $15 million to pay for the basic station box.

The emergence of the Market Street Development Association, an organization devoted to bringing about a renaissance to the street that was once the spirit and spine of San Francisco, was also a strong signal that change was on the doorstep. One of the early primary goals of the association was to continue to raise money to build the Embarcadero Station at Davis Street. At the association's behest, several private developers kicked in $500,000 for initial design work a few months after the ground-breaking.

Problems between BART and the city over the aesthetics of the Market Street stations popped up when the city demanded that the stations have skylights. This concept created several issues. It would have required the unscrambling and additional relocation of utility conduits, an assortment of pipes and sewer lines crossing Market Street not far below the surface and just above the roofs of the stations, and indeed the structures themselves would need to be redesigned, thus causing delays and adding to unplanned costs. The city's position on the skylight issue was that they would open up the stations' concourse levels to natural light. Further, the city would not allow BART to build protective canopies over the entryways, nor to post station-identifying signs, again citing aesthetics, particularly after the Market Street beautification plan was adopted. It involved widening sidewalks, landscaping, and general sprucing up. Interestingly, that plan would eventually influence the city's quest for the skylights.

Meanwhile, soil studies had begun under Market Street in 1963 with the drilling of 5-inch bores to 100- and 200-foot depths. The engineers weren't sure exactly what they were going to find, but they had a hunch it was not going to be good. The permeability of the soil, particle size, settlement behavior, and other factors gave clear warning of the complex construction problems ahead for PBTB engineers and project contractors.

Actual work on the Market Street subway did not begin until the day after the "dig-in," on Tuesday, July 25. With the first dig, contractors encountered a maze of utilities of one kind or another about ten feet below the surface. Over the past hundred years, more than two hundred utility companies had planted lines, many of which had been abandoned long before and did not even show up on plans provided by the city's public works department. Threading through them, contractors found live high-voltage wires, conduits of all shapes and sizes, high-pressure fire hydrant lines, and steam pipes, all of which presented an ever-present danger. They would have to be moved or suspended in place while the work went on around them. It was critical that the lines be kept intact so that service to surrounding office buildings would not be interrupted.

The work consisted of building twin double-decked tunnels for BART and Muni, which followed Market Street to Van Ness and then split up into single-deck tunnels. The BART tunnels would swing south along Mission Street; the Muni tunnels would continue along Market. The San Francisco line would include twelve completed stations, including three specifically for the San Francisco Muni system. There was no money at that time for Phase Two work—the fully detailed completion of the Embarcadero Station's interior. The shell was a placeholder until additional funding could be found.

The contractor for that portion of the Mission–Market Street line was a joint venture made up of Morrison Knudsen, Brown & Root in conjunction with the Perini Corporation. Morrison Knudsen also got the contract for excavation of the 700-foot space for the Embarcadero Station.

Cut-and-cover construction along San Francisco's Market Street was the primary method used to build the mammoth subway stations.

While Market Street was being torn up for cut-and-cover construction, one of the biggest challenges was relocation of the utilities, which one foreman referred to as an underworld of spaghetti.

Contractors first had to excavate enough to provide a staging area for their work, and then they decked over the hole so that streetcars, buses, and general traffic could continue to move freely. Two Calweld oscillating tunnel-boring machines were used for soft-earth tunneling. Eighteen feet in diameter, they were employed to bore twin mile-long tunnels between the Mission Street lines and the Market Street lines. The late Harre Demoro, an acclaimed transit reporter and writer, once described the shield boring machine as something like a giant cookie cutter.

The tunnel-boring machines were the first of their specific kind ever used in the United States. Each weighing 93 tons, they were lowered by a giant crane into a huge shaft more than 75 feet deep, at 15th and Mission Streets. BART quickly picked up on the nickname of the machine, "the Mole"—which was how these machines were affectionately referred to in tunnel digs around the world—when it commissioned a film about the machine titled *We Call It the Mole.* Each machine had a tail shield, which was like a monster cylinder extending out behind the Mole. During the construction of the overall project there were thirty-six different tunnel headings, making up one of the greatest concentrations of tunneling work in history.

As the shield boring machine pushed forward with a system of 115 hydraulic jacks, rotating cutter arms with sharp steel teeth knifed through the soil, moving at an average rate of 4 to 4.5 feet an hour, or 35 feet a day, depending on the soil type. The cost for this form of excavation was $2,142 per foot; today that cost would be more like $50,000 to $60,000 per foot.

The shield behind the Mole provided limited protection from potential cave-ins to the "sandhogs," tunnel workers who labored in the extremely hazardous conditions. The sandhogs also had to work in air pressure of at least 12 pounds per square inch (psi) along the Mission Street dig. The high air pressure was another safeguard against the soft earth, sand, and mud collapsing during the work. Like the Transbay Tube divers, workers leaving the bottom of the subway construction had to go through a decompression tank before emerging from the depths to prevent getting the bends.

The dirt and mud from the bore was mixed with slurry, put on a conveyor belt, dumped into a mud cart, and removed by a heavy crane from the shaft. Integral to the boring process, large robotic erector arms would then place specially forged steel rings to line and reinforce the tunnel walls and ceiling. Each ring was almost 3 feet wide and weighed 3 tons. It took six rings to line one segment of a tunnel, and a smaller ring to act like a keystone. Workers bolted the rings together, then a form of grout and gravel was forced in between the raw mined walls and the liners to minimize ground-moisture leakage. A total of 27,700 tunnel liners were produced by Kaiser Steel in Napa County specifically for the project's tunnels at a cost of $27.5 million, or about $975 per ring. Overall they lined approximately 65,000 feet of tunneling.

THE SHIELD'S FASCINATING HISTORY

As mentioned in Chapter 1, a shield was employed to tunnel some of the New York City subway system. While it was much cruder than the ones used by BART almost seventy years later, it served the same basic purpose: protecting the sandhogs working behind it from cave-ins as it dug and pushed forward. The tunneling shield was first invented in

The shield tunnel-boring machine is 18 feet in diameter and here works almost 80 feet under Mission Street in San Francisco. Working at that depth and under high air pressure to prevent cave-ins meant construction crews were required to go through decompression when they resurfaced after their shifts. Development of this technology began in the mid-1800s with the observance of a naval shipworm.

London by architect Marc Isambard Brunel to excavate a tunnel under the Thames. Charles Dickens wrote about this strange contraption in his newspaper columns around 1843.

Brunel and his partner, Thomas Cochrane, patented the first such machine in January 1818 but did not begin using it until 1825, when they excavated a pedestrian tunnel under the Thames. That tunnel was 1,300 feet long, at a depth of 75 feet. At one point it was flooded, delaying the work, but it was finally completed in 1843. Although the tunnel was originally built for pedestrians, it is now part of the London Underground. Brunel's inspiration for that early design of the shield came from a seagoing worm called *Teredo navalis*. The *Teredo* is a nightmare for owners of wooden ships because of its ability to bore through wood hulls from underwater. As this kind of saltwater termite moves through the timber, it secretes a substance that hardens and forms a shield behind it. Thousands of them working at once could destroy a ship's hull. While the main concept developed by Brunel has remained the same over nearly two hundred years, the shield has, of course, seen major technical improvements, and it continues to be used today for major tunneling projects in the United States and abroad.

LOWER MARKET STREET WORK PRESENTS WORST CONDITIONS

A contract for the lower Market Street tunnel segment approach-way was awarded to Perini–Brown & Root for $14.6 million. Because the San Francisco waterfront was mostly fill from Montgomery Street to the Embarcadero, the water table was high, and the deep, soft bay mud made subway excavation under Market Street particularly challenging and dangerous. The shell of the Embarcadero Station was completed in 1969, and years later, during the inauguration of the station's finished interior, Bill Cummings, one of the architects of the Embarcadero Station, talked about the design issues he and chief architect Tallie Mahl had faced. "Hell, the shell, which was really nothing more than a concrete box, was practically floating, like a submarine," Cummings said. He also noted they had had to squeeze the design to be slightly narrower than the other downtown stations due to adjacent structures and the high water table.

Excavating the Market Street stations was like digging holes for three-story buildings. These stations had to be constructed with three levels: a bottom twin-track level for BART trains, a middle twin-track level for eventual Muni light rail trains, and a mezzanine or concourse level that would contain entry gates, fare collection/ticketing machines, agent booths, information racks, bathrooms, and commercial vendors' kiosks. To accommodate ten-car trains, the stations were 700 feet long—longer than the Bank of America Building is high—and 60 feet wide, except for the Embarcadero Station, which was 50 feet wide.

THE GREATEST CHALLENGE OF MARKET STREET

Even more challenging was the tunneling work necessary to connect with the caisson ventilation structure 400 feet offshore. The structure contained double trackways submerged 85 feet under the bay waters, waiting to be tied in. The vent building trackways were sealed by bulkheads on the west side. Like the Transbay Tube on the east side of the vent structure, these bulkheads would be removed once the connection with the subway approach was made. Excess water that accumulated during the process would then be pumped out.

During the excavation work the contractor encountered a jungle of old, deeply embedded timber piles that had to be removed. Some of the pilings, about nine hundred in all, had supported the original ferry building wharf and slips that had been used back in the early 1900s, when ferry service was the only cross-bay mode of travel. Also discovered were the carcasses of three old sailing ships from the gold rush days, as well the bones of early Indian inhabitants. One rumor had it

These views show San Francisco's Civic Center BART station, first during construction and then at its gleaming finish, ready for passenger service in 1971.

that the partial remains of a Barbary Coast speakeasy, including a bar, had been found during the dig, but this story has never been verified.

As the early stages of the dig progressed, the contractor, Perini–Brown & Root, encountered bay mud 100 feet below the water table in some places. While this was expected based on the deep soil samples taken at the foot of Market Street in 1963, such excavation was considered unprecedented. Another major challenge during the digging of the lower Market Street subway was the discovery of yet another network of utilities and sewer lines below the surface, which in some places looked like a pile of spaghetti that had to be untangled. The relocation work was costly and time consuming but ultimately successful. That effort alone was considered an amazing feat.

SUPERSTITION

At one point the subway construction was made accessible for special tours and visitors, both domestic and foreign, who had heard about this futuristic new system being built. Descending into the catacombs of the deep subway construction held a certain fascination that made it a popular venture. Kay Springer, an early employee of BARTD who held a number of jobs during her long career at the transit district, arrived in 1966, when the staff was still relatively small and employees were often called upon to perform a number of tasks outside of their official job descriptions, such as giving slide show presentations to community organizations (mostly in the evenings, on their own time) or taking visiting public officials to outlying construction sites. On one particular day, Springer was assigned to give a tour for a group of male visitors interested in the subway construction techniques being employed by the BARTD project. When she reached the access entrance, the foreman on the job told her that she herself could not go down into the construction area. The sandhogs were superstitious about women being in the tunneling area during construction.

"Why's that?" Springer asked.

The foreman shook his head. "Because it's considered bad luck," he said. "There's no way you're going down there with your group."

Springer asked her group to wait while she went to the nearest pay phone and called headquarters to report the problem. The issue reached general manager Stokes's desk and, through PBTB, he ordered that Springer and her group be allowed access, thus breaking a long-standing taboo.

SPECIAL PRECAUTIONS TAKEN

Because of the tremendous hydrostatic pressures from the watery bottom and deep mud of the subway excavation, extraordinary measures had to be taken between Montgomery Street and the vent building. The contractor was concerned that the excavations in the alluvial soils along the lower end of Market Street could endanger some of the long-standing buildings. Slurry walls had to be built, and heavy-duty soldier pilings were sunk down more than 100 feet on each side of the open cuts to shore up structures along both sides of the street. Here again, the contractor employed hydraulic-driven shields to bore through to the caisson at a very slow rate of about 2 to 3 feet per hour. The sandhogs had to work in air pressure of 36 psi, which slowed the operation considerably. For every hour of actual work, the sandhogs had to spend three hours in a compression chamber and three more hours in a decompression chamber to avoid getting the bends. In addition, 7-foot-thick reinforced concrete bedding for the trackways 80 feet down had to be poured to accommodate the weight of the trains. This bedding was almost three times the thickness of the typical track beds being constructed elsewhere on the system. All of the work along Market Street had to be conducted while streetcars, buses, and automobiles continued to roll along overhead, often making officials nervous that some disaster might befall the traffic flow.

A THEATER LAWSUIT WITH FAR-REACHING IMPLICATIONS

During the digging and construction of the Civic Center Station, as with the other stations, temporary pilings were driven to shore up adjacent buildings. One of those buildings was the Orpheum Theatre. Its owners later sued BART for damages in the amount of $900,000, a key part of the lawsuit claiming that the proximity of the BART station had impaired pedestrian access to the theater. After six weeks of trial in San Francisco Superior Court, a jury determined that not only were the theater owners not damaged by BART's construction, but the value of their property had actually increased from between $5 and $10 per square foot, based on appraisals that had been testified to by real estate experts. The jury's decision carried significance beyond this particular lawsuit; it established a precedent that proximity to a rapid transit station has a beneficial rather than negative impact on real estate values, a contention that the District had always promoted.

SHIFTING GEARS

The basic Phase One work was completed along Market Street without a major disaster, and one can imagine a great sigh of relief coming from all concerned. This might have been particularly the case for the officials of San Francisco, who were vulnerable to the least perturbation that might have taken place. Their signatures were on the many agreements that had to be worked out between BARTD and the city for the project to move forward.

Following closely on the heels of Phase One—the shell construction of the San Francisco BART line—was the enormous amount of detail work to be completed. Numerous contracts were let for such things as station finish (using marble from North and South American quarries), electrification, plumbing, track laying, fare equipment installation, and, finally, the installation of the automatic train control equipment.

Two separate systems were set up for electrification. One system was dedicated solely to the 160 miles of the third rail throughout the system, including storage yards. That system used strategically located substations to energize the third rail with 1,000 volts of direct current to power the trains. The early testing program had shown that using 1,000 volts instead of the traditional 650 volts would be essential both for the high speeds called for and for negotiating inclines of up to 4 percent (that is, a rise of 4 feet for every 100 feet traveled). The second electrical system provided general power to support everything else, from station lighting and equipment to three maintenance shops and storage yards (the Daly City shop and yard came much later), the control center, and the newly constructed headquarters building in Oakland, over the Lake Merritt Station.

What next? Aerospace was about to enter the ground transportation market.

CHAPTER 13

THE CONTRACT FOR TRANSIT CARS GOES TO AN AEROSPACE COMPANY

The temporary half-cent sales tax would become effective in April 1970. In July 1969, with the money to complete the basic system now ensured, BART officials opened the bids they had received two years earlier for its revolutionary transit cars. The initial contract for 250 cars, with an option to purchase 200 more if funds were available, was granted—as required by law—to the low bidder, Rohr Industries, an aerospace company in Chula Vista, California. The price tag was a shocker. The original estimate for a fleet of 450 cars, as outlined in the Composite Report, was $71 million, or roughly $158,000 per car. Rohr's bid for the first 250 cars was $80 million—$9 million more than the initial estimate for the entire fleet—which brought the unit cost to $320,000. In 1972, as the first order was coming to an end, the BARTD board was under the gun to approve picking up the option for the final 200 cars at another $80 million, or $400,000 per unit, without any prospect for the needed funding. The total contract, with escalation, was for $160 million. As it turned out, federal grants from the Urban Mass Transportation Act paid for about 64 percent of the total cost. Today's sticker price is between $2 and $2.5 million per car and climbing.

(By 1975 BART had received a total of $315 million in federal assistance, covering about 20 percent of the $1.6 billion cost of the system when all was said and done. Ironically, even though BART was the catalyst for the creation of the federal Urban Mass Transportation Administration and its grant program, it did not receive the large percentage of funding awarded to later systems. Had BART been built in the 1970s, it would have been eligible for 80 percent federal money. That said, the system probably could not have been built at a later point because freeway medians would have been swallowed up by the state highway system, and needed land and exclusive rights-of-way would have been extremely difficult, if not impossible, to obtain.)

The Rohr contract called for the first ten vehicles to be prototypes that would be used for extensive testing. Over the next year and a half, the prototype cars were operated day and night, putting many thousands of miles on them. This intense testing was designed to ferret out as many bugs and manufacturing issues as possible before production cars started to come off the assembly line. Rohr Industries had never built a transit car before, but since aerospace contracts were beginning to thin out at that time, the company had decided to take the opportunity to diversify its product base and jump into the transit vehicle supply business. Lawrence D. Dahms, a former BART assistant general manager, interim general manager, and later executive director of the Metropolitan Transportation Commission, recalled numerous change orders with Rohr during those years.

Frederick Rohr, the founder of the company, had gotten his start back in 1927 building airplane parts, particularly fuel tanks for the *Spirit of St. Louis* as Charles Lindbergh readied it for his transatlantic flight. In 1940, Rohr founded the Rohr Aircraft Corporation, as it was originally called. During the war years, Rohr's company grew exponentially as government contracts came along in great numbers to help meet the demand for aircraft parts. In 1971 the company's name was changed to Rohr Industries. Mr. Rohr died only two years before Rohr Industries bid on the BART cars.

Many industry observers questioned the viability of an aerospace company building transit cars, but from BART's point of view, the fact that the new transit cars were coming from an aerospace company lent credence to the image the District had portrayed for years: that of a futuristic space-age system. The District also expected that a company like Rohr, with a solid reputation in the aerospace industry, would produce the dream vehicle.

CONTROVERSY SPARKED OVER THE CONTRACT

Once again controversy came knocking with criticism of the Rohr contract. Railroad aficionados, who were to some degree being played by some of the local press outlets, hammered away at the fact that Rohr was an aerospace company and said BART should have gone with tried-and-true rail car providers, such as the Budd Company of Philadelphia or other venerable and experienced businesses. What did an aerospace company know about producing rolling stock?

Meanwhile, Stokes, with board approval, had a full-scale model of an A car (with a sloped-nose cab in front) built by Sundberg-Ferar Industrial Design, a Michigan-based company whose task was to come up with the design and look of the car. The model was shipped to the Bay Area and displayed all around the three-county district, mostly in shopping malls and similar venues. The public was invited to inspect the model, touring its comparatively lush interior to get an idea of what the actual cars would look like when they finally arrived. According to spot surveys, visitors to the model were, for the most part, very impressed with the cushioned seats, the carpeted floors, and the clean, wide body. Some visitors remarked that it was a little like being on an airplane, only with picture windows.

The contract with Rohr specified that, of the first 250 cars, 150 would be A cars and 100 B cars, or flat-nosed cars without the operator's cab. Two A cars would be needed for each train consist. The A cars were to be 75 feet in length and the B cars 70 feet. At 10 feet, 6 inches wide, the cars would be roomier than traditional urban rail cars, and both types would seat seventy-two passengers. Each car was to be equipped with four 150-horsepower motors, one mounted on each axle, and specially built wide trucks with steel wheels. The wider trucks were for the wide-gauge rail at 5 feet, 6 inches instead of the standard 4 feet, 8.5 inches. A major innovation was the incorporation of the "chopper" system, which chopped the current to the traction motors during acceleration and deceleration in order to create a smoother ride than traditional rail lines offered. The chopper system was totally new at the time, but it has since been adopted by other systems both domestically and internationally.

Above: A mockup of the future BART car was put on display at various locations around Alameda, Contra Costa, and San Francisco Counties for public inspection. Here the model is on display at the San Francisco marina, with the Golden Gate Bridge in the background.

Left: In August 1970, BART officials, dignitaries, and members of the press gathered at the system's Hayward storage yard for the unveiling of the first BART prototype car to be delivered from Rohr's Chula Vista plant.

The skins of the transit cars would be brushed extruded aluminum along the full length of the car, to keep them as lightweight as possible, and therefore more efficient in terms of power consumption than the conventional stainless steel. The sloped-nosed cabs on the A cars would be constructed of fiberglass and would contain the operators' consoles and communications equipment. Since the trains would be fully automated, the operators' primary role would be to act in emergencies, operate the train manually when called for, announce stations, and occasionally do "fingertip" maintenance—that is, fixing something on the spot during the train's operation. In case of power loss, all cars were to be equipped with emergency backup batteries to provide light.

An early model of a lead BART car by Sundberg-Ferar, a Michigan-based industrial design firm.

All maintenance, both preventive and repair, would be done at one of the three shops, located in Richmond, Concord, and Hayward.

A CRITICAL NEWSPAPER SERIES

During the late 1960s, Scott Newhall, the managing editor of the *San Francisco Chronicle,* questioned the wisdom of the sloped-nose car as a practical matter, as well as voiced various other concerns about the management of the project. In particular, the paper had received complaints that BARTD was not responsive to community concerns, among which were grumbles stemming from the protracted battle with the City of Berkeley over putting the tracks underground. Newhall decided to follow up, and in 1966 he sent veteran reporter Michael Harris to other parts of the world to look at various long-established urban rail transit systems, all of which had flat-nosed lead cars that could be interchanged with mid-train cars. Harris went first to Canada and observed and interviewed officials at the Toronto subway system. From there he headed for Europe, where he visited systems in London, Paris, and Leningrad, looking at the organizational structures of these systems as well as the general experience and backgrounds of their top executives. On his return, Harris authored a series of critical articles about the management decisions concerning the design of the cars and other aspects of the system, such as the decision to not use rubber tires, which were being employed successfully in Toronto and Paris. PBTB, in making its original recommendation to go with steel wheels, had considered but rejected rubber tires because of the shrill noise they made, particularly on curves, and because they would not have the traction needed for the 4 percent grades. Maintenance issues also influenced the decision.

The *Chronicle* also seemed to have a fair amount of animosity toward Stokes's management style, often implying that he bulldozed the early board, which for the most part had little collective technical expertise, and criticizing the time it took to settle the underground issue with the City of Berkeley. In the early 1970s, in a television panel discussion that included B. R. Stokes (representing BART) and Michael Harris (representing the *San Francisco Chronicle*), the moderator asked Harris why his stories were generally negative about the new system. Harris replied that he believed BART was in fact a great project, but he questioned whether it should be managed by a former journalist. Stokes shook his head, puffed on his signature pipe, and replied: "Mike, you don't think much of journalists, do you?" A letter to the editor a few days later by someone who had seen the broadcast noted that the late president John F. Kennedy had also started out as a journalist.

As for being responsive to community concerns, it was well documented that fifteen of the original station locations, as well as track alignment in some areas, were changed from the original plan in response to local community input. In addition, the stations were enhanced architecturally and aesthetically at greatly increased cost as a direct result of community desires. Landscaping was also added to soften the often looming presence of the system's suburban stations. Adrien Falk, the BARTD board president for eight years, never faltered in his backing of Stokes; he believed that Stokes was a man of his time and the right man for the job. Stokes's children have noted that during the period when cost overruns were being publicized in the media and the financial crisis was looming, the family received bomb threats. A few years later, during intense labor negotiations, pickets began showing up in front of their house and yelling catcalls. As a result, twenty-four-hour gun-toting security personnel were stationed around the family home in Orinda.

As for the *Chronicle*'s criticism of the sloped nose of the A cars, the transit district strongly defended the design, which was an important component of marketing the space-age concept in the early days of the system. While BART in later years developed the C car, a flat-nosed lead car that provides more operational flexibility, more than forty years later one can still see the old sloped-nose cars leading numerous trains.

A LEAP IN THE STATE OF THE ART

One outstanding issue was that an initial fleet of 450 cars would be only barely adequate for the 71.5-mile BART portion of the 75-mile project. Much would depend on the travel patterns of each weekday, with peak travel times expected for the morning and evening commutes. Eight-, nine-, and, at maximum, ten-car trains would be needed to meet that demand, but midday traffic would be a question mark for a time. From a marketing standpoint, attracting midday ridership would be the key to achieving an economy of scale and a positive overall utilization rate of seat miles to passenger miles.

Upon receiving the BART transit vehicle contract, Rohr Industries was responsible for engineering and final design based on the aesthetics of the full-scale model built earlier by Sundberg-Ferar. The requirements of the contract were unprecedented in that the work to be done was based primarily on performance specifications and not individual component specifications or off-the-shelf components, which were highly reliable. Although this bold and progressive approach would come back to haunt system operations during the early years, it also advanced the state of the art in the ground transportation industry, which had been working with skimpy budgets for the past sixty years and had stopped calling for research and development during a time when major industry suppliers had little incentive to modernize their technology. However, research and development to create innovative technological advances was the bread and butter of the aerospace industry, and Rohr's empirical approach to innovation for the BART project moved the industry a great distance ahead of standard rail transit technology. BART was demanding extremely high performance standards—unheard of in the industry—that only major advances could meet. (As an example, one of many problems that plagued the maintenance of the new cars in the first years of operation was the solid disc brakes. In order to replace a disc, the entire brake assembly of the undercarriage truck had to be dismantled at great cost of time and money. Eventually the fix for this particular problem was a "split disc" designed by BART engineers, which is still used today.)

In a background information piece, Rohr Industries described its production methodology as "a systems management concept" commonly employed in the aerospace industry. Under this approach, vehicle systems were broken down into subsystems and components, each with its own specification standards. For instance, the propulsion system for the cars, designed by Westinghouse Electric under a subcontract, had to meet speed performance requirements, which in this case were the ability to accelerate from a standing position to 50 miles an hour in 20 seconds and decelerate from the top speed of 80 miles per hour down to zero in 27 seconds. It was advertised as one of the most advanced propulsion systems in the world.

System integration was another key consideration: newly designed components had to interact well with other components. Similar to airplane fuselage construction, the BART transit cars would be constructed on the assembly lines using a semi-monocoque design, in which the body is integrated with the chassis for maximum strength by creating a kind of dynamic tension between the materials. In addition to body strength, this construction method allowed for the seats to be cantilevered out from the walls, which in turn offered better legroom for passengers.

AUTOMATIC TRAIN FUNCTIONS

Rohr subcontracted with the Westinghouse Electric Corporation to supply the onboard controls that would have to work in congress with wayside controls and track circuitry, which were also to be supplied by Westinghouse under a separate contract with BART. Solid-state circuit boards were used for the first time in developing the speed codes for the cars. Eight performance levels would be used in the operation, each level representing a specific speed and programmed to kick in at given locations on the system. The train would receive its speed command by "listening," that is, interpreting the special frequency of the signal in the rails, each coded sequence of frequencies representing one of the eight speed or performance levels. Speed commands would begin with zero, then increase to 6, 18, 27, 36, 50, 70, or 80 miles per hour. As an example, trains approaching a station at 36 miles an hour would slow down to 18 miles an hour under dynamic braking. Mechanical braking would kick in at 18 miles an hour and slow the train to a complete stop, or "zero speed code." While cars were in dynamic braking mode, the motors would turn into generators and produce electrical power that would go back into the third rail.

CAR INTERIORS

Like the mockup model, the specifications for the interior of the cars called for a well-lighted and comfortable environment for traveling. The cushioned seats, picture windows, and wall-to-wall carpeting not only added comfort to the rider's experience but also reduced potential noise. The cars would be temperature controlled, and a special intercom system would be added so that passengers could communicate directly with the train operator in case of a problem or emergency.

The new cars would not, however, have any overhead handholds or hand straps, such as might be found in the older Eastern systems. Each seat would have a handhold, just in case someone had to stand. BART's early public relations materials suggested that there would be a seat for everyone. Many years later, as passenger loads increased dramatically, ceiling handrails were added, and today one can look down the aisle of a BART car and see the gentle swaying of hand strap loops. BART also advertised that the new cars would be "virtually noiseless and vibration free." Transit writer Harre Demoro often referred to that phrase in a mocking way when reporting on the system.

AUTOMATIC TRAIN CONTROL AND TRAIN PROTECTION

In May 1967, about the time bids were first received for the transit cars, a contract was awarded to the Westinghouse Electric Corporation for the low bid of $26.1 million to build BART's automatic train control system. Again, the idea was to break new ground in propulsion and control systems for rail transit. Westinghouse had participated in the early research and development on the Diablo Test Track during 1965 and 1966, and the feasibility and desirability of a fully automated system were an outgrowth of this program. BART's automatic train control system was heralded as something that had never been attempted before; according to the engineers, the system would be a new paradigm in the history of mass transit. It would also be a major leap that industry observers would eventually criticize as reaching too high too fast. It might be likened to jumping from a Stanley Steamer car of 1897 to a 2016 Cadillac or Prius in one swift motion, not only transcending but completely revolutionizing traditional rail transit systems both in the United States and abroad.

Other bidders for the contract included the General Railway Signal Company, Philco Ford Company, General Electric Company, and Westinghouse Air Brake, a separate entity from the Westinghouse Electric Corporation.

To compete with the automobile in a geographic area that had a predominating car culture, BART management, in conjunction with the consulting engineers, determined early on that this new system had to be special in order to attract and keep riders. It had to offer high speed, close headways (the spacing between trains), conveniently located stations, and comfortable, spacious cars. It also had to be safe, and to achieve that parameter in particular, BART sought to eliminate the potential for human error.

Statistically, over the course of history, human error has always been the most common cause of accidents on rail transit systems, and so to reduce that chance, an advanced automatic train control and propulsion system had to be at the apex of BART's operation. According to a Westinghouse paper, a human operator in a train traveling at 80 miles per hour would need to be able to estimate about 1,800 feet ahead for a safe stop—something that could not be done reliably and consistently. And braking distances were just one factor that influenced discussion about the train control system. The original concept had been to eliminate human operators entirely, but it was later determined that it simply wasn't feasible to have no one in the cab, particularly for long distances between stations, where both mechanical and nonmechanical incidents might require human intervention.

The ambitious concept of fully automatic train control was revolutionary; it would supervise all functions of the operation, from starting and stopping the trains, opening and closing the doors, scheduling route alignments that might require automatic switching of tracks, and precision station stops. All these functions and more would be monitored and operated by employees from a central control room, to be located at Lake Merritt. An 85-foot-wide control board, or console, backlit with LEDs (light-emitting diodes) displayed a schematic of the entire system for monitoring train movements and interacted with a central computer.

Similar schematic boards in the same room would represent the electrification of the third rail and its support facilities in blazing red. If a segment lost power, the red light would go off, indicating the location of the problem. If maintenance needed to be done in a specific location along the trackway, the control center would be able to shut off power along that section. Each of the three consoles would have accompanying keyboards that would be staffed by train controllers, who could press buttons to make changes or operational corrections as needed.

One of the most critical components of the automatic train control project was train protection. For this part of the control design, the tracks themselves, in addition to sending signals for speed commands, would also act as electrical signal conductors to keep trains a safe distance apart. An antenna on board the front of each train would pick up the track signal and decode it into appropriate speed commands. Using the tracks to conduct signals was not in itself a new concept, but as in other areas, BART improved on what came before. Whereas older systems had used single amplitude-modulated (AM) radio signals, which were subject to electrical noise interference, BART would use frequency-modulated (FM) signals, virtually eliminating the possibility of outside signal interference. Another advancement incorporated into the control system was "multiplexing" the signals, which meant several signals could be transmitted through a pair of wires at the same time.

The train protection itself was done through a system of blocks—about 1,500 of them system-wide—each one designated by an individual track circuit ranging from 200 feet to 1,500 feet in length. Once a train was detected by the current running through the tracks of a specific block, it would signal a transmitter at the front of the block that would in turn cut off, or short circuit, the current to the back of the block, thereby sending a zero speed code to the train behind. This series of signals would cause the following train to stop until the block was no longer occupied by the leading train, creating a buffer zone. Specific speed commands would be determined by track configuration and the length of the given block, and would be automatically adjusted for the distance between trains. Each speed command would be repeated three times every second, and if the train did not receive them as designed, the train would come to a halt. If for some reason a failure occurred, the engineers had designed the system to fail in a "safe mode."

While the speed signals are mostly transmitted from wayside equipment, the different speed codes correspond to various track configurations, switches, grades, and station stops. The signals also give the command to position the train at a very specific location along the station platform so that the doors always open at the same spot. Today those spots are marked by black squares of hard rubber tiles, at which people often line up to board the trains during rush hour. The technology was cutting edge and forward thinking, but the testing leading up to opening day revealed one serious problem, causing yet another roadblock that once again inspired a field day for BART's career critics and the media.

CHAPTER 14

THE BART BOARD VS. STOKES

The dynamics of the BART board began to change dramatically beginning in 1969, as new appointees were named to fill vacancies created by some departing directors. One of those directors was Adrien J. Falk, who had served as the board president for eight years. He had been a major force from the beginning, continually pushing the project forward, come hell or high water, and his departure left a wide gap in the political leadership of the transit project. Other members of the board looked to Falk for leadership and, for the most part, deferred to his judgment. In particular, he was always able to get fellow directors to coalesce in support of general manager B. R. Stokes, even in times of controversy, of which there were plenty. In Falk's absence, Stokes would find it harder and harder to keep the board on track, especially in terms of getting the needed votes for approving complex contracts without a lot of teeth gnashing. Conflict on the board was reflected in press coverage, which tended to make it look to the public as though the organization were in chaos.

Although the environment in the boardroom had become highly charged politically, Stokes was still fully in charge and working toward the day when the massive construction project would transition to an operating railroad. He had an open-door policy, which meant that any staff member from the bottom up could always come and see him personally if they had a problem. That said, an employee might have felt too inhibited to break standard business protocol and go around his or her immediate supervisor to see Stokes. Without question it was a blurry line, but in any case Stokes was generally loved by the staff, and many of them felt comfortable engaging with him directly. In one incident in the late 1960s, Kay Springer, a staffer who had come to work at the District in 1966, wrote a memo to Stokes about what she observed as a period of low morale among employees. The money was running out, there was a lot of uncertainty about the future of the project, and dissension was building among the board members. The memo became famous when *Oakland Tribune* writer Harre Demoro somehow got ahold of it and printed it verbatim under the headline OH KAY CAN YOU SEE.

Meanwhile, Stokes's reputation as a kind of visionary transit guru was growing both nationally and internationally. In addition to his job as the BARTD general manager, Stokes was also named a special consultant to the U.S. secretary of transportation as a member of the Department of Transportation's Urban Transportation Advisory Council. In 1971 the secretary of transportation, John Volpe, appointed Stokes to chair the three-person steering committee of the council, which periodically met in Washington, D.C. He also served in a similar capacity to the U.S. Department of Housing and Urban Development and to Governor Ronald Reagan's California Task Force on Transportation. Prior to his Department of Transportation appointment, Stokes was one of fifteen Americans selected to join a similar number of British experts in the 1969 Anglo-American Task Force on Transportation held at Ditchley Park, England. To round out his resumé, Stokes was also named a director of the American Transit Association (a national trade organization for bus service providers) and a vice president and director of the Institute for Rapid Transit (a trade organization representing rail transit agencies). A few years later, Stokes would play a major role in the merger of these two organizations to form the American Public Transit Association, a powerful trade and lobbying group headquartered in Washington, D.C.

NEW DIRECTORS BRING OMINOUS CHANGE TO THE BOARD

Meanwhile, new directors coming in from all three counties of the District brought with them different agendas, some strictly parochial, others concerned about the overall project and the final price tag, which had not yet been projected. All of the new directors seemed to come into the boardroom with a mandate to challenge management, and this new dynamic was the beginning of a crack in the strong support Stokes had received from the directors since becoming general manager in 1963. While he still had the preponderance of votes needed to get the job done, his backing was no longer unanimous. Some of the new directors groused a lot about cost overruns, and one of them believed that they amounted to a runaway cost-plus contract with PBTB and that the new system was clearly not going to open on time. (The original estimate for opening the first segment of the BART line in 1969 was no longer realistic, as the cars had not been built and the fully automatic train control system was far from ready. At the earliest, an opening date might be possible in mid- or late 1971.) Some of the new directors asked questions that seemed inspired by Michael Harris's series of negative *Chronicle* articles, which had begun appearing in 1966. Inside the boardroom, people were demanding answers.

Stokes deftly defended management's approach, including its decision to maintain a minimum staff during the construction years and rely heavily on the consulting engineers. This was the strategy that had been recommended by early consultants and agreed on from the beginning; it made sense to not have as many as 1,000 employees on the payroll at the start only to let them go at the completion of construction. Also, Stokes noted that, in the mid-1960s, he had brought in a small cadre of experts in both construction management and rail signal technology to ensure the District had its own source of expertise to bring to the table when dealing with the consortium of consulting engineers.

Two of the relatively new members on staff had been colonels in the Army Corps of Engineers: David Hammond was named assistant general manager of operations and engineering, and Erland Tillman was appointed director of engineering and construction. Considered highly competent and among the best in their field, they would interface with PBTB, monitor contract progress and issues, and make recommendations when appropriate. (Both men would also eventually find themselves embroiled in a major controversy over the firing of three engineers employed by BART, a story that comes later in this chapter.) A former marine colonel, Bill Benedict, had also been brought in to head up administrative services, and together the three men were soon referred to as "the Colonels Club" by other employees. In many ways the BART organization pyramid itself was based on a military model;

DIRECTORS

ALAMEDA COUNTY

ARNOLD C. ANDERSON | RICHARD O. CLARK | H. R. LANGE | GEORGE M. SILLIMAN **President**

CONTRA COSTA COUNTY

NELLO J. BIANCO | JAMES P. DOHERTY | DANIEL C. HELIX* | JOSEPH S. SILVA

SAN FRANCISCO CITY AND COUNTY

WILLIAM C. BLAKE | WILLIAM H. CHESTER **Vice President** | THOMAS F. HAYES** | WILLIAM M. REEDY

In 1972, the appointed twelve-member BART board, frustrated that completion of the construction was over budget and more than two years behind the original schedule, pushed staff to settle on a firm opening date.

according to then–assistant general manager L. A. Kimball, "We successfully resisted being set up under Civil Service and instead chose to operate as a top-down organization, much like a small military base, but with an open-door policy."

Stokes was clearly sensitive to the change in tone on the twelve-member board. Nevertheless, he felt secure that he at least had the seven votes, and maybe more, required to get done what needed to get done as the countdown toward opening began. "If they want to play hardball, we can do that," Stokes quipped one day on his way into what was expected to be a contentious board of directors meeting.

One of the new directors appointed by the Contra Costa board of supervisors was Nello J. Bianco, a Richmond businessman who had served on the City of Richmond's Personnel Board and was active in Democratic politics. He and his wife, Betty, owned a very successful delicatessen and catering service in Richmond. Bianco, who became not only one of the longest-serving directors on the BART board but also one of the most influential, was not in the Stokes camp from the very beginning. Before taking his seat on the board, he vowed to look critically at all aspects of the project, particularly the relationship between PBTB and the transit district.

Bianco was one of six candidates nominated for selection by the Contra Costa board of supervisors. Among the other candidates were Joe Silva, an incumbent who was easily reappointed to his seat, and Roy Anderson, a member of the Diablo Chapter of the California Society of Professional Engineers. Gilbert A. Verdugo, also a member of the Diablo Chapter and himself a nominee for a board position, gave a nomination speech for Anderson. During the selection process, each candidate was asked to give a presentation on why he wanted to be on the BARTD board and what he thought he could bring to the seat. The incentive was certainly not money, since board members received a stipend of only $50 per meeting, up to a maximum of five meetings per month, plus expenses.

Anderson, who worked for the California Division of Bay Toll Crossings, had been nominated as a candidate for the BARTD board by his chapter of the California Society of Professional Engineers, as was Verdugo. Anderson seemed to be loaded for bear when he was interviewed by the Contra Costa board of supervisors, and his lengthy presentation caused a real stir. He was extremely harsh in his criticism of how the project was being managed and even called for the firing of the general manager, a change in the makeup of the transit district board, and a detailed audit of the project by the state. The thrust of his words was that no one at BARTD had any experience, either technically or in the managing of such a mammoth project, and so everything was left up to the consulting engineers, who ran the show while lining their own pockets with public money. Anderson also lambasted BARTD for the deficit and in essence accused management of a cover-up of what he believed was the real reason the project had run out of money. All of this, of course, was after the state legislature had passed its bailout bill.

On September 24, the *Richmond Independent* published the gist of Anderson's presentation, particularly the parts that targeted the BARTD board's choice of a general manager. According to the book *Divided Loyalties: Whistle-Blowing at BART* (written by Robert M. Anderson, Robert Perrucci, Dan E. Schendel, and Leon E. Trachtman; Purdue University, 1980), Anderson was called on the carpet by his supervisor at the Division of Bay Toll Crossings because of the publicity surrounding his publicly expressed attitude about BART, which was creating an awkward situation for the state. Anderson was told in no uncertain terms to knock it off, because it would look as though there were competition for funding between the BARTD project and the proposed Southern Crossing, the latter of which the bridge authority was pushing and which eventually failed at the ballot box. All of this would become relevant two years down the road.

Meanwhile, Bianco was focused not just on getting the BART system launched as soon as possible but also on future extension lines. These were already on the board's radar and beginning to be discussed, even though the basic system was not yet completed. The board was committed to prioritizing any future extensions within the three counties before spending a dime outside of the district, and in the years to come, this issue would create a volatile division among members of the board, who sometimes became involved in public shouting matches. Bianco's concern that the board might seek an extension to the San Francisco airport before first meeting the District's commitment to building East Bay extensions prompted strong support from the *Contra Costa Times*. This led to special legislation by state assemblyman Daniel Boatwright, who was from Concord in Contra Costa County. The Boatwright bill, authored in 1976, very specifically prohibited BARTD from spending any money outside the three-county district before meeting its extension commitments within the original boundaries.

Soon after signing the Boatwright bill into law, then-governor Jerry Brown took his first ride on BART from Daly City to the Embarcadero Station, accompanied by the general manager at that time, Frank C. Herringer, and me, as director of media and public affairs. While getting

In the late 1970s, Governor Jerry Brown buys a ticket to take a ride on BART from Daly City to the Embarcadero Station in San Francisco.

a briefing inside the operator's cab of the train, Brown asked when BART would be going to the San Francisco airport, exclaiming that the extension should be a priority. He was then reminded that he'd just signed a bill that would prevent that from happening anytime soon. "Was that a bad bill?" the governor asked. "Well, it prevents us from going to the airport," Herringer responded. The governor looked at Herringer and then at me. "Hmm," was all he said at that point.

Also in 1969, the San Francisco board of supervisors appointed William C. Blake to replace Adrien Falk on the BARTD board. Blake, formerly a San Francisco supervisor and a director of the Golden Gate Bridge and Highway Transportation District, soon began hammering away at the delay in opening the system. "What the hell is going on?" he would often be heard saying in board meetings. "When are we going to open this system?"

Another new director was Richard O. Clark, a former mayor of Albany and a member of the city council who was appointed to the BARTD board in 1970 by the Alameda County Mayor's Conference. Clark was also skeptical of Stokes's management, and in fact all of the directors were now feeling the pressure from an unhappy public. Much of the dissatisfaction came about during the late 1960s when it looked like the District was going to run out of money and not complete the system at all. Ironically, the cost overruns were in many cases the result of delays due in part to the transit district's responsiveness to community demands for changes and improvements. The other significant factor was the huge rate of inflation—caused in some measure by the Vietnam War—which had more than doubled the projected expenses.

While critics continued to be skeptical of these reasons, Lawrence Dahms, a young man working at the time for legislative analyst A. Alan Post in Sacramento, had been assigned to review the project's well-publicized shortfall and concluded that it would in fact take $150 million to finish construction of the system (see Chapter 8). "I believe I did as thorough an analysis as possible of the situation and the causes for the shortfall and recommended my conclusions to Post, who in turn made his recommendation to the legislature," Dahms said. Dahms would later be recruited to join the BARTD staff as the assistant general manager of planning, budget, and marketing.

THE MARGARET THATCHER VISIT

On March 11, 1969, a youngish member of parliament from North London, Margaret Thatcher, visited the BART construction site, accompanied by a friend and San Francisco resident, Bryan Hemming. Thatcher, an outspoken fiscal conservative who then had the title of Shadow Minister of Transport, wanted to see this new space-age system in its development stage. (A "shadow minister" is a member of a "shadow cabinet" of the minority opposition, ready to take

England's future prime minister, Margaret Thatcher, visits a BART construction site in 1969 accompanied by her friend Bryan Hemming. At the time, she was the minister of transportation for the shadow government.

over in case the majority government fails.) During the tour, a representative from BART's Information Department explained what the frequency of the cars entering the station would eventually be. "You call them cars?" Thatcher exclaimed. "Don't you get confused with cars on the street? In London we call them trains." The information officer nodded and noted, "We call them trains, too." She was shocked when told by the representative that tunneling 2 miles under Berkeley would cost $20 million. "Ten million a mile?" she reacted, not surprisingly, with horror. Of course, the information on the cost was erroneous. It was $12.5 million per mile and included two stations. That said, in today's dollars it would cost somewhere in the vicinity of $100 million per mile.

After taking a tour, Thatcher, the future prime minister of the United Kingdom, did not want to speak to reporters who had gathered at BART headquarters to interview her. Instead, she met privately with general manager B. R. Stokes in his office at 814 Mission Street in San Francisco. According to Hemming, she told Stokes, "It will never work and it costs too much." She was not alone in that view, as local project watchers, career critics, and newspaper pundits were grumbling the same thing, some even going so far as to suggest the work stop and no more money be invested. That, of course, is what the naysayers had said about the cost of building the New York City subway system, which essentially saved New York and made it one of the great cities of the world. Our history is replete with cynics who have opposed so many other great and now iconic structures that have been built since the founding of this country.

MORE CHANGES ON THE BOARD

Also new to the board in 1970 was William H. Chester, who was appointed by San Francisco mayor Joe Alioto. As vice president of the International Longshoremen's and Warehousemen's Union, he served on the mayor's Labor Advisory Committee and was a member of the San Francisco Human Rights Commission. He would play a major role in union contract negotiations and minority hiring. Chester was a moderate where Stokes was concerned, and for the most part was a supporter of BART management.

In 1972, Thomas F. Hayes was also appointed by Mayor Alioto to serve on the BARTD board. Hayes, who had emigrated from Ireland in 1949 and eventually settled in San Francisco, was a successful businessman and very active in civic affairs. He was a strong Stokes supporter. Also in 1972, Daniel C. Helix, the mayor of Concord, was appointed by the Contra Costa County Mayor's Conference. He came to the board with a critical view of management, making for a total of four board directors who were not supporters of Stokes. While Stokes continued to maintain a strong grip on the wheel of the project, his detractors were growing in number. His primary goal now was to get the system up and running, and once that was accomplished, he indicated that he would be ready to move on. But as was par for the course for the project, things did not go smoothly. A crisis on the twelve-member board came into the spotlight over concerns about technology and, on the personal side, loyalty.

THE UNFORTUNATE SAGA OF THE THREE ENGINEERS

The loyalty issue began with an incident involving three BART engineers, each with a specialty on the technical side of the project. The book *Divided Loyalties* was, in fact, devoted to examining the ethics of the incident, which involved whistle-blowing at BART in the early 1970s. At the time, the incident was well publicized, and once again it put the BART organization, and particularly its management, in the hot seat. The three engineers were Holger Hjortsvang, a systems engineer; Max Blankenzee, a programmer; and Robert Bruder, an electrical engineer.

The work being conducted by the three engineers was interrelated technology. Hjortsvang had started with the project in 1966 and worked directly with Westinghouse on developing maintenance for the automatic train control system. He had spent almost a year in the Westinghouse headquarters in Pittsburgh, Pennsylvania, working on the project. During that time, he felt that significant problems were not being addressed and that the sense of urgency to produce the product so that BART could be ready to open soon was leaving gaps in the work. In 1969, working back in Oakland at the Lake Merritt facility, Hjortsvang began to express his concern about Westinghouse's approach to the work. He believed that the training program for maintaining the automatic train control system was inadequate and that not enough documentation was coming from Westinghouse. He expressed his concerns in a series of memos sent between 1969 and 1971 to his supervisor, Edward Wargin, the superintendent of maintenance and engineering. Wargin in turn reported to Charles O. Kramer, the general superintendent of power and way, who in turn reported to director of operations E. John Ray. Ray then reported to the assistant general manager for operations and engineering, David Hammond. In his communiqués, Hjortsvang also said he felt that the monitoring of the Westinghouse work was not adequately structured by either BART or the consulting engineers of PBTB. He predicted a mean time between train failures would occur somewhere around every three and a half hours. According to Hjortsvang, he received little or no response to his concerns.

During 1971, Hjortsvang found a compatriot in Max Blankenzee, also an engineer and a senior programmer analyst, who himself had similar concerns from another perspective. Blankenzee was a former employee of Westinghouse who had worked on the BART automatic train control project. He had joined the BART staff in May 1971 and also reported directly to Wargin. While Hjortsvang was primarily concerned with the development of the automatic train control maintenance procedures and training to be provided as part of the Westinghouse contract, Blankenzee was highly critical of the automatic train control development. He, too, had written memos expressing his concerns to his supervisor, apparently with little or no response. He had worked on the simulator, which was supposed to show what a train would do in actual operation under automatic train control. He felt the software people had not delivered a completed product, saying that so far nothing really worked and that BART would be left holding the bag, so to speak, dealing with a high failure rate.

The third member of the trio was Robert Bruder, an electrical engineer who had been working for the transit district since 1966. He had major concerns about the quality control of the work on communications installations. By November 1971 the three engineers determined that they were on the same page with regard to PBTB's ability to monitor the technical products from the contractors.

THE FAMOUS UNSIGNED MEMORANDUM

On November 18, Hjortsvang circulated an unsigned memorandum describing the many problems he believed needed to be dealt with. In it he suggested that management as structured was not competent to understand the problems and that what was needed was the creation of a Systems Engineering Department. The memorandum was surreptitiously distributed throughout much of the organization. Management found the memo of great concern and invited the author to come forward and discuss the issues. It wasn't clear whether the invitation came from Stokes or another higher-up. Hjortsvang, more than likely fearing for his job, chose not to reveal himself.

About this time, the three engineers decided that they needed to find a way to get their message directly to Stokes. The question was how to do so without infuriating their immediate bosses, Wargin, Kramer, and Ray. Even though the memo had been circulated through the company, they simply didn't know whether Stokes was aware of the full extent of the problems with the automatic train control. They were certain Kramer knew of the issues, and they speculated that he might be keeping bad news from the boss on the basis that things would eventually be fixed. Meanwhile, the anonymous memorandum was being seen more as an attack on BART and PBTB management than an attempt to shine a spotlight on potential problems.

At this point, the three engineers felt they were facing a significant ethical dilemma. On the one hand, whatever action they might contemplate could very well put their jobs on the line, which was the last thing they wanted to do, according to statements they made later. On the other hand, as professionals, did they have an obligation to broaden their communication beyond their immediate superiors? In other words, was there a public interest that needed to be addressed, given their views? They had been told in no uncertain terms by their supervisors that they were not to go above their heads to a higher level in the organization's hierarchy. In the case of Hjortsvang and Blankenzee, Kramer, whom Wargin reported to, was the firewall. Kramer was a crusty, rough-and-tumble guy who had practically grown up as an old-time railroad man. He knew rail "power and way" like the back of his hand. In other words, his experience and longevity in the field trumped any play that might be made by so-called troublemakers.

One big problem was that Hjortsvang, Blankenzee, and Bruder had no documentation to back up their claims. Initially Kramer suggested that the concerns being raised by these lower-level engineers were more subjective than substantive. According to interviews with the engineers by the authors of *Divided Loyalties,* an organizer for the Service Employees International Union (SEIU) by the name of Gil Ortiz somehow got involved with the three engineers, possibly having met them in the course of trying to organize employees. In any case, Ortiz apparently offered to set up a secret meeting with a couple of the board members, namely Bill Blake and Nello Bianco. The engineers weren't sure how to present their case to the board members, who were not technology savvy, yet they nevertheless realized that the meeting could be the avenue they had been looking for to get to Stokes. But they saw another problem. The three engineers expressed the fear that their names might come out in such a meeting. Ortiz apparently told them they would be protected.

Still, toward the end of 1971, the three engineers decided to hold off on such a meeting until they felt they had their act together. In a phone conversation with Blake, Hjortsvang got the impression that the board member was suggesting he get some help to back him up. This translated into getting an outside party to confirm the legitimacy of their fears, someone who could articulate the issues for the board members. For this the three engineers contacted a consulting engineer named Edward Burfine, who had been recommended to them. During the meeting with Burfine at the Lake Merritt offices, the engineers turned over copies of their memos to him for review, including the unsigned memo of November 18, 1971, which Hjortsvang had written. They did not want Burfine to put his conclusions in writing—more than likely they feared a potential paper trail that might lead back to them—and at this point the operation had all the appearance of a cloak-and-dagger operation with clandestine meetings and communiqués. The three engineers believed, and rightly so, as it turned out, that it was imperative their names be kept out of it.

Meanwhile Bruder managed, through Phillip Ormsbee, a public relations official whom he had buttonholed, to get a meeting with general manager B. R. Stokes, who in turn brought in Hammond and Erland Tillman to listen to what Bruder had to say. However, from the engineer's perspective, while Stokes and the others seemed to listen with interest, nothing concrete came out of this meeting. They did express some surprise at what Bruder said about the extent of the problems he saw and what he felt was a lack of oversight of PBTB's work, especially as he emphasized that the problems would come back to haunt the project.

THE BURFINE REPORT

What happened next was this: Burfine wrote a seven-page report based on his conversation with the three engineers and the copies of the memos they had given him. Although a meeting with Blake and Bianco did not come together, a secret meeting with a new director, Daniel Helix, the mayor of Concord, did in fact take place in early January 1972. The meeting took place at SEIU Local 350's headquarters, an old English Tudor house on Grand Avenue in Oakland. Gil Ortiz had arranged for use of the facilities. Helix was very interested in what problems might be lurking for BART behind the scenes that would benefit from transparency, especially with regard to management. He was briefed by the engineers about the problems they saw with the automatic train control system, as well as the fact that they wanted to bring the problems to the attention of Stokes and the top managers. They gave Helix copies of various memoranda, mostly written by Hjortsvang, plus a copy of the Burfine Report, which was titled "Review of BART Operations" and dated January 12, 1972.

Not long after the meeting with Helix, the *Contra Costa Times* printed the contents of the memoranda, to the apparent horror of the three engineers, particularly Hjortsvang, who had been the author. Next, Helix distributed copies of the memoranda and the Burfine Report to the other eleven members of the board and BARTD top management for review. Management was, of course, nonplussed by the Burfine Report, which caused a buzz throughout the organization as well as the entire Bay Area. Both radio and television news picked up the story, and other newspapers followed up; the Burfine Report, in today's vernacular, went viral.

The managers of the three engineers immediately began questioning their subordinates about who might be behind the leaks. Who were the troublemakers in the organization? Hjortsvang, Blankenzee, and Bruder were among those questioned, and all three denied any knowledge of the report or of the anonymous memorandum of November 1971 titled "BART System Engineering." Management saw that memo as a fifth-column attack, and one that was political in nature rather than intended as a vehicle to bring technical problems to management's attention. Without question, once Stokes was aware of the memo, he was angry at the clandestine path someone inside the organization was taking. From his point of view, the memo was clearly designed to discredit BARTD's management hierarchy along with PBTB; as far as he was concerned, this covert scheme had been hatched to create havoc within the engineering division.

Helix put together a meeting in Concord and invited two other directors, Richard Clark and Nello Bianco, as well as Hjortsvang, Blankenzee, Bruder, and Burfine. The purpose of the meeting was to go over the Burfine Report and to bring Clark and Bianco into the loop before Helix took the report to the BARTD board's Engineering and Operations Committee. Burfine's initial seven-page report would be expanded into a twelve-page presentation. Hjortsvang was worried. He did not think Burfine could adequately present their case, believing Burfine simply didn't know enough about the issues, particularly if he got hit with questions. And Hjortsvang was proven right.

The Engineering and Operations Committee meeting was held February 22, 1972. The meeting room at BART's Lake Merritt headquarters was packed with members of the media and interested observers along with staff. Burfine was given several minutes to make his presentation. As it turned out, however, Burfine was shot down pretty fast and ended up being little more than a footnote to the meeting. The committee rejected the Burfine Report outright, and its perceived attack on management was defended by various parties. Dr. Woodrow Johnson of Westinghouse, who headed up the automatic train control project, came all the way from Pittsburgh, Pennsylvania, to give a very glowing report about the progress his people were making. A PBTB representative also gave a similarly positive review. Helix and others probed with various questions, but all in all the board committee seemed satisfied that everything was under control.

Following the failure of the Burfine presentation at the committee meeting, Helix decided to bring the three engineers themselves to the board meeting that was scheduled to take place two days later, February 24. Helix apparently believed the engineers could do a better job of explaining their concerns and had to convince them to go public. Burfine again spoke, and again did not impress the board. At this point, the three engineers, who had not yet been identified and whom Helix wanted to bring out in the open at that time, were not allowed to make a presentation. The board instead rejected the Burfine Report outright and gave B. R. Stokes and the BART project a vote of confidence, though it was not unanimous. The vote on the resolution was 10 ayes, 2 nos. I was present at the time, and I recall that when the board president asked Stokes about the contents and reliability of the Burfine Report at the open board meeting, he replied, "I find it passing strange that someone from outside the organization could, in one day, come up with such a report about the organization and the advanced and very complex technology BART was employing." Later a couple of the board members said management should try to find out who the malcontent engineers were.

When I interviewed him for this book in 2012 about the Burfine Report and the three engineers, Stokes recalled that he thought at the time that the Burfine Report was simply an incompetent piece of work, even childish in some respects. He also recalled that, while he was angry at the subterfuge behind the whole episode, he also felt sorry for the three engineers, whom he believed had been misguided and used for political purposes.

The engineers, whoever they might be, were then invited by management to come forward with their concerns. While it is not certain what would have happened had they done so, it has been suggested that they would more than likely have been reprimanded for the way they went about sharing their concerns (that is, going around their supervisors to reach upper management), but they at least would have kept their jobs. They still did not come forward.

As for the technical problems themselves, Stokes was unconcerned. "Like any new technology," he said, "there were bound to be numerous problems, most of which we were aware of, and that fixes were being worked on which BART was demanding of the contractors." Stokes said that it seemed there was also a self-serving aspect as to why the engineers, at least Hjortsvang and Blankenzee, had instigated their "conspiracy" to challenge the work being produced by Westinghouse and to level accusations that PBTB was not providing enough oversight. It was well documented that they had tried to recruit other engineers to join them with a promise of reward if they were successful in creating a Systems Engineering Group with Hjortsvang at the head. There were no takers. When interviewed later, some of the engineers who had been approached said that the three engineers' undercover efforts had had a negative effect on morale, particularly with the release of the bashing newspaper stories over the leaked documents.

At the time, the three engineers were still under the radar. But when push came to shove, their continued denial of involvement with the unsigned memo, the Burfine Report, and Director Helix ultimately determined their fate with the project. While Helix never divulged their names, the agency eventually figured out who they were without much difficulty.

AN UNHAPPY DENOUEMENT

On March 2, 1972, Holger Hjortsvang was called into John Ray's office, where he was confronted by both Ray and Charlie Kramer. At this meeting, Hjortsvang was asked to resign. He refused. Ray then informed him that unless he resigned he would be terminated. Hjortsvang, taking stock of his position, changed his mind and resigned. He was not given a reason, only that it was ordered by Stokes. He was escorted by a security person to his office, where he was allowed to take his personal items, and then was escorted out of the building. Later that day, Blankenzee was terminated after refusing to tender his resignation. The next day, March 3, Bruder was also terminated after refusing to resign. After receiving recommendations from their supervisors that they be terminated, Stokes had directed that they be offered the chance to resign first.

In 1974, the three engineers filed a wrongful-termination suit against the District, asking for $885,000 in damages. In 1975, against the wishes of the then former managers who had given depositions in the case, the BARTD board elected to settle the matter out of court. In a closed executive session, the District's general counsel apparently advised the board that he believed the agency would prevail if the case went to trial, however, the trial might open many doors and become a distraction during a period when great effort was being made to correct various early problems. Thus, the board agreed to pay out a total sum of $75,000, giving $25,000 to each of the three engineers.

In a private conversation with David Hammond at a transit conference following the settlement, I had the distinct impression that he was very unhappy with the board's action, which undercut the staff's view that the firings were the correct and only reasonable action to take. Hammond, of course, understood the public relations issues that could be generated by a trial. By this time he was no longer working for BART, having taken a position with the internationally recognized engineering firm of Daniel, Mann, Johnson and Mendenhall. In the final analysis, the whole affair involving the three engineers had a troubling effect on the employees throughout the District as it geared up for picking a firm date to open. The pressure was building.

CHAPTER 15

DAYS OF THE LONG KNIVES

The long knives were growing longer and getting sharper in the wake of the episode involving the three engineers, and they were aimed primarily at Stokes and his management team. People were upset not just because of the firing of the engineers but also because of the continued delays in opening the system. New questions were being thrown out about contracts and the costs associated with the PBTB contract, plus the numerous change orders for the transit vehicle contract. Politically, the atmosphere of the boardroom was highly charged and thick with rancorous rhetoric. Management was coming under constant attack by the minority contingent of the board, which had distanced itself from the Stokes camp. At the time, it seemed as though almost every day some new revelation was being pursued, while the media outlets, primarily the *Contra Costa Times* and the *San Francisco Chronicle,* were salivating over the controversies. Among the questions, which sounded more like charges, were: Why have there been cost overruns? Why have there been so many delays in opening the system? Why does the project have a general manager who is not an engineer? Where was the accountability?

Bill Stokes's resolve and toughness kept his critics at bay during the early 1970s as the pressure was building to announce a firm opening date for the new system. At that point the start of service was about two and a half years late, according to the estimated date in the original Composite Report. Some critics reiterated the old theme that BART was simply aiming too high in its quest to advance the state of the art in transit-signaling technology and automation. "We want BART to be the most efficient system operating in today's world, and full automation is the key to achieving that," Stokes said in answer to the critics. "If you don't aim for the optimum, you won't achieve the optimum." To him, efficiency meant having a minimal number of employees to run the system, lower power requirements (in part thanks to lightweight trains), and the ability to carry as many as 750 seated passengers on a ten-car train with one operator at the helm. (In actuality, these days it is not unusual to see as many as 2,000 passengers packed into a ten-car train.)

Meanwhile, an anxious public wanted to see the doors open and those promised silver trains gliding along. And an anxious public also meant anxious politicians, who were putting pressure on the appointed board members. Everyone was pushing for a commitment to an official opening day. A tentative date was picked for the spring of 1972, but even that turned out to be optimistic. One of the events that scuttled a spring opening at the time was a strike at the transit car supplier, Rohr Industries.

ROHR HITS THE BRICKS

In the early hours of November 15, 1971, the workers at Rohr's Chula Vista plant walked off the job; they would stay away for nine weeks. It was my first day as a BART employee, then as an information officer. I was the first one to receive news of the strike, which came from a reporter at the *San Diego Union* seeking comment. The question was "Will this delay the system opening?" I did not know the answer and said I would call back. The reporter was on deadline and pressed for an answer. I then roamed around looking for someone and eventually wandered into general manager B. R. Stokes's office and, addressing him as Mr. Stokes, nervously told him of the strike. He said to tell the press, "We'll keep an eye on developments." As I was leaving his office, he said, "By the way, call me Bill."

The strike, of course, held up the delivery of the production cars needed for the start-up of revenue service. All the District had so far were the prototype test cars. Next was an incident that received plenty of media attention and further exacerbated the board's growing concern over the delayed start date. Earlier that year a two-car test train traveling at about 25 miles per hour under manual control ran into another test train parked on the Fremont line near the Coliseum Station. It was believed the train operator fell asleep at the control panel, but he claimed he simply couldn't stop the train. Inspectors investigating the accident found that the emergency braking system was fully operational. However, the first stories of the incident speculated about whether the train had been operating under automatic control, fueling rumors that the system would not work as planned. In another freak incident, gophers had been eating up the train control cables running underground along the track near BART's Hayward storage yard. The gophers apparently found the cable quite tasty, and PBTB had to re-lay the cable within concrete conduits for protection against any further invasion.

Meanwhile, Daniel Helix, who had been powerless to protect the three beleaguered engineers, was quoted in the *Contra Costa Times* as saying that he believed their firings had had a muzzling effect on others inside the organization who might want to come forward. He had allies in two reporters from the *Times,* Justin Roberts and Rick Vogt, both of whom wrote extensively about BART, mostly negative stories that targeted Stokes. A new story about one thing or another seemed to appear in the *Times* every day. Helix was also quoted as saying that he thought the transit district's twelve-member board had "whitewashed" the issue of the automatic train control system as reported by Burfine. The board's 10–2 vote to reject the report and assert full confidence in management had a lingering political effect. Still, Arnold C. Anderson, a longtime member of the BARTD board from Alameda County, said after Helix's remarks that, if he'd been Stokes, he would also have fired the engineers for not following the proper chain-of-command protocol in getting recognition for their concerns. The fact was that initially they *had* tried to convey their concerns to their immediate supervisors but saw no response.

Another longtime director, George Silliman, who was named president of the BARTD board by his fellow directors for 1972, agreed with fellow director Anderson. While more often than not he disagreed with Stokes, he said that he, too, would have fired the engineers had he been in Stokes's place. However, he said that he did think that in some respects BART had taken on the mantle of a military-style organization, primarily because of the two highly placed former army colonels, David Hammond and Erland Tillman, and their influence on the personnel structure. But Silliman also felt that the management had a leading edge that encouraged creative thinking among its staff from the bottom up. He attributed this positive element to Stokes for setting the overall tone, even though he was not one of the general manager's biggest supporters.

A FIELD DAY FOR CARTOONISTS

From the beginning of the project, BART provided grist for newspaper cartoonists during different stages of its development. In 1972, one cartoon in particular from the *San Francisco Chronicle*'s Robert Graysmith was inspired by a quote in the *Chronicle* from director Nello Bianco. At one board meeting, the general counsel complained that he was not certain whom he should be taking direction from—he sometimes got direction from the general manager, who was in conflict with the board, which was his client by statute. The board made it clear that the general counsel should take his direction from the board. Bianco then likened Stokes to an emperor, with BART as his empire. The cartoon depicted Stokes sitting on a throne with a crown and fur cape, holding a scepter and governing by fiat. Even Stokes got a chuckle out of the portrayal; privately he remarked in his office one evening that if he had had that much power he would have had the system built and delivered to the people of the Bay Area years before.

Still, his critics were becoming more and more strident as 1972 pressed on with no firm opening date. Observers could see the change in the board as it transitioned from having a passive role, which it had assumed over the years, to a more active role, in which it would begin harsher questioning of contracts and, under new authority granted by the state, set administrative policy, in effect eroding the general manager's authority. But Stokes, true to his nature, was hanging tough, ready to play hardball. With a voice that suggested power but was modulated by a slight Oklahoma drawl, he had a very commanding presence. Since Stokes had begun running the show in 1963, he had gained the respect of the industry worldwide as a visionary pathfinder, and his stature was not lost on the board of directors. Despite the mounting criticism and attacks, he was still very much in charge.

SAFETY CONCERNS

Even though board president George Silliman had agreed with the firing of the three engineers, he was still very concerned about the safety of BART, and he did not want the system to open if there were any question about it being safe to operate. Silliman urged Stokes, Hammond, and John Ray to join him on a visit to Westinghouse in Pittsburgh, Pennsylvania, to discuss the automatic train control system. After meeting with the top people, including the chairman of Westinghouse, and witnessing a successful test of the system, Silliman was satisfied enough to be able to report back to the board that the project was on track and that the Westinghouse people had assured him the system would be safe. This visit helped staff and the board to begin looking at an opening date, possibly in September.

FINALLY, A FIRM OPENING DATE

When the nine-week Rohr strike ended in mid-January 1972, sleek silver production cars finally began to roll off the assembly line in Chula Vista. The cars were then trucked up to the Bay Area and delivered to BART's Hayward yard and shop, where they were detailed and made ready for eventual revenue service. Before the Rohr strike, a tentative opening date had been set for sometime in April, but the strike had made that time frame impossible. As spring approached, and with the assurances from Westinghouse that it could deliver the completed automatic train control system, staff recommended a firm opening date of September 11, which the board readily adopted. One could sense a collective sigh of relief coming from the board upon adjournment from one of its regularly scheduled meetings that spring.

BART, the baby of the transit industry and the first all-new system to be built in the United States in almost sixty years, would finally see the light of day. On a national level, the U.S. Department of Transportation and its funding arm for public transportation grants, the Urban Mass Transportation Administration (UMTA), viewed BART as a grand laboratory, paving the way for new, modern systems to be built in the capital and other parts of the nation. The Washington Metro had begun its building phase in 1969 and adopted the Westinghouse automatic train control system designed for BART. The Metropolitan Atlanta Rapid Transit Authority (MARTA) soon followed. Those later systems also benefitted from 80 percent federal funding, as compared to BART, which was primarily a locally funded project and received only 20 percent federal assistance.

AUTOMATIC TRAIN CONTROL PROBLEMS ARISE

Getting the automatic train control system ready for revenue service did not prove to be smooth sailing. After it had been fully installed, a series of tests was begun in the summer to determine the reliability of the train protection system. The goal was to ensure 100 percent detection of a train or a maintenance vehicle anywhere on the track. At this point, there was no redundant or backup automatic train control system; the theory was that this super-modern primary train control at the heart of the BART network would be adequate and never fail, or, in an extraordinary circumstance, would fail safely. The testing involved dragging a "dead" car around to various points on the tracks to see if it could be detected by the system. The tests, which were monitored by representatives of the California Public Utilities Commission (CPUC), the system's safety oversight authority, could be viewed in the Lake Merritt control center on the giant display board.

Unfortunately, initial tests showed a 1 percent dropout of detection, a very serious matter. The way the system was designed to work, when a block of track receives a signal that it is occupied by a train, it cuts off the current to a receiver located at the tail end of a block, which prevents another car from entering that portion of track (see Chapter 13 for more information). The 1 percent loss of detection meant that for 1 percent of the time the wheels and axle of the dead car were not performing as a shunt of the low current being sent through the rails, and thus a following train might be allowed to enter an occupied block. Anything less than 100 percent detection was unacceptable.

There were several theories as to why this glitch was happening. One was that the tracks themselves had developed a film of rust over time from lack of use, which minimized the wheel-to-rail contact and thus impeded the shunt. BART and Westinghouse engineers believed the problem could be solved quickly, but the CPUC observers told BART it could not open as planned. This news sent a wave of depression throughout the organization. Management was desperate to find a way to make the opening day. Finally it was suggested that BART would have to come up with an alternative plan to mitigate this problem if the system were to open on the September date. The board, of course, was not happy to hear about this new setback, and even questioned whether the CPUC was being too heavy-handed. But the CPUC, using a worst-case scenario as its guide, was adamant: opening

BART in its current condition would be unsafe for passengers. So the question was, how should the District proceed? What was the solution going forward to be?

After some hand-wringing, the BART operations department came up with what was called a "manual block" system to satisfy the CPUC and ensure that the system could safely operate until the automatic train control protection problem could be fixed. The plan worked this way: A BART transportation supervisor would be placed on the platform of every second station and call to alert the supervisor two stations down the line about the position of the train coming through. That supervisor would then release the following train to go on to the next station, and so on. This extra precaution would keep trains separated at all times by at least two stations. It was a safe solution, but, critics noted, under this kind of operation the service would be anything but rapid. This setback was, of course, played up in the press as an embarrassment—the promised space-age system had to resort to a hundred-year-old procedure, similar to a conductor holding up a lantern to signal the engineer to let a train proceed.

SACRAMENTO UNHAPPINESS

As rumors about safety issues and questions about contract management persisted, the angst increased in Sacramento about whether BART's new trains were ever going to operate. Again the media pounced on whatever was being said, regardless of whether the criticism had merit. Amid the growing hysteria, it was difficult to sift what was real from what was political hyperbole. One question emerged about the possible need for an operating subsidy, something that had never been considered in the original planning, since the assumption was that this modern system would pay for its operating costs out of the fare box. But this view may have been unrealistic from the beginning, given that many municipalities were taking over private transit systems in the postwar years because they simply couldn't be sustained by passenger revenue. In any case, it was clear from projections that, once in operation, at least initially, the shortfall in fare-box revenue would have to be made up out of diminishing capital. BART's staff planners and economists were already scratching their collective head as they projected worst-case scenarios when the system began operating. The capital set aside to help fund start-up costs would be eaten up within two years, according to the best estimates.

In June 1972, as the BART organization was gearing up for the September opening, all hell seemed to break loose at the state capitol. John Nejedly, a highly respected state senator from Contra Costa County, demanded that the Senate Committee on Public Utilities and Corporations conduct an investigation of BART and how it was being managed. Nejedly, who had been a county district attorney before successfully running for and entering the state senate in 1969, may have been spurred partly by the negative stories written by Justin Roberts appearing in the *Contra Costa Times,* as well as partly by a long-simmering attitude that all was not right with BARTD.

Dean Lesher, the publisher of the *Contra Costa Times* and various other papers, who was not a Stokes fan, may also have helped spur Nejedly's concern. One could speculate that his issues had their roots in the 1962 vote to approve the BART project. It was no secret that many Contra Costa County residents felt they had been dragged along by Alameda and San Francisco Counties, which had brought the combined vote to 61.22 percent. And Stokes had been the linchpin of the overall campaign. Because Contra Costa County had fallen short of the required 60 percent approval, a festering resentment was prevalent, particularly in the outlying areas.

The Senate Committee on Public Utilities and Corporations agreed to conduct an investigation of BART and assigned legislative analyst A. Alan Post to carry it out. Post, who had served in that position since 1949, had developed a strong reputation for integrity and in general was highly trusted. His job was nonpartisan; his primary mission was to review and analyze the state budget and expenditures. In that role, he also made recommendations involving legislation designed to provide funding for state agencies. In the case of BART, he had recommended the temporary half-cent sales tax to bail out the project in 1969. The sales tax increase, levied only in the three BART counties, generated the needed $150 million to help complete the basic system.

When notified of the Post investigation, Stokes at first bristled but then wisely ordered full cooperation on the part of staff, noting in interviews with the media that he welcomed the review by the analyst's office on behalf of the senate committee. Soon operatives from the analyst's office began showing up at the transit system's Lake Merritt headquarters, where they pored through various documents and interviewed key staff members. Meanwhile, my then colleague Bob Krae and I were being inundated by the press daily for comments on the meaning of the senate hearing and our official reaction to what was being said.

FINAL PREPARATIONS

Meanwhile, BART continued to gear up for the opening. Preparations included not only the final checklist of technical and physical work to be done on the system but also the first marketing and public information efforts for revenue service. Tours of the transit stations and the control center were conducted as part of an extensive community outreach program. The overall communication program included ads in local newspapers and the creation of a special full-color rotogravure titled "A Bright New Day for the Bay Area." The rotogravure, paid for with ads from contractors, would appear as a newspaper supplement on Sunday, September 10, in the Bay Area's three major metropolitan newspapers, which had a combined circulation of between 2 and 2.5 million. The supplement contained a variety of information segments about how to use the system, its automatic fare collection machines, danger areas like the third rail, and the very first fare schedule, which had been adopted by the board for the overall system. The minimum fare was 30 cents and the maximum would be $1.25 for the longest ride, although it would cost only $1.00 from end to end for the initial segment. Even the marketing effort received some criticism from a couple of the directors, one of whom stated, "Once in place, the riders will come. Why do we need to advertise?"

"Most of the early marketing was informational in nature," said Larry Dahms, the assistant general manager of planning, budget, and marketing. "It was important to make the public as aware as possible of the different facets of the system prior to opening. Of particular concern was getting customers familiar with how the fare machines worked. Under a $7 million contract, IBM designed and manufactured the new fare machines, the arrays of fare gates, and the magnetic-striped ticket, which is still used today. The plan was to have trained passenger service representatives to help." The passenger service representatives, four young women in orange uniforms, were to be proactive

The opening of the system caused a great deal of excitement in the business community, as evidenced by numerous ads in the area's major newspapers.

in providing help to riders. Taking a page out of the Disneyland model, if a passenger even looked as though he or she had a question, the passenger service representatives were to approach and offer to help. Other employees were stationed around the system with large round badges that said simply: "Ask Me."

As transit cars arrived from Southern California, the staff felt some trepidation as to whether or not Rohr would be able to deliver enough of the new vehicles to provide a reasonable service by an early August due date, leaving enough time for online testing. By July, only fourteen cars had been delivered. Stokes personally went down to the Hayward maintenance yard to inspect the cars, sometimes followed by the news media to get his perspective on BART preparations for the opening day. On Sunday, the day before opening, Stokes was visiting the Hayward facility when he was asked by Ed Arno from Channel 5 if he expected any problems. Stokes grinned and said, "Lots of them. But we'll have people out there to troubleshoot." As it turned out, BART would have eighteen cars available for the opening. A total of eight trains—six two-car trains and two three-car trains—would operate along 28 miles of track between Fremont in southern Alameda County and the MacArthur Station in North Oakland. The initial service would include twelve stations.

OPENING DAY

At ten o'clock on Monday morning, September 11, 1972, fifteen years after it was created by the State of California, BART held a grand and colorful ribbon-cutting ceremony at its Lake Merritt headquarters plaza. The celebration was kicked off by a local high school band, and thousands of people gathered to hear speeches by numerous local dignitaries, including San Francisco mayor Joe Alioto and Oakland vice mayor Frank Ogawa, among many others. At each stop between the Fremont and MacArthur Stations a ribbon-cutting ceremony was held, with local officials from each city participating. Following the individual ceremonies, trains positioned at every other station began moving northbound from Fremont and southbound from MacArthur in a rolling opening.

Service would be provided fourteen hours a day from six o'clock in the morning to eight o'clock in the evening, Monday through Friday.

Left: Gertrude Guild of San Leandro made history by being BART's first paying customer when the fare gates opened for revenue service at 10:00 A.M. on Monday, September 11, 1972.

Below: Following the opening of the system, BART management gathered at the Elegant Farmer restaurant in Oakland to celebrate. Left to right are Joan Stokes, Bill Stokes, Rosella Brady (Stokes's administrative assistant), and the author.

The fact that trains could travel up to 80 miles per hour was well publicized, which prompted an amusing question: a novice reporter from a local weekly called the public information department one day to ask how BART could run trains at 80 miles per hour when the California speed limit was 65 miles per hour. Another questioner asked whether or not train operators had special driver's licenses.

Within the BART organization, the deadly third rail was given special attention with a full-blown information campaign focused on

Following the system's opening on September 11, 1972, officials gathered in the central control room for a photo op. The man on far left is unidentified. Next to him, from left, are director Richard Clark, board president George Silliman, director Nello Bianco, secretary of transportation John Volpe, directors Thomas Hayes and Arnold Anderson, the author with a mustache, and directors Harry Lange, William Chester, and Joe Silva. At the far right, almost out of the picture, is general manager B. R. Stokes.

safety. As part of the campaign, a cadre of staff visited all schools close to the right-of-way to inform students and school personnel of the dangerous 1,000-volt third rail. Years later an inebriated man in Chicago climbed down into the trackway at a Chicago Transit Authority Station and urinated on the third rail. As the story goes, the man was electrocuted.

During that first week of operation, journalists from across the country and around the world came to cover the dramatic story of this newest of urban transit systems. More than 10,000 press kits were given away during that first week. All of the major U.S. radio and television networks, side by side with local outlets, covered the story. A large cartoon by Ken Alexander appeared in the *San Francisco Examiner* in which a wide-eyed, nervous-looking nose of a BART car is peeking through a curtain. The caption was: "Holy Smoke, the Whole World Is Watching!" And indeed it was, as accolades poured in from all corners of the globe.

SOME STRANGE HAPPENINGS

Plenty of eccentricities were reported from the field as service entered its second week. A middle-aged man with a craggy face, his countenance fixed in an alarmed expression, wandered into the Public Information Office one day and demanded to have an audience with the general manager or president of the board. He then warned in a loud voice that the devil was riding BART trains and all system employees had to purge themselves of sin before the start-up problems, of which there were many, could be fixed. He was thanked for his input and ushered out. Another report came from a line supervisor that a man on the platform at the 12th Street–Oakland City Center Station kept throwing coins on the floor and screaming something about how the I-Ching would determine where BART fit into the universe and if the next train was going to arrive on time. People were also doing horoscopes on the birth of the system and submitting them to the newspapers. One astrologer said that BART being born under the sign of Virgo meant that it was full of mystery, energies, and promise.

A young female flasher was escorted out of the system by BART police when they finally caught up with her. Her modus operandi, as the story goes, was to get on a train naked under a long coat, knock on the train operator's door, which was mostly glass, and, when she had the attention of the operator, open her coat and press herself against the glass. She was sent for 72-hour observation and eventually merged into obscurity. On another occasion, not long after opening, a young couple had their marriage ceremony performed on a Friday afternoon on a BART train between the

During the early years of BART operations, this poster by well-known Berkeley artist and printer David L. Goines could be seen on BART trains and in larger displays in transit stations. It was commissioned by BART to promote the system's information center.

19th Street and MacArthur Stations. *Chronicle* columnist Herb Caen wrote about the marriage in his column the following week, reporting that the couple had gone to Las Vegas for their honeymoon but that by Monday they were seeking a divorce; he called it just another unreliable story from BART. Over the years it would become clear that BART was like a microcosm of the world at large, a kind of city on wheels.

THE PRESIDENT AND FIRST LADY TAKE A RIDE

On the morning of September 27, President Richard Nixon and the First Lady made what was termed a surprise visit to BART. In actuality, several weeks of meetings with the White House advance team went into planning the visit, although it was kept hush-hush. I was assigned to be the liaison with the White House staff.

At first, everything seemed very loose and almost casual as details were being worked out, often over informal lunches. The advance personnel were friendly and open. But as the time approached, the net began to close tighter and tighter until the event became a Secret Service show and security was the top priority. Anyone who might get close to the president had to make his or her social security number available to the FBI, who in turn did background checks. This restriction included reporters, who learned of the visit a day or two before and had to request clearance to cover the president's arrival.

The secret service gave me the job of identifying which members of the working press could come to the airport to cover the president's visit. It was a unique position to be in. I set up a table on the tarmac of Oakland International Airport and handed out press packets and secret-service pins to reporters who had already been vetted. Fights almost broke out between two competing factions jockeying for position: the local working press versus the national press who were traveling with the president.

The Nixons landed on Air Force One at the Oakland airport, where they were officially greeted by Oakland vice mayor Frank Ogawa and then driven as part of a motorcade to BART's San Leandro Station. There, the president and his wife were met by Stokes. While Stokes showed President Nixon the station, I instructed the First Lady, Pat, on how to use the fare machines and how the tickets worked in the fare gates. She was very impressed. Stokes then accompanied the couple on a train to the Lake Merritt headquarters. Interestingly, I was on

A few weeks after opening day, BART hosts President Nixon and the First Lady. General Manager B. R. Stokes chats with the couple on a train from San Leandro to Lake Merritt Station in Oakland.

the same car in the background with White House Press Secretary Ron Ziegler and Chief of Staff Bob Haldeman, who was taking home movies. I couldn't have guessed at what was to come for these men, as the Watergate scandal was at that time still in its embryonic stage.

At BART's Lake Merritt headquarters, the president and his wife were given a tour of the control center and introduced to BART directors and staff. Before leaving for a rally, President Nixon presented the transit district with a check for $38 million, from a federal grant from UMTA earmarked for the completion of the system. At that point there was still a shortfall in funding for the second half of the transit car order: the final 200 cars to make up the total of 450. Sometime soon the transit system would have to exercise the option to purchase the remainder of the order before the Rohr assembly line shut down.

THE FREMONT FLYER

During its first week of operation, the BART trains carried 100,000 people. Service was becoming routine, except for being plagued by reliability problems with the cars themselves. Often they had to be taken out of service and replaced by newly delivered cars.

Then, less than a month after opening, on the morning of Monday, October 2, 1972, a BART train went off the end of the track at the Fremont Station. The lead car ended up in the station parking lot, and the train was dubbed the "Fremont Flyer." There were passengers aboard, but luckily no one was seriously injured. The incident did, however, take place as A. Alan Post was nearing the end of his investigation for the California State Senate Committee on Public Utilities and Corporations. As might be expected, the Fremont Flyer set off a whole new firestorm of probes and accusations that were further fueled by wide press coverage. As one might imagine, the senate committee's concerns about BART were looming larger than ever in anticipation of Post's conclusions.

Just a week later, on Monday, October 9, 1972, Post published and distributed his 106-page report, which contained thirty-one specific recommendations. A critical recommendation was that the transit system should not operate merged lines, such as in the Oakland Wye, where the Fremont, Richmond, and Concord trains came together, because of alleged deficiencies in the automatic train control system. A copy of the report was sent to BART for review and response, and copies were distributed to the press upon request. At that time, it was anticipated that BART would begin transbay service through the underwater tube the following year, with September 24 as the tentative starting date.

A few days later, on Wednesday, October 11, a long-planned special dedication of BART was held. This event was attended by U.S. Secretary of Transportation John Volpe, Urban Mass Transportation Administrator Carlos Villarreal, and several other federal and state officials. During his speech, Volpe characterized BART as being on the leading edge of technology, a pioneer and benchmark for the country's transportation progress, and tangible proof that the challenge of urban mobility could be met. When asked by reporters about his thoughts on the Fremont Flyer and the automatic train control problems, he responded by noting that all great technical achievements are not without start-up problems. He predicted that BART would be everything promised to the Bay Area residents who had paid for it, and then some. Then, on the heels of the grant check from President Nixon, Volpe announced a $27 million grant specifically to help pay for the new transit cars.

STATE SENATE HEARINGS HELD

Post's report called for a thorough technical review of BART's automatic train control system and recommended that the CPUC prohibit the transit system from opening any more lines until a fix corrected the problems. The timing of the Fremont Flyer, of course, could not have been worse, since it reinforced the Post report's basic premise. As it turned out, the incident was caused by a crystal that had come loose in an onboard circuit board, causing the train to speed up rather than go into a braking mode. In addition to inspecting all circuit boards, sandboxes were placed at the ends of the tracks as an extra precaution. Meanwhile, board meetings got a little wilder than normal as various speakers ranted about a variety of issues, from labor organizing, which had been going on for some time, to BART's technical problems. The board did go ahead and order the last 200 transit cars.

One speaker who became a regular at the meetings was Dr. Willard (Bill) Wattenburg, an electrical engineer who at the time was on the faculty of the University of California at Berkeley. He attended several meetings during which he often called Stokes a liar and accused him of giving the board a snow job about the technical issues. He was a factor at meetings for almost two years. Wattenburg was a colorful figure, having written a successful book, *How to Find and Fascinate a Mistress,* under the pseudonym Will Harvey, and later hosting a popular talk show on KGO radio out of San Francisco.

Countering Wattenburg's attacks was Dr. Woodrow Johnson, a Westinghouse vice president and top manager for the automatic train control project. He also appeared before the BART board and reported that BART was, in fact, receiving everything the contract called for, and, moreover, that the automatic train control worked.

On November 14, 1972, the first of five hearings was held in Sacramento by the Senate Committee on Public Utilities and Corporations, chaired by Senator Alfred Alquist. In testimony before the senate committee, BART board president George Silliman, general manager Stokes, and John Asmus, the automatic train control managing project engineer from PBTB, were adamant in their contention that the system was safe. Stokes went on the offensive. He said that, while he agreed with some of the recommendations of the Post report, he took issue with the overall assessment: "We are disappointed in the report and the manner in which it was prepared and that it has created a cloud concerning the safety of BART. It's not only disappointing but deplorable as well. BART is safe." He went on to testify that, with the manual block system on top of the primary train control system, "no two trains could get closer than two stations apart in our present operations." Stokes further noted that the goal of detecting a dead car on the rails 100 percent of the time was being worked on and that when the solution was found BART would be able to operate converging lines with absolute safety.

Others testified before the committee, including Wattenburg, who strongly contested the BART testimony: "There is no such thing as absolute one hundred percent safety," he said. "This is simply baloney!" Wattenburg did, however, say he believed that the track circuits would eventually work.

Roy Anderson from Contra Costa County, who was president of the Diablo Chapter of the California Society of Professional Engineers at the time, testified that he, too, believed BART to be unsafe and cited a story he had heard about a supposed accident at BART's Union Station that could not be verified and for which there was no record. He claimed that BART had tried to hide the incident from the public by not documenting it. He, too, accused Stokes of lying. A few years earlier Anderson had unsuccessfully sought a seat on the BARTD board (see Chapter 14), and he had also written extensively in defense of the three engineers who were fired in connection with the Burfine Report.

Those critics who were testifying along with the senate committee members were astonished to learn that BART did not plan to have a backup train control system. According to the plan, once all of the bugs were worked out of the primary automatic train control system, there would be no need for redundancy. This acknowledgment, seen as a revelation, only set the stage for continued political histrionics as the controversy raged on.

Meanwhile, on December 12, 1972, BART service hit its first milestone by marking the millionth passenger to enter the system.

CHAPTER 16

A CRITICAL DECADE AHEAD AS ATC CHALLENGES PERSIST

The 1970s have been some of the most critical and turbulent years in the system's bumpy history thus far. On December 19, 1972, as an outgrowth of the Post report and the testimony presented, the State Senate Committee on Public Utilities and Corporations created what was referred to as an ad hoc Blue Ribbon Committee, with $10,000 allocated for its expenses. The committee's charge was to investigate and review BART's automatic train control system and determine the validity of the allegations that either it simply didn't work or at least it didn't work as specified by the contract. Another critical question was whether the automatic train control should have a backup train-protection component. While Westinghouse did not believe a backup system would be necessary once the bugs were worked out, others were not so sure; in any case, a redundant system had not been included in the original specifications of the $27 million contract. A couple of years later Bill Wattenburg, who at the time of the state senate hearings said he was absolutely astounded that there was no redundant fail-safe component to the Westinghouse primary train control system, would refer to BART as "Watergate on Wheels."

Wattenburg continued his harangue at just about every meeting of the District's board of directors, which met twice a month, with committee meetings in between. Some of the directors did not want to let Wattenburg speak, calling his diatribes nothing more than over-the-top histrionics from a self-appointed critic. Wattenburg always identified himself as a concerned citizen who wanted to see the system succeed. At the end of the day, the minority contingent of directors who did not support Stokes insisted that Wattenburg be allowed to express his opinions and that, as board members representing the public, they should listen. He could shed some light on the path that BART engineers should be taking, they said. Some of the anti-Stokes directors, including Bianco, who was vice president of the board during 1972, argued that it didn't hurt to listen to Wattenburg, and, since he was certainly knowledgeable, perhaps he could identify possible fixes to the automatic train control system. Stokes argued that this was like having one more unneeded cook in the kitchen. He emphasized that very competent engineers were working on the fixes.

Dr. Woody Johnson, the Westinghouse vice president and overall automatic train control project head, was adamant that everything was going to work. With his feisty personality in high gear, he went even further and admonished the board for considering the opinions of outside gadflies, without necessarily pointing any fingers. Bianco and others did not take kindly to being lectured at by Johnson. George Silliman, president of the board during 1972, agreed with Bianco and the minority contingent that Wattenburg should be heard, and with their backing Wattenburg pursued the same general line of attack that he had used at the senate hearings, basically denouncing the competence of those working on the project and again condemning BART management oversight. He also accused Westinghouse of giving the BART board a lot of bambosh concerning the efficacy of the automatic train control.

The rancor over the automatic train control issue and Wattenburg's diatribes went on for almost two years, until around mid-1974. Mostly Wattenburg attacked Westinghouse, whose representatives were always there to rebut his arguments. Also, Wattenburg rarely failed to verbally attack Stokes in person at the meetings for what he believed was Stokes's stubborn refusal to back away from Westinghouse's contention that all was well. Stokes never denied that there were problems, but he made it clear that he felt certain the basic concept was sound, continuing to underscore his contention that there were fixes in the works that would allow BART to operate as intended. Stokes never failed to take a moment to emphasize that the system was safe, which Wattenburg, when present, always countered with cries of "Malarkey!" or "Nonsense!" At one point it looked as though a fistfight might break out in the boardroom as charges and countercharges flew.

The press, of course, was enjoying a bumper crop of material with the circuslike goings-on, but the working reporters were not always exactly sure where the truth lay. Without doubt, Wattenburg was a compelling personality as he presented his arguments and solutions before the board, and he was very quotable. Michael Harris of the *San Francisco Chronicle*, who was now covering BART extensively, worked almost as a tag team partner with Wattenburg. Other reporters covering BART on a regular basis, including Harre Demoro from the *Oakland Tribune*, a nationally recognized transit expert who had written several books on the subject, and Hank Kusserow, a venerable reporter from the *San Francisco Examiner*, could not be certain about what was real and what wasn't as the controversy about the automatic train control raged on. Demoro always called it as he saw it, but for the time being this was a "he said–he said" battle. He did believe that in the end Stokes would prevail and that the system would work as intended.

Wattenburg suggested several antidotes to the alleged automatic train control problem, one of which was a device in a box designed by some of his students at the University of California. Westinghouse, however, declared that the use of any special devices, such as what Wattenburg proposed, could, and more than likely would, jeopardize the warranty on its deliverables. Wattenburg did demonstrate that a film of rust on the tracks accumulated from lack of use impeded the low-voltage current from being picked up by the wheel-axle shunt, which was a key component of the train protection system. If the current was not shunted, a receiver in a following track zone or block would not indicate that the block ahead was occupied and thus a following train would not go into a braking mode. Braking would then depend on a train operator, who could manually bring his or her train to a halt upon a visual sighting of the train ahead. During the initial operation of BART, the manual two-station separation of the trains worked as a backup, but that solution was only a temporary fix.

Meanwhile, BART management, Westinghouse, and PBTB engineers were already aware of the rust problem on the tracks and had begun looking at cleaning the rails as one factor toward solving the problem. Eliminating the rust would lessen impedance, enhancing wheel-rail contact, which in turn would ease the flow of low current through the axle shunt. But even with this approach there would be a great deal more to do before the system could work fully off of the primary train control. And what else could be done besides cleaning the rails for better contact? A staffer came up with an idea.

HYSTERIA AND PANIC

Along with Westinghouse, BART engineer Charlie Kramer, who had been involved in the forced resignation of Holger Hjortsvang, one of the three whistle-blower engineers, was now under excruciating pressure to come up with some immediate answers. Feeling stampeded, Kramer and his team determined that they should attack the problem of the film of rust on the tracks as soon as possible. Primarily as a result of the dead-car test, they knew that the rust did in fact impede the flow of current between rail and wheels, and it was no wonder considering that the track had been sitting unused and exposed to the weather for years. Westinghouse was also working on the problem, and it was one of its engineers, Howard Miller, who finally came up with a possible solution. In an effort to improve the wheel-rail contact, he developed the idea for something called "wheel scrubbers," which were attached to the axles.

The scrubbers, specially molded out of solid aluminum, would act like brushes and clean the wheels as the trains moved along the tracks. Charlie Kramer's team directed the implementation of the scrubbers, but with some skepticism; Kramer simply wasn't sure the scrubber scheme would work. BART invested in the idea only as a short-term experiment, and only a few cars were outfitted with the scrubbers. They worked intermittently but were clearly not the long-term answer to the problem, and the idea was soon dropped. Even more important in the debate at the time was the nagging question of whether there should be a permanent backup system in place, even though management still insisted that the primary train control system would work.

THE BART BOARD CREATES ITS OWN BLUE RIBBON COMMITTEE

To answer some of the critical questions being raised, the BARTD board decided to create its own blue-ribbon approach to review existing technical issues and evaluate management's ability to deal with them. While the dynamics of the board had, since 1969, been trending toward greater involvement, it still pretty much rubber-stamped most items brought to it for approval by staff. Up to that point the board had been more or less passive as Stokes, a strong general manager, ran the show virtually unchallenged. While mistakes had been made during the construction years, on balance no one could argue that Stokes didn't get things done.

By the 1970s, Stokes's reputation nationally and internationally as an expert on urban transit was solid. Still, in the face of the criticism coming at the District from all sectors—public, political, and technical—the board, including Stokes's longtime supporters, was beginning to take a more active role in the decision-making process. The board determined to also be proactive in setting policy for the administration, a move that followed recent legislation designed to give it more authority in that area. Under the original enabling legislation, the administration had been almost wholly under the purview of the general manager. Stokes, of course, was not happy about the board's action to bring in more outsiders.

For its own blue-ribbon effort, the board contracted with the Arthur D. Little Company (ADL) as a consultant. ADL in turn contracted with a systems engineer named Robert A. Profet, on loan from the McDonnell Douglas Corporation, to serve as a technical analyst. ADL and Profet were charged by the board with conducting an investigation of the automatic train control and with reviewing BART management and the organization's technical ability. Profet concluded that BART did not have the desired level of technical expertise at the management level, that the systems engineering was deficient, and that problems would persist under the current leadership at the top. Like the earlier Burfine Report, Profet's report spurred a fair amount of resentment for what some saw as a quick-and-dirty review. It became the butt of some internal joking: one BART executive began calling it the "non-Profet report." Profet was eventually removed from the work, but ADL continued to review the overall management structure and, in the fall of 1973, delivered to the board its own report, which was highly critical of both management and the board for not exercising more control of the District's functions.

THE SENATE BLUE RIBBON COMMITTEE GETS TO WORK

Meanwhile, the state senate's Blue Ribbon Committee would be made up of three men with expertise in the field of electronics. One of the three was Dr. Bernard Oliver, a vice president at Hewlett-Packard, who did not believe the automatic train control was as deficient as it was being made out to be. He testified at the senate hearings and noted that he believed the necessary corrections would be implemented as stated by Dr. Woody Johnson and Stokes. Senator Nejedly was not happy with Oliver's benign testimony and tried to press him into a more critical mode, which did not work. Oliver did, however, say he believed that such a complex system should have an extra measure of safety assurance with some sort of fail-safe mechanism or redundant train protection.

The Blue Ribbon Committee began its work in early 1973. BART's assistant general manager for planning and budget, Larry Dahms, who acted as the transit system's liaison with Oliver, said he was impressed with Oliver's low-key style and believed he was something of a genius in his field. With Oliver setting the tone, the Blue Ribbon panel began working quietly behind the scenes in an effort to separate itself from the politics and individual state senators looking to make political capital on BART's back. Oliver also began working on a secret project that he believed would be the key to full system operation.

With the volatile senate hearings ended, at least for the time being, the new year was already full of turmoil and contentious debate among board members. Continued daily press coverage magnified the myriad start-up problems and the political infighting. Two new board members took their seats, but Stokes's balance of power was maintained. Tom Hayes, a San Francisco businessman appointed by Alioto, supported Stokes; San Francisco supervisor Quentin Kopp, appointed by the San Francisco board of supervisors in 1973, did not.

Even with the changes on the BART board, Stokes still maintained the solid support of seven of the twelve directors when it came to a vote of confidence. This was tested when Dan Helix called for a resolution to fire Stokes in an open board meeting. The boardroom, with its hundred blue-cushioned seats filled and standees along the sides, suddenly became electrified with silence. You could hear a pin drop. Richard Shephard, the district secretary, called for a vote. Many interested attendees and staff leaned forward to make sure they did not miss the count. There was a long, pregnant moment up at the curved dais when it was not clear exactly what was happening or how the vote was going to come out. Stokes sat stoically in his usual place at the end of the staff table, leaning back and calmly sucking on his pipe, while board members gathered their thoughts. Some of the directors looked shocked or taken aback at hearing the resolution as stated read back to them by Shephard. Shephard then tallied the votes. There were 5 ayes and 7 nos. Stokes survived, even though it was becoming clear that his tenure as the guiding force to get the system built and running was being shortened by the day.

NEW LINES OPEN AS POLITICAL TURMOIL CONTINUES

On January 29, 1973, BART opened the Richmond line, which extended 11 miles north from the MacArthur Station through Berkeley and El Cerrito. This brought the total system miles to 39 and added six new stations. With more cars now available for service, BART was now able to add additional trains. Ridership on average prior to opening the new line was running at 12,000 daily, on a fourteen-hour-day operating schedule from 6 A.M. to 8 P.M. With the opening of the new line, ridership jumped to 27,000 per day. The system wasn't running at top efficiency—the trains were still operating under the manual block system, getting no closer than two stations apart, which lengthened the headways—but the system was able to operate on fifteen-minute headways that kept the trains moving smoothly and safely.

On May 21, the MacArthur to Concord line opened, adding 19 miles and six more stations to the operation, bringing the total system miles in operation to 58. The Concord line, along a freeway median, was perhaps the most scenic of the system, running through rolling, grass-covered hills, with eastern vistas of Mount Diablo, which in winter sometimes sported snowcaps. With this line now operating, ridership jumped again, to 38,000 daily, with trips almost evenly divided between peak and off-peak travel. This division of travel times by riders was an excellent sign that BART, which was primarily a long-distance trunk-line system, would be used for a variety of purposes and not just for commuting. This factor would be important for achieving an economy of scale in terms of full utilization.

Since the CPUC would not allow BART to operate through merged lines until the automatic train control system was operating at 100 percent, the start-up of revenue service between San Francisco/Daly City and the East Bay could not take place in April 1973, or at all that year, as had been planned. This setback not only deprived potential customers, and particularly transbay commuters, of available service at the earliest possible time but also negatively affected anticipated essential revenues. While the system had reached 95 percent of the ridership projections for the services being provided thus far, service between Oakland and San Francisco/Daly City was the key to achieving optimum revenue levels. Historically, with the Transbay Tube at the very heart of the system, it had been projected that one day BART ridership would see as many as 250,000 passengers each weekday, operating at ninety-second headways.

LABOR ISSUES BUBBLE UP

Controversy over the automatic train control system was not the only cause for concern at BART headquarters. With the opening of the new lines, BART fully activated both its Richmond and Concord maintenance shops and storage yards to support the new services. In the summer of 1972, before the initial start of revenue service, a herculean effort had been made to recruit and train new personnel for the multitude of jobs required to support operations and administration. A hiring freeze imposed by the state from June 18 to July 15, 1972, shortened the hiring window just as the system was gearing up for its opening. The jobs included positions for train operators, station agents, mechanics, carpenters, electricians, engineers, and a variety of other disciplines. It was estimated that about 55,000 hours of specialized training were administered to new employees in a very short period of time before the September 11 opening.

The state had appointed Sam Kagel, a highly respected professional labor lawyer and arbitrator, to establish the framework for determining the collective-bargaining units that would eventually represent the District's rank-and-file employees, including some staff at the mid-management level. Kagel was an old hand at how unions and management functioned, with experience going back to the docks of the San Francisco waterfront in 1934, when he worked with Harry Bridges, president of the International Longshoremen's and Warehousemen's Union (ILWU). Years later, in 1982, he would gain national attention when he helped settle a fifty-seven-day strike by National Football League players against team owners, thus saving the season.

An essential element of Kagel's charge concerning the BART labor force was to determine what jobs should be included for collective bargaining and under which bargaining umbrella. He organized two separate collective-bargaining units and determined they should bargain together on general issues common to both unions and separately on supplemental issues pertaining specifically to each unit. Employees were then lobbied hard by organizers from different well-established unions to vote for their representation. In the end, Service Employees International Union (SEIU) Local 390 was voted in as the umbrella bargaining agent for mechanics, various crafts personnel, groundskeepers, janitors, and some professional staff. Amalgamated Transit

The Richmond maintenance shop is one of four facilities built to service the system's fleet. Here transit cars are brought in for both scheduled and unscheduled maintenance, and this is also where they are regularly washed and vacuumed before being sent out on runs.

Union (ATU) Local 1555 won the vote to represent train operators, station agents, and certain clerical and other operations staff.

On June 18, 1972, with the state's department of labor behind him, Kagel imposed a four-week hiring freeze until the requirements were satisfied for Amendment 13(c) of the Urban Mass Transportation Act of 1964 and its reauthorization in 1970 (see Chapter 7). Amendment 13(c), to which BART was a signatory, was an important amendment sponsored by big labor. It required a new agency like BART, receiving federal funds, to offer positions to employees from other local carriers that would be negatively affected. In this case local carriers included public agencies, such as San Francisco's Muni and Alameda–Contra Costa Transit in the East Bay, and private companies, such as Greyhound, Peerless Stages, and the Southern Pacific Railroad's commuter lines. BART went through between 1,100 and 1,200 applications from other agency employees to satisfy the amendment's requirements.

Most of the jobs being offered were for train operators, station agents, and maintenance personnel. BART train operators were making $12,000 a year, while drivers from the other agencies who had put in twenty years or more were making as much as $20,000 a year, thus creating a significant disparity. Several employees from the other agencies exercised their option to make the move and came over to BART. Kagel red-circled those employees with higher salaries until their lower-paid colleagues could catch up. This, of course, set the stage for BART negotiating its first labor contracts. The union leaders were already calling for equal pay for equal work, or parity. In the spring of 1973, Paul Varacalli, executive director of the SEIU Local 390, spoke at board meetings with some urgency about the need to sit down soon at the bargaining table to exchange proposals now that the employees were represented.

BART'S FIRST STRIKE

After ten weeks of contentious bargaining at the Claremont Hotel in Berkeley, the two unions, representing a combined 1,100 employees at the time, went on strike around the beginning of July 1973, an action that halted service for the entire month. After a couple of weeks on the bricks, the striking employees were getting frustrated, and some members of other unions were recruited to picket general manager Stokes's home in Orinda. Armed security guards had to be placed around the house for a time. When it was clear that the union and BART management negotiators were at an impasse, the unions demanded that the board get involved at the table.

Board president William H. Chester stepped in to see if he could help break the deadlock. Chester, who was also vice president of the ILWU Local 10 in San Francisco, had first joined the union in 1938 in order to get work on the docks. He was the first African American member to become an officer in the International. Like Kagel, he had worked closely with ILWU president Harry Bridges, who was a mentor as Chester rose to the top of the ILWU hierarchy. He was joined at the BART-labor bargaining table by board vice president Nello Bianco and fellow director William M. Reedy, business manager of the San Francisco local of the International Brotherhood of Electrical Workers.

After several days of hard bargaining, an agreement with the union negotiators was finally reached that gave the young BART union chapters a three-year contract. This first contract included full cost-of-living adjustments indexed to the Consumer Price Index, paid quarterly and compounded annually at the end of each contract year, ending June 30, concurrent with BART's fiscal year. A wage increase of 9.5 to 12 percent was front-end-loaded for the first year, and second-year increases of 6 to 12 percent were included as part of the package, which also compounded on top of the base wage at the end of the contract year. The agreement—the transit district's first labor contract—was an important milestone and would set the stage for one of the transit district's most contentious labor disputes in its history a few short years later. The new contract, retroactive to July 1, 1973, added $19.6 million in additional labor costs over its three-year life and would add to the District's dire financial situation, which was growing at a steady rate. Projections showed that the transit system would be faced with a $100 million deficit over the next five years. At one point it looked very much as though the system might actually have to shut down because of the significant shortfall in the fiscal year operating revenue. So far, a permanent solution to the money woes had not been found.

THE FIRST TRAIN THROUGH THE TUBE

On August 10, 1973, BART recorded another historic event by operating its very first train through the Transbay Tube from Oakland to

San Francisco. The non-revenue train got up to speeds of 80 miles per hour. Even though it was supposedly not carrying anyone, in fact a stowaway was on board. *San Francisco Examiner* cartoonist Ken Alexander had heard about the test train and decided to sneak on at the West Oakland Station to commute to the city. BART found out and dubbed Alexander the first unofficial transbay commuter. This transbay run was a prelude to beginning the operation of intra–San Francisco satellite service sometime in the next couple of months. The service was planned for the 7.5 miles between the Daly City and Montgomery Street Stations. The Embarcadero Station would not be completed for another three years. On September 11, one year after opening, BART recorded its five-millionth rider. When the intra–San Francisco line opened on November 5, ridership doubled to 76,000 daily trips.

THE SORS SOLUTION AND GHOST TRAINS

At the first board meeting in December, Dr. Oliver showed up at the system's Lake Merritt headquarters with a demonstration model of a proposed solution for a backup to the automatic train control system. He had built a model train line on an eight-by-ten-foot sheet of plywood and used a model replica of a BART train that ran on HO-scale tracks. (BART had licensed a company in Los Angeles to manufacture and market the model train.) In the lobby outside the boardroom, Oliver and some assistants set up the demonstration.

Oliver showed how once a train entered a block its detection would be locked in until it entered a new block down the line, thus a following train would always be prevented from getting any closer than one block or "buffer zone." He called it a "sequential occupancy release system" or SORS for short. It was basically a check in–check out program. The demonstration was a success, and BART contracted with Westinghouse to implement the backup based on Oliver's concept, which would take from about six months to a year to install. Once implemented, full transbay service could begin.

While SORS was the answer to operating at closer headways, it would also contribute to operating problems. Since opening for service, the system had been plagued with what were termed "ghost trains," or false occupancies. When the detection system indicated that a ghost train was occupying a block, a following train would then have to go through in manual mode at no more than 25 miles an hour, thus negatively affecting service schedules. Before SORS was used, a train might have to go through only a portion of a block before resuming full automatic speed, but after SORS was implemented, a false occupancy would lock up an entire block. It was eventually determined that the ghost trains were caused by heat, which affected the wayside multiplex boxes, or equipment boxes for the automatic train control.

I remember on one particularly hot day around the mid-1970s we sent crews out on the line to put ice packs on top of the wayside equipment boxes to cool them down. In the employee newsletter, *Inside Track*, we joked that it was a "no-sweat operation." It was primitive, but it did in fact help. In any case, the solution of SORS felt like two steps forward followed by one step back. In the years ahead, the ghost train problem was pretty much eliminated through modifications to the equipment. SORS is still operating today with its own backup.

The view from the Rockridge Station in Oakland shows trains heading east and west at dusk, with the San Francisco skyline in the background. A similar picture appeared in *Life* magazine in 1972.

CHAPTER 17

THE SPECTER OF BANKRUPTCY

As the tepid days of spring 1974 began to wash over the San Francisco Bay Area, major changes were in the air for BART, still struggling toward full service. The transit system's problems were being heralded daily by the media, giving the impression that this new space-age system might be ephemeral because of its overly ambitious technology.

Now that launching transbay service had been put off once again, the board concentrated on the system's continuing financial drought, as well as the imperative need for technical fixes. The board had already voted to stop delivery of transit cars from Rohr Industries because severe reliability problems had been encountered. There were door problems, coupler problems, electronic-equipment problems, even problems with the cushioned seats. By this time 291 cars—144 A cars and 147 B cars—had been delivered, with 159 still on order. Little more than half of the delivered cars were working on any given day, and the high maintenance cost of keeping the new cars available for service was certainly one of the factors driving the increasing deficit.

Earlier in the year, as projected operating deficits were growing under the five-year plan for fiscal years 1973–1974 to 1977–1978, the board had given serious consideration to closing down and declaring bankruptcy or something like it. This, of course, was a shocking revelation. It was simply hard to believe that this behemoth system, which was just getting started, could possibly shut its doors. Stokes remained optimistic that things would settle down and the trains would keep rolling, but the District was facing a $13 million shortfall in operating money for fiscal year 1974–1975, with no income source in sight to make up the deficit. Modification work on both wayside train control and car components continued. BART maintenance also introduced a computerized program to enhance its preventive maintenance.

Nello Bianco, who had been the BART board's vice president during 1973, was elected by his fellow directors to be president in 1974. This fairly routine rotation method had been adopted by the board following the departure of Adrien Falk, who had served as the board's president for seven years. Yet the year ahead would be anything but routine for the new board president. The numerous challenges the District faced were now dumped into his lap, and while the management team led by Stokes continued to pretty much run the show, the pressures were mounting, and the detractors were about to strike.

Following the recommendation of legislative analyst A. Alan Post, the Senate Committee on Public Utilities and Corporations hired the University of California's Lawrence Berkeley National Laboratory (LBL) to conduct a thorough technical review and analysis of the fixes to the automatic train control system being carried out by Westinghouse, PBTB, and BART engineers. Dr. Theodore Scalise was put in charge of the study team. Board president Bianco was a strong proponent of bringing LBL in to assist BART in getting the automatic train control to operate at an optimal level. Of primary concern to all on the operating side was demonstrating that the system could operate transbay service safely. Bringing in LBL was seen by some staff as a rebuke of Stokes's confidence in Westinghouse's efforts. Moreover, it was also an example of changing the attitudes of several board members.

THE BOARD BEGINS USURPING MANAGEMENT

The following is another example of the shifting dynamics of the board.

As president of the BART board during the calendar year 1973, Bill Chester appointed an affirmative action officer to report directly to the board. This move was unprecedented and clearly bypassed the management. Some even questioned its legality. While Chester was generally a strong supporter of Stokes, he also had a long history of being a human-rights advocate, and he was particularly bullish on minority hiring, going back to his early days with the ILWU. Stokes already had a strong affirmative action program under way, but Chester wanted direct involvement on the part of the board. With support from other members of the board, he wanted to see the makeup of the BART workforce reflect the ethnic makeup of the population of the system's service area in the three counties. In addition to being an advocate for minority hiring, the new affirmative action officer was responsible for conducting seminars on management objectives for hiring minorities across the workforce spectrum. The key was to ensure that hiring supervisors had top-of-mind awareness of the District's affirmative action goals. By 1974, BART had achieved a 37 percent ethnic minority representation, which was reported as being 5 percent above the minority population ratio within the District's three counties. Another emerging aspect of this work was encouraging more participation by minority contractors or subcontractors on work being put out to bid by the District.

From the beginning of the new fiscal year on July 1, 1973, and on into 1974, the total District staff increased from 1,400 to 1,696 as the system continued to gear up for full revenue service. As staff grew overall, the number of department heads decreased, based on recommendations of the report submitted to the BART board and management in September 1973 by consulting firm Arthur D. Little Company (ADL). Those positions were cut back from nineteen to ten, mostly through attrition and title shifting. The reason for this change was two-fold: some of the positions were made obsolete during the transition from a construction project to an operating railroad; in other positions, responsibilities had diminished or changed. Finally, ADL recommended that a highly technical engineer be placed at the executive level, such as in systems engineering, to evaluate and monitor the work ahead.

From an organizational perspective, these changes symbolized the evolving relationship between the board and management—specifically, the board was taking a more aggressive role in the District's administration. Assistant general manager of operations and engineering David Hammond had resigned in March 1973 to take a job in the private sector, leaving a hole in the hierarchy of the engineering management, and following his departure the position was reconfigured as the assistant general manager of operations. Meanwhile, the head of the new Systems Engineering Department came on board in early November. He would be responsible for the automatic train control system and closely monitoring Westinghouse.

Foremost on the agenda for 1974, in addition to finally launching transbay service, was saving the system from financial collapse. The project had come too far, with too much at stake, to let it falter now. But the state had few options for securing a source of funding for an ongoing operating subsidy. Several options mentioned were simply politically untenable. In January, the BART board passed a resolution to advise the state legislature, the governor, the Metropolitan Transportation Commission, and the U.S. Department of Transportation that the District needed timely relief. The reasons stated were higher-than-projected labor costs (referring to the new labor contract), the fact that the District had to have its own police department, continued inflation, and the high level of unscheduled maintenance on the transit cars.

The original operating-cost projections had not included police. The early planners as well as the District directors had assumed that each of the local jurisdictions would make its police resources available to BART to perform duties that would include patrolling stations, the rights-of-way, and trains passing through individual communities, as well as providing a quick response in emergencies. But when these needs were negotiated with the various police departments, the answer was always the same: there were scarce resources available. BART would have to pay for more officers in some of the jurisdictions and could have no guarantee they would be ready to respond on a moment's notice. Another issue was the potential for jurisdictional overlapping and potential territorial disputes. Frustrated with the response from local jurisdictions, the transit district determined it would need its own force. The board sponsored legislation to empower the District to have an autonomous police force and hired a former FBI agent to head it up.

On March 19, BART board president Bianco testified at the fourth hearing of the State Senate Committee on Public Utilities and Corporations that, in order to keep fares low, and without some form of operating subsidy, the system was in danger of having to be closed down. His testimony was met with another blast from Post, who gave a lengthy report castigating both the BART board and management concerning the way business was handled by the District and the deficiencies in the automatic train control, which he stated were still not being addressed. Moreover, he contended that the system was unsafe and referred to the Blue Ribbon panel's report, which had recommended a backup system, and a statement by Dr. Oliver that suggested a validation of Post's assertions. Oliver, however, was unhappy with Post and charged that the legislative analyst had misrepresented his remarks. Overall, Post's report was one of the most critical yet, now calling for the outright dismissal of Stokes as general manager. Some believed that Post had it in for Stokes for attacking his first report at an earlier hearing.

THE STATE HOLDS BART HOSTAGE OVER STOKES

During 1974, several hearings were conducted by the Senate Committee on Public Utilities and Corporations specifically on the issue of BART's projected operating deficit. Post urged the senate committee to make it clear to the BART board that until Stokes was removed there would be no money forthcoming to continue operations. Senate committee chairman Alfred Alquist and the committee members agreed. In other words, the California State Legislature was going to hold BART hostage until the present general manager was out. At this point Stokes was down to a 6–6 vote on the board, which meant he still had enough support to retain the position he had held for eleven years, if he wanted it. His supporters were not about to be bullied, even as Alquist warned that if the system went broke and shut down it would be on them.

Unbeknownst to most, Stokes had been planning to move on for some time. He was working closely with a powerful figure in the industry, his friend Dr. William J. Ronan, chairman of the New York Metropolitan Transportation Authority, to merge the transit industry's two giant trade organizations—the Institute for Rapid Transit and the American Transit Association (representing bus operators)—into an amalgam that would be called the American Public Transit Association (APTA). The deal had not quite gelled yet, but it was getting close. While Stokes could still count on enough votes to conduct the District's business, more than likely he was aware of just how close his nemeses were getting to a showdown. Nevertheless, his resilience seemed to insulate him from the continued threats.

ESTIMATED SHUTDOWN OF THE SYSTEM

BART staff estimated that without financial relief the system would have to be shut down sometime around the end of September, or by October 1. Such a crisis facing a major regional transit system was unprecedented. Historically, most of the early metropolitan transit systems were privately owned and made a profit, but this all changed around midcentury as the automobile became king. As major cities across the country took over these private systems that could no longer operate solely out of the fare box, the reality was that subsidies were required to keep them running.

On April 2, Senator James Mills (D–San Diego) introduced Senate Bill 1966, coauthored by Assemblyman Leo McCarthy (D–San Francisco), to extend the half-cent sales tax levied in the three BART counties for two years, or until December 1977. Given all of the controversy surrounding the system, the question was whether the bill would pass and, if it did, whether the governor would sign it. Even with this uncertainty, BART moved ahead with preparations for transbay service.

THE FIRST MAJOR CHANGE IN 1974

As the general frenzy over BART continued, there was a strong movement to make the transit system's board of directors elected rather than appointed by county supervisors and city mayors within the District. Various critics asserted that elections would make the directors more accountable. This notion gained a lot of traction in Sacramento, and soon California Assembly Bill 3043, authored by assembly speaker pro tempore Carlos Bee, called for a vote to determine whether the BART board of directors should be elected instead of appointed, as had been the case since the District's creation in 1957. Prior to the election to decide the issue, a great deal of public debate took place on the merits of elected versus appointed representatives on the BART board of directors. Most of the push was for an elected board, which proponents argued would make that body more responsive. On June 4, voters living in the three BART counties voted overwhelmingly to approve what became Measure A on the ballot to change the twelve-member appointed board to a nine-member elected board from nine election districts. This outcome was no surprise to anyone who had been following the press reports covering the transit district's many controversies. BART had been called everything from a boondoggle to a white elephant. Potential candidates for the board would now be gearing up their campaigns for a fall election.

THE SECOND MAJOR CHANGE

Bill Stokes resigned as general manager of BART effective July 1, 1974, ending a volatile era in the transit project's history. He had been with the transit district for sixteen years, eleven of those as general manager. His supporters, including BART directors Harry Lange and Bill Chester, would say he had accomplished something of a miracle in managing to overlay the 75-mile project onto an already much developed topography. Not many observers in the early days believed it could be done or even should be done—and of course there were those naysayers who had done everything they could to scuttle the project before it ever started. But most who knew the history would say Stokes's belief and drive made BART happen. Someone likened the whole recent episode of hysteria and frenzy as being like the inner tube of a tire being blown up bigger and bigger until it almost bursts, and then someone lets the air out of it just in the nick of time. In this case, Stokes's resignation defused the political powder keg the transit district was facing as it contemplated potential bankruptcy. But for some of the directors and most on the staff it was a sad moment. Stokes was beloved by the organization he had built.

"I was very proud of what had been accomplished and of the many talented people who contributed to bringing BART into reality," Stokes said in a 2012 interview. "We beat the odds in getting the system built, and back in 1974 I was ready to take on a new job. I had no doubt that the BART system was going to be among the world's best in the years to come." When asked if he had any regrets, he said, "Sure, we made some mistakes, but we did a lot of things right. No regrets."

One of Stokes's final acts in terms of getting additional federal funds to partially pay for the final construction phase of the basic system had been to testify before the U.S. Congress, an act that resulted in BART receiving $181 million. Stokes also praised the Mills-McCarthy bill and urged the state legislature to pass the temporary extension of the half-percent sales tax, which had been levied in the three BART counties since 1970 to generate $150 million, also

This early rendering from 1969 depicts BART trains racing the 6 miles between San Francisco and Oakland in a tube 132 feet below the surface of the bay.

earmarked toward completing the system. State Senate Bill 1966 was passed by the legislature in September, though the governor had not indicated whether he would sign it.

Upon Stokes's departure, assistant general manager Larry Dahms was named by the appointed board as the interim general manager. BART board president Nello Bianco announced that a nationwide search would be conducted to find a new general manager, and an executive search firm was retained.

Stokes went on to become the first executive director of the newly formed American Public Transit Association, headquartered in Washington, D.C. Bill Ronan became its first president. Ronan, along with Henry Kissinger, had formerly been an aide to New York governor Nelson A. Rockefeller, who appointed Ronan to be the chairman of the New York MTA. The new amalgam of APTA, a nonprofit industry trade organization, had more than six hundred member organizations and associate members, including private suppliers across the nation and in Canada. APTA's primary mission was to be an advocate in Washington for the advancement of public transportation interests in its many forms, from rail to bus operations, and to bring industry leaders together to share information on advances in technology, administration, and marketing. Today, APTA (whose original predecessor, the American Street Railway Association, was founded in the late 1800s) has more than 1,500 members. The amalgam combined the Institute for Rapid Transit, representing rail operators, and the American Transit Association, representing bus operators. Stokes is credited with being a prime mover in getting the federal government to greatly expand its funding commitment for public transit across the nation, much as it does through the Highway Trust Fund.

After six years, Stokes left APTA to become the director general of the Saudi Arabian Public Transit Company for American Transportation Enterprises (ATE), which had contracted with the Saudi government. In this new role, Stokes oversaw the development of public transit within and between seven cities. Following his work in Saudi Arabia, he continued as a consultant on various projects around the world. He passed away on May 15, 2013, in Sammamish, Washington.

TRANSBAY SERVICE FINALLY IN THE OFFING

During the summer of 1974, progress was frantically being pushed as BART and a cadre of consulting engineers worked day and night toward implementing the system's key link: transbay service. In August, testing for transbay service was being evaluated by the Lawrence Berkeley Laboratory along with observers from the CPUC. While installation of the automatic train control backup—the sequential occupancy release system (SORS)—was under way by Westinghouse, an interim method of ensuring extra train protection had to be put in place before a new date to begin transbay service could be set. September was now the target month.

In June, BART demonstrated that the primary train control system could hold trains at one station apart. Earlier in the year, the CPUC had permitted the transit system to rely on the automatic train control to keep the trains two stations apart and eliminate the need for supervisors on station platforms to release trains. In order to provide optimum service between San Francisco and the East Bay, a pseudo station was created in the middle of the tube; this strategy meant that once a train was released from the middle of the tube, a following train could be released from the Oakland West Station (now West Oakland Station), thus providing a closer headway of ten minutes between trains.

At noon on Saturday, September 14, 1974, a gala ceremony was held at BART's San Francisco Powell Street Station to celebrate the official beginning of revenue service through the Transbay Tube. Dignitaries from around the Bay Area attended the festive occasion to help cut the ribbon. East Bay members of the BART board, along with San Francisco mayor Joe Alioto and New York mayor Abraham Beame, entered the Oakland West Station, where they boarded the first of two special non-service trains. As luck would have it, the first VIP train broke down. Everyone was then herded onto the second train, which headed under the bay at 80 miles per hour for San Francisco and the Powell Street Station, where the main event would commence.

Following the celebration, work continued through the weekend in final preparation for sending passenger-filled trains through the 3.6-mile underwater tube. Tension mixed with excitement was high among staff as everyone wanted to make sure that the first day of transbay revenue service came off without a hitch.

On Monday, September 16, 1974, transbay service was finally launched. It was a history-making event for BART, the culmination of twenty-two years of struggle, beginning with the early engineering work of the Bay Area Transportation Commission. The workday began at 4:15 A.M. It was black and wet outside, mostly from early morning fog and dew. The first train had been dispatched from the Hayward yard south to Fremont and, with the operator changing ends, made ready to head north. Meanwhile, in the deep, dimly lit temperature-controlled central control room beneath the system's Lake Merritt headquarters, a needlework sign hung on the wall that read "Pamper the Passenger." You could see that legend from almost anywhere in the room. Made by a supervisor's wife, the sign was intended as a reminder that there were people out there depending on what went on in that room. As the early hours wore on, men and women sipped their morning coffee while working feverishly in preparation for finally opening the key link of the system. They knew this was a historic occasion. Working with hushed voices, train controllers and power and support facility personnel checked consoles and computers as the system charged up in preparation for the first day of transbay revenue service.

"Just think, part of the FIRST peak-hour crush! I feel like Evel Knievel"

BART was the subject of numerous such pundit cartoons in the local newspapers before and after opening.

Reportedly, 6,000 people rode the trains through the tube on that first day. System-wide, ridership immediately jumped from 68,000 per day to 120,000 per day. Three of those hopeful first-day riders didn't quite make it: Rachel Abelson's parents, Richmond attorney Howard Abelson and his wife, Janet, were looking forward to being first-day riders, but Rachel decided it was time to be born. Instead of racing to a BART station they raced to Kaiser Hospital in Oakland, where Rachel arrived pretty much on schedule. Her father called and told me the story. We stayed in touch, and ten years later I invited Rachel to the Embarcadero Station to cut the ceremonial cake marking the anniversary of transbay service. She did so again for the twentieth anniversary. Today she is an assistant district attorney in Northern California. Several years later, in 1988, Rachel's father, a former mayor and city councilman from the city of El Cerrito, was appointed by the BART board to fill a vacant seat. He joined a voting block supporting both

BART's general manager Keith Bernard and, most importantly, a serious get-down-to-business move on the extension program.

Even as transbay service was under way, with the financial crisis still on the doorstep, some initial preparations were being made to shut the system down. Fortunately, the crisis was averted on September 26, when Governor Ronald Reagan signed Senate Bill 1966 into law. This legislation at least allowed for two years of breathing room until a permanent operating subsidy could be put in place.

One of the last official acts of the appointed board was to vote affirmatively on filing a lawsuit seeking $237 million in damages against Parsons Brinckerhoff–Tudor–Bechtel, the Westinghouse Electric Corporation, Rohr Industries, the Bulova Watch Company, and their respective surety companies. Bulova Watch was included because it supplied the speed control crystal oscillators that had contributed to the Fremont Flyer accident back in October 1972. The lawsuit was filed November 18, 1974. Its outcome would be left to the new board.

On November 5, with 138 candidates running, a new board of directors was elected, three from each county, although there was some overlapping of districts. Three of the former appointed members were elected: Nello Bianco of Richmond, Richard O. Clark of Albany, and James Hill of Walnut Creek. The first woman to serve on the BART board, Ella Hill Hutch, was from San Francisco. Other members of the newly elected board included Robert Allen, from Livermore; John W. Glenn, from Fremont (some thought he was the former astronaut); Dr. Harvey Glasser, from Alameda County; Elmer Cooper, from San Francisco; and John H. Kirkwood, also San Francisco. The new board was sworn in on December 2 by Alameda County presiding judge Spurgeon Avakian. The terms of office would be four years, but in order to stagger the terms it was determined by lot that directors representing odd-numbered districts would serve only two years initially.

A top priority for the new board was to find a permanent general manager.

CHAPTER 18

THE 1970S: PRECARIOUS TIMES CONTINUE

While BART was making the front pages of the Bay Area's major metropolitan newspapers on an almost daily basis, usually with bold banner headlines above the fold, the system did take a back seat to several terrible events that made news during the 1970s.

On November 6, 1973, the popular Oakland Unified School District superintendent Marcus Foster was ambushed and assassinated, and his deputy, Robert Blackburn, seriously wounded. The year before, Foster had been one of the key dignitaries riding BART on opening day, accompanied by Alameda County presiding judge Robert Bostick. Bostick, who a few short years before had ordered the BART Ashby Station underground, remembered how Foster had marveled at the sleek, shiny new trains and how glad he was to be a part of the Oakland community. The story of his assassination went national and international.

As it turned out, the killing of Foster, which outraged the community, was carried out by a small ragtag band calling itself the Symbionese Liberation Army (SLA). They mistakenly thought Foster was a proponent of requiring students to carry school identification cards. One can only speculate that the SLA saw this as a form of oppression. On February 4, 1974, the SLA kidnapped Patty Hearst, heiress to the Hearst newspaper conglomerate, a story that filled the pages for the next few years. Other major news events included the death of Elvis

Presley in August 1977; the killing of Congressman Leo Ryan in Guyana and the Jonestown mass suicides on November 18, 1978; and, following soon after, on November 27 of that year, the assassinations of San Francisco mayor George Moscone and city supervisor Harvey Milk by former San Francisco supervisor Dan White at San Francisco City Hall. These stories permeated the media during the 1970s along with the still-fledgling BART system; BART was and still is considered one of the single major news subjects of the San Francisco Bay Area. One former editor from the *San Francisco Chronicle* put it very succinctly when asked on a radio show, "What is it that makes news?" He said, "Let's take BART for example. BART is big. And one way or another it touches all of our lives, whether we are riders of the system or not. So, when something occurs and it involves BART in any way, shape, or form, it's news. And even if it's something happening close to a BART station, it's news." The late three-dot columnist Herb Caen (so called because he wrote his daily column in snippets separated by ellipses) loved to take jabs at the system from time to time. In one of his famous columns, he wrote that I had written a movie down in Hollywood called *The Dirt Gang,* but he made sure to specify that it was *not* about sandboxes at the end of the BART lines (that is, to keep trains from ending up in parking lots).

ANOTHER SERIOUS BART INCIDENT COSTS A LIFE

At 10:15 P.M. on Sunday, January 19, 1975, a nine-car test train crashed into a maintenance vehicle that was on the same track. Arthur L. Briggs, the driver of the maintenance vehicle, was tragically killed. A lengthy investigation of the incident and several hearings determined that the accident was due to human error: the maintenance vehicle had somehow gotten onto the wrong main-line track. It was also determined that alcohol may have been a factor. Once again, the media had a field day, heralding the accident as another crack in the space-age system's troubled image.

The incident did raise a critical question: Why didn't the train protection system detect the vehicle on the track? The explanation turned out to be fairly straightforward. The maintenance vehicle in question did not have steel wheels like the train cars but rubber tires that ran along the tops of the rails, with guides to keep the vehicle on the track. The rubber, of course, would not conduct the low-voltage current in the tracks that triggers the train protection system. Without the conductivity from the wheels through the axle, the current could not be shunted to send a signal to an approaching train that the track ahead was occupied and automatically bring the train to a stop. BART immediately set to work finding a solution to the problem.

Then, a little more than a week later, on Monday, January 27, at around three in the afternoon, a lead A car somehow separated from the rest of its train. The out-of-service train was being stored just south of the MacArthur Station, and because it was not properly secured with chocks, the lone free-wheeling A car rolled south along the main-line subway through the 19th and 12th Street Stations before coming to a stop just short of the Lake Merritt Station. Another investigation ensued.

Once again, with the two incidents offering grist for the pundits' mills, there was political fallout and copious finger-pointing. The train couplers were now suspect, and every car coupler went through a rigorous inspection to see whether there was a flaw in the design or whether this incident was an anomaly.

A NEW GENERAL MANAGER

Meanwhile, finding a new general manager that the directors could agree upon was no mean feat. Several potential candidates were brought in by the headhunting firm, but after a series of interviews the new board of nine could not find enough votes among themselves to agree on a permanent successor to Stokes. Larry Dahms, the interim general manager, was perhaps the strongest of the candidates being considered. Some members had favorites, but it would take five affirmative votes for any single candidate to be confirmed.

General managers of public transit systems were a breed unto themselves once they achieved that status; job longevity is not an industry long suit at the higher echelons, and the men and women in those positions seemed to be itinerant soldiers of the transit industry, moving from system to system, job to job. The turnover in the field is unsurprising given the politics of public transit, which might be likened to a human-shredding machine. And while the job was tough, the candidates were in many cases even more so. I remember one case in the late 1970s in which a candidate was taken out of the running after demanding certain perks, including a paid membership to a local country club, a chauffeured limo, and an interest-free or low-interest loan to purchase a house. Before making these demands, the candidate had been the top choice for the position.

Almost six months of wrangling over the appointment passed without success. Then Elmer Cooper—an urban planner from San Francisco, the BART board president for calendar year 1975, a current board member, and chairman of the ad hoc General Manager Selection Committee—had an intriguing idea. He wanted to amp up the potential field, and although he was not sure his idea would fly, he thought it was worth a try, since the board was at an impasse. One thing was certain: for the time being, Cooper's plan called for secrecy.

On behalf of the majority of the BART board, President Cooper went to Washington, D.C., where he met with and recruited a young man named Frank C. Herringer to accept the position of BART's third permanent general manager. Herringer was the administrator of the federal Urban Mass Transportation Administration (UMTA), a division of the Department of Transportation. In that capacity, he was responsible for overseeing the allocation of $1.5 billion in federal monies for a renewed mass transit system program nationwide, as well as issuing grants for research and development. At thirty-two years of age, Herringer, who was viewed as a "wunderkind," had been a rising star in the Nixon administration and was well thought of in the transportation industry at large. While he had never been a transit system operator, board members figured that in addition to bringing a fresh new point of view to BART, Herringer would also know where to find money in Washington. On April 25, 1975, the BART board announced the appointment of Herringer, effective July 1, at the astounding salary of $68,500 per year, more than the governor of California made at the time, and about $28,000 more than he had made in Washington. The salary, of course, was controversial all on its own. "Whenever my name was mentioned," Herringer quipped in a recent interview, "the $68,500 was tacked on as if it were a part of my name."

The salary revelation reached Sacramento, where Senator Alfred Alquist held a hearing on the matter and threatened to introduce a special bill to cap Herringer's salary at $50,000, which would have been an unprecedented move. When asked by board members what he would do in that event, Herringer told them that he would quit, end of story. However, it never came to that. As the head of media and public affairs and the chief spokesperson for the District, I found myself constantly being interviewed on every conceivable issue, Herringer's salary included. When I was asked by a reporter to comment on how it was that the BART general manager made more than the governor of the state, I simply replied, "The governor should make more." The following year, Elmer Cooper resigned from the board when he found himself knee-deep in an expense account scandal.

Meanwhle, Larry Dahms, who had been acting as interim general manager, eventually went on to be named executive director of the nine-county Metropolitan Transportation Commission (MTC), where he presided over solving critical transportation-funding and land-use issues for the next twenty-five years. As a key player in the now balkanized transportation scene in the nine Bay Area counties, he would often walk a political tightrope as small upstart bus systems, like birds in a nest, demanded to be fed. In the years to come, Dahms as executive director of the MTC would be instrumental in BART's $2.5 billion expansion program.

Upon officially moving into his new fifth-floor office at BART's Lake Merritt headquarters in the summer of 1975, Herringer wasted little time in assessing the organization and how it was functioning. At a press conference during which he was introduced to the Bay Area media, he was asked by one reporter what he personally intended to do to tackle the system's problems. "I don't plan to get a wrench and get under the cars," he joked. "But I will be working to bring some knowledgeable and creative people in to fix the system."

Earlier in the year, the California

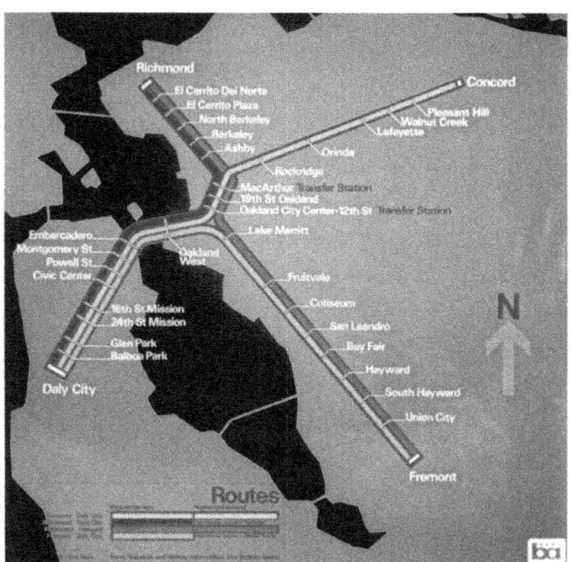

When BART officially opened for service, this map could be found on trains, in stations, and in "All About BART" brochures.

Public Utilities Commission, following A. Alan Post's last report, had hired a nationally known consulting firm, Cresap, McCormick & Paget (CMP), to conduct a management audit of the District. Coincidentally, Herringer had once worked for CMP prior to his UMTA job, a connection that helped establish a good working relationship with the consulting firm's team. The audit was done through a series of workshops held with BART managers.

One of the recommendations was a deferral of night service. At the time, BART was still operating only from 6 A.M. to 8 P.M., Monday through Friday; it had yet to fully transition from a construction project to an operating railroad. The Embarcadero Station was still under construction, and work was continuing on the 3.5-mile San Francisco Muni light rail line, which from the beginning had been part of the overall BART project.

A multitude of challenges, both mechanical and political, faced the new general manager. Tackling the myriad technical fixes needed to bring the system to its full operating potential was, of course, the first priority, and reliability problems were of paramount concern. Ghost trains still plagued the rolling stock on a daily basis, creating numerous delays, and when a train broke down because of mechanical problems on the main line, all trains behind it were impacted as well. The scarcity of bypass or run-around tracks on the system added to operational headaches. On average, 219 cars, or 54 percent of the fleet (at that time a total of 408 cars), were available on any given day for service. About 15 trains a day were taken out of service for one problem or another. This was unacceptable.

On the political side of the ledger was the challenge of balancing the parochial issues of individual directors, each elected and each needing to satisfy local constituent demands. The directors were often in conflict with one another, sometimes in a very volatile way, over such issues as extension priorities or some other scheme that benefited one community at the expense of another. Often such conflicts put staff right in the middle. A special task force of engineers was established to work specifically on the reliability problems with assistance from the Lawrence Berkeley Laboratory. This approach in time paid off. Over the next few years, numerous modifications made to the transit cars and wayside control equipment would stabilize the operations, with a marked improvement of on-time performance.

As the 1970s rolled on, BART once again faced a projected operating deficit, even with the temporary half-cent sales tax to supplement the shortfall in fare-box revenue. Austerity was going to be the name of the game for the foreseeable future. In his June 16, 1975, report to the legislature, legislative analyst A. Alan Post expressed grave concern over the projected deficit and strongly recommended that the BART board implement deep budget cuts, staff reductions, and fare increases, as well as continued deferral of additional service. For fiscal year 1975–1976, the board approved a threadbare budget of $65.6 million and a fare increase averaging 21 percent.

One of Herringer's first major acts was to hire a new assistant general manager for administration, Robert D. Gallaway, whom he recruited from the airline industry. Next, Herringer and Gallaway implemented a reorganization of management, which included a planned purge. Several top managers were terminated and replaced with a cadre of new managers, most of whom came from other industries. One manager called up to meet with Herringer returned to his office ashen-faced and announced to his staff that he'd just been terminated. "I walked into his office, sat down, and looked into those steely blue eyes of Herringer's and I knew in that instant I was going to get my walking papers," the manager recalled. "He wished me luck."

When questioned by members of the media about why he would hire executives from outside the transit industry, Herringer said that, in his view, strong management skills could be transferred from one industry to another. He also felt the airline industry came closest to rail transit, particularly in BART's case, where much of the technology had come out of the aerospace industry. The key position of heading up maintenance and engineering was filled by a former manager of maintenance for United Airlines. Over time these changes proved to be effective, as concrete improvements were made and fewer trains were taken out of service on a daily basis. Still, technical issues persisted, and on one very hot day in the summer of 1976, some of the wayside train control boxes overheated and created a fleet of ghost trains on the Concord line. The nontechnical solution was to rush out and put ice packs on the boxes that housed the sensitive electronic boards, a fix that seemed to work. Later, sun shields were designed and installed over the boxes to shade them like umbrellas.

THE BART IMPACT PROGRAM REPORT

Since BART was the newest of the country's modern systems, it served as a model and laboratory for proposed future rail systems, and it was thus of great interest to know what impacts BART might generate. Sponsored by the U.S. Department of Transportation and the U.S. Department of Housing and Urban Development, the BART Impact Program was a study to develop a vital information bank for federal decision-making, as well as an information exchange with the nine-county Metropolitan Transportation Commission. Of particular interest, in addition to ridership demand and usage rate (the ratio of seat miles to passenger miles), was information about land-use management, an array of social issues, and the environment. One important question was, how efficient was BART compared to the automobile and bus transport, in terms of energy use? Mostly an academic document, the BART Impact Program Report also looked at how key decisions came about in the creation of the Bay Area Rapid Transit system. Was it created less for the purpose of easing congestion caused by post-war population growth and more to serve San Francisco business interests (i.e., the Manhattanization of the city as the gateway to the Pacific Rim and growing Asian markets)? Or was there simply an amalgam of a grassroots push for a new regional system together with the interests of the high-powered members of the Bay Area Council?

For a time the BART Impact Program Report made the news not only in the Bay Area but also in Washington, D.C., and Atlanta, Georgia; the new Washington Metro had just opened, and a new regional system similar to BART was being developed in Atlanta.

Following on the heels of the BART Impact Program Report, Melvin Webber, a professor of transportation studies at the University of California, Berkeley, published his own study in the fall of 1976. He basically called BART a white elephant. Since he was a highly respected academic and, ironically, an early BART planner, his study was met with great interest by the media. While referring to the system

Opposite page, top: This aerial view shows San Francisco with a fairly flat downtown skyline before BART. Bottom: This view underscores the significant impact BART had on San Francisco, particularly along the Market Street corridor, which saw the growth of billions of dollars in high-rise office space and mixed-use development. In the years since this photo was taken in the early 1970s, billions more have been invested in development both along and south of Market Street, including the AT&T ball park.

as a public relations success, he viewed its effectiveness with much skepticism. While these reports were instant grist for newshounds, they were for the most part premature. BART in many ways was like an adolescent who simply had acne and was still growing.

A NEW STATION OPENS

On Thursday, May 27, 1976, BART's Embarcadero Station in San Francisco opened to great fanfare, with mayor George Moscone joining BART directors for the official ribbon cutting. Located at the heart of the city's redevelopment, the thirty-fourth station of the system immediately rivaled the Montgomery Street Station as a primary destination. Hailed by many observers as BART's finest architectural achievement, the Embarcadero Station was considered the jewel in the crown.

SOCIAL DYNAMICS AND THE NEW MINORITY ACTIVISM

Two significant issues were now facing the transit district in addition to its ongoing operational and technical problems. Affirmative action in hiring was taking a front-row seat politically as the board continually received one complaint or another from community leaders saying BART was unresponsive to the demand for work. Predominantly minority communities, including Richmond in northern Alameda County, the Fruitvale neighborhood in Oakland, and West Oakland, generally had a high unemployment ratio of eligible workers compared to the predominantly white urban and suburban communities nearby. Minority activism had begun to emerge from these communities in the late 1960s as displacement occurred to make way for urban renewal and the new BART rail line.

West Oakland was a prime example. In addition to BART, other displacement factors were the mammoth new U.S. Post Office building on 7th Avenue and the Cypress Street Viaduct, or Cypress Freeway. The double-decked Cypress structure, which connected the Nimitz Freeway with the Oakland Bay Bridge and the Eastshore Freeway, created a social dividing line between West Oakland and downtown Oakland. Some at the time described West Oakland as being like an island cut off from the mainland. (On October 17, 1989, the Loma Prieta earthquake would cause the collapse of the Cypress Freeway. When

Caltrans wanted to rebuild it on the same route, the community rose up in protest and eventually triumphed. Instead, a parkway named after Nelson Mandela was built, and the freeway was rerouted to the west.) BART's "Oakland West Station," a name that the community did not like, became the centerpiece of the area and very much a symbol of change for the residents.

West Oakland had a rich history long before the Cypress Freeway and BART were built. The neighborhood was once a major hub for transportation not only across the bay but also on a national level. In 1869, as noted in Chapter 2, the West Oakland Long Wharf, or Mole, became the terminus for the transcontinental railroad at the foot of 7th Street. Operated by the Central Pacific Railroad (later Southern Pacific), the new line soon brought new settlers to the territory from the East. From the Mole, ferryboats took travelers on to San Francisco.

A widely diverse population eventually settled in West Oakland, and the ethnic representation included Mexicans (many of whom immigrated as refugees from the 1910 Mexican revolution), African Americans, and people from Portugal, China, and Japan, to name a few groups. The railroad and the emerging Port of Oakland spurred

A BART train heads south on the Fremont line toward Fruitvale, with the Oakland skyline and its iconic Tribune Tower in the background.

growth as the area's major employers. In many ways West Oakland was a boomtown microcosm of the city of Oakland. Businesses of all kinds sprang up as the community grew. The writer Jack London spent much of his youth in West Oakland and wrote about it years later as a partial setting for his novel *The Valley of the Moon,* about a young fighter and his wife who are determined to find a better life up north in Sonoma County. The place of their dreams was the Valley of the Moon, just outside Glen Ellen.

World War I brought new migrants to West Oakland to work in the shipyards and as porters for the railroad, and the community grew exponentially. Up until the Depression years of the 1930s, the area was flush compared to other parts of the city, and quaint little houses sprang up by the bushel to accommodate demand. By then the West Oakland population had risen to well over 200,000, now predominantly made up of African Americans, many of whom had migrated from the South for work and a new life. World War II brought even more new workers to the shipyards, and the demographics shifted yet again as many of the Hispanic residents in the community moved to the Fruitvale area along 14th Avenue (now International Boulevard) and to points south in East Oakland.

By the mid-1960s, the bulldozing of old neighborhoods to make way for urban renewal projects and public housing became the target of community wrath. In addition to the mammoth Nimitz Freeway cutting a wide swath through the community, BART had taken up a necessary right-of-way to build its thirty-foot-high aerial structure along 7th Street and built the "Oakland West Station" as the gateway to the Transbay Tube. The Black Panthers were to a great degree a product of the anger over the displacement of longtime residents to make way for these various projects, and as part of a general backlash against the establishment, the Panthers invaded the state legislature, an act that instantly brought them into the national spotlight. BART board meetings were often attended by representatives of the Black Panther Party, along with both West Oakland and East Oakland community leaders, to see that their issues were being addressed. In addition to land-use concerns, minority employment and hiring by the District was also being monitored, and by late 1975, over 39 percent of BART's 1,900 employees were minorities, a number above the District population minority ratio of 32 percent. The system was, in fact, developing a reputation for having one of the strongest equal rights and affirmative action programs in the industry. At the same time, part and parcel to minority issues was the name of the "Oakland West" station. Community leaders leaned on the board to change the name to the West Oakland Station, basically calling the old name disresepectful, primarily because the historical name of the neighborhood had always been "West Oakland." The BART board did vote to change the name.

SUMMER SUMMARY

By June 1976, weekday ridership averaged 131,000, an 8.3 percent increase over the year before. The ridership increase took place despite a 21 percent fare increase, which had been put into effect in November 1975. For those who want to look back at the good old days, the minimum BART fare in downtown San Francisco was actually lowered from 30 cents to 25 cents, although it remained at 30 cents in suburban areas of the system. The fare for the longest trip of almost 50 miles, from Fremont to Daly City, went from $1.25 to $1.45. Initially the system saw a 5 percent drop in daily patronage resulting directly from the increase, but the ridership loss was quickly offset by significant increases during December. In January 1976, with the help of some gas-tax money from the state, BART extended its hours of operation from 6 A.M. to midnight, Monday through Friday. Previously, the system had shut down at 8 P.M. After its opening, the Embarcadero Station immediately became the second-most popular destination on the system; the Montgomery Station—at the heart of the downtown business district—was clearly number one in terms of daily passenger trips.

THE BART POLICE

Since the BART system first opened for revenue service on September 11, 1972, the BART Police Department has evolved into a full-service law enforcement agency with more than 200 sworn officers and 90 civilian support personnel. BART police officers' uniforms are now the traditional navy blue, making them indistinguishable from any municipal police officer, but it was not always that way. Originally the officers' uniforms consisted of royal blue blazers, dark slacks,

In 1972, BART employees could be easily identified by their uniforms, from the jumpsuit of the train operator at left to the light-blue blazers worn by the BART police officer at right. While the softer look of the BART police was well intentioned, management eventually determined that traditional dark-navy uniforms were more effective.

a light-blue shirt, and a striped tie. The idea was to present a softer image, and indeed officers were at that time perceived more as customer service employees, as if for an airline or a car-rental agency. As it turned out, however, the original uniforms were an interesting experiment that just didn't work as intended. Experience showed that perpetrators simply didn't respond as well to someone in a blue blazer as they would to an officer in a traditional uniform.

"This was really a conditioned response kind of thing," said former BART police chief Gary Gee, who first came to the District in 1973 as a young officer from the San Rafael Police Department. "The public had long been conditioned to recognize the authority of a uniformed officer with gold badges and gun belts in plain view, which in many ways helped to avoid and defuse confrontations," he said. "We found there was simply a lack of respect and credibility, particularly on the part of the criminal element, for someone in that original blue blazer outfit."

BART police officers are sworn California peace officers, academy trained, and have the same full authority to arrest as any city police officer or sheriff's deputy anywhere in the state. In fact, the majority of BART police officers hired in the 1970s came from various police and sheriff's departments.

The first task of the BART Police was to ensure a safe environment for the riding public. To that end they kept a watchful eye in the stations and on the trains, and provided security for all other system facilities. Fare evasion was one of the more common scams, and over time numerous misdemeanor citations, which required a court appearance, were issued to perpetrators. The BART Police also broke up a major pickpocket ring operating on the system and chased down bank robbers who tried to use BART trains for escape. In this respect, the system was very much like a medium-sized municipality on wheels, dealing with all of the issues a small city might encounter. Certainly the daily police log looked like a microcosm of the adjacent communities BART served, if not also the world at large.

Several tragic incidents of officer-involved shootings have occurred over the years. Two of the more high-profile cases include one on November 15, 1992, at the Hayward Station, in which a robbery suspect, Jerrold Hall, a young black man, was shot. He later died at Highland Hospital in Oakland (see Chapter 22). Seventeen years later, another high-profile tragedy occurred. Very early on New Year's Day of 2009 at the Fruitvale Station in Oakland, twenty-two-year-old Oscar Grant III, also a black man, was shot dead by an officer as he was returning from celebrating with friends in San Francisco (see Chapter 25). Both cases were wrenching for all involved. They were also watershed incidents that greatly impacted police training and procedures. Because the officers in both cases were white, racial overtones were heralded by black community leaders in both the Hall and Grant cases.

In July 2011, another fatal incident took place at the Civic Center Station in San Francisco. Riders reported a man, Charles Hill, acting erratically as people tried to board the trains. The responding officers tried to calm Hill down, but when he attacked with a knife, he was fatally shot. Once again there was public outcry, and two demonstrations were staged inside the station in an attempt to disrupt service.

THE BIG STING

Getting back to earlier days, the transit district made headlines again when, on the bright Thursday afternoon of August 17, 1978, I was called to come upstairs and meet with BART general manager Frank Herringer. My secretary took the call. When she asked Herringer's secretary what it was about, she was told it was confidential. She relayed the message to me and I went up to the fifth floor, where I was immediately ushered into Herringer's office. He nodded for me to shut the door, and I took a seat opposite his desk. He glanced at some papers on his desk and then looked up at me and shook his head.

"What's going on, Frank?" I asked.

"You are not going to believe this," he said.

Luckily, I'd brought my coffee with me so I could sip and listen to the tale he was about to unfold.

Herringer then told me about a covert BART Police investigation that had all the makings of a thriller. It had been going on for almost a year and was about to surface, and surface big. A major drug-dealing operation was being carried out by somewhere between twenty and thirty employees of the District. The employees allegedly included train operators, station agents, and maintenance personnel at the system's three shops, and the operation involved transporting the drugs on the trains.

(This story would certainly be more intriguing than when BART was accused of secretly transporting polychlorinated biphenyls [PCBs] on midnight trains from Richmond to Hayward for hazardous-materials disposal. PCBs were widely used as a coolant for transformers, capacitors, and motors until the late 1970s, when researchers discovered their toxic properties could cause cancer. A certain hysteria ensued until their manufacture was banned. BART caught some heat on that one, even though the material being transported was contained in solid ballast products and carried in closed barrels. Also, the system managers in charge of the work had verbal permission from the local health department, which later denied it.)

Soon after my meeting with Herringer, I was escorted by an officer in a police car to a secret office specially set up as the command post for the coming drug bust. It looked like something out of an action movie. A few uniformed officers and detectives in civilian clothes were milling about discussing various aspects of the case *sotto voce* and marking a large system map partially covering one wall. Here, BART police captain Tommy Sowell, who was heading up the special unit carrying out the investigation, introduced me to a young woman he called Carole. He immediately informed me that Carole was not her real name and that she was an undercover operative working at the Richmond shop as a janitor. She had been brought in from out of the area especially for the operation. Her role, as it was revealed to me, was to purchase drugs from dealers inside the organization. According to her later testimony, she was able to purchase about $10,000 worth of drugs from contacts she had managed to cultivate inside the workplace.

The next step was to set up a press conference to take place in the board of directors' room at BART's Lake Merritt headquarters. Assignment editors at all Bay Area television and radio stations, plus newspaper city editors and beat reporters, were notified that at ten the next morning, Friday, August 18, a major announcement would be made. Of course, some of the working press made a strong attempt to wheedle a clue out of my office as to what it was about. But the firewall was up, and the press turnout the next morning practically filled the hundred-seat boardroom. BART's assistant general manager for operations, Robert Gallaway, strode to the podium and, after scanning the room for an instant, announced that at that moment BART police officers were arresting some twenty employees for involvement in the selling of narcotics on District property. He then introduced Captain Sowell, who went on to explain the use of undercover operatives to help in the investigation.

One of the undercover operatives, calling himself Ed Britt, was posing as a train operator. The year before, he'd been brought in from the Alameda County Sheriff's Office and given a job as a train operator, for which he received full training and certification. During his tenure undercover, he was so outspoken about criticizing management that he was elected shop steward. In fact, several of his fellow union members even urged him to run for president of the local. "He was always asking where he could get some dope," one of his fellow train operators told the press. "I thought he was a big junky." Later, when it came out that Ed Britt was a phony name and that he was actually an undercover police officer, the union told the press that the whole affair was a frame-up aimed at union busting, that this was BART's way of getting rid of the troublemakers, particularly in the shops. Speaking for the District, I, of course, denied this allegation when asked for a comment by Pearl Stewart, the writer of the story for the *Oakland Tribune.* The sting story was real, and the sooner we got out in front of it the better. It was no surprise, and maybe even a smart move on the part of the union, that they counterattacked.

Coincidentally, not long after the sting, I played against Stewart in a mixed-doubles tennis tournament. She turned out to be a formidable opponent, though we did not talk shop. I will note as an aside that, in general, cultivating good, candid communication with members of the working media is, I believe, paramount in the role of advocate for an organization such as BART, or any organization that impacts the public.

GOOD NEWS FOR ONCE

The temporary half-percent sales tax, which was put in place to subsidize BART's fare-box revenue, was rescued at the last minute by California assembly speaker Leo McCarthy. His bill, A.B. 1107, would replace the original temporary bill, AB 3785, which passed in 1976 and was due to expire in June 1978. An amendment to the bill added a caveat: revenue from the sales tax collected in the three BART counties would now be shared between BART, Muni, and the Alameda–Contra Costa Transit District (AC Transit). BART would, however, get the lion's share—75 percent—while 25 percent would be divided up and allocated by the Metropolitan Transportation Commission to the other two agencies.

SUPPLIERS SETTLE A LAWSUIT

On another important front, BART's multimillion-dollar lawsuit against its major suppliers, filed back in December 1974, was finally settled after extensive negotiations with the defendants, Parsons Brinckerhoff–Tudor–Bechtel, the Westinghouse Electric Corporation, Rohr Industries, and the Bulova Watch Company. The case was heard in the San Joaquin County Superior Court in Stockton, California. The overall settlement, valued at $34 million, called for the defendants to pay $15 million in cash to the District, as well as for the release of claims against the District in the amount of $13.7 million, and for the defendants to make available critical technical documents and patent licenses, which Westinghouse had considered proprietary intellectual property. The BART board and staff were pleased with the settlement for several reasons. First, a lengthy trial would be a distraction, and in the end it probably would not serve any party's best interests. Second, and more important than the cash payment, was obtaining the technical documents and patent licenses. Without them, BART maintenance work would be beholden to Westinghouse, and BART's efforts to reverse-engineer some of the components that might eventually have to be modified would be hampered.

A lot had happened in just ten short years, but the 1970s were not through with BART yet. The end of this decade brought turmoil that would nearly become a stake in the heart of the system. Still to come was one of the most horrendous and critical periods in the transit district's comparatively short history.

CHAPTER 19

1977 AND 1978 SEE SEVERAL IMPROVEMENTS AND ADDED SERVICE

Equipment failures were in decline and train car availability on any given day had increased through a concentrated engineering and maintenance effort. Overall, reliability and on-time performance were on the upswing. There were some slip-ups, however. On one occasion, a revenue train heading south on the Fremont line inadvertently switched off the main track and took an unscheduled detour into the Hayward storage yard. The quick-thinking operator announced over the public address system that this was a special tour that riders would not likely have the opportunity to see again. Some passengers apparently thought it was actually intentional. But someone, of course, snitched. Naturally, San Francisco columnist Herb Caen was tipped off and made the most of the item. Needless to say, there were a few red faces in the control room as supervisors scrambled to figure out what had happened. Such glitches are always taken very seriously and thoroughly investigated, and in this case it turned out the cause was human error, which, it should be noted, is the preferred error. Glitches in technology generally tend to be more worrisome because automation is the hallmark of the system and confidence in the technology is therefore critical to its success. In the case of the errant train, someone in the field had forgotten to unlock the switch that otherwise would have automatically set the right course.

THE HUNDRED-MILLIONTH PASSENGER FIASCO

Based on computer analysis, it was projected that BART would see its hundred-millionth passenger stride through the fare gates on January 26, 1977. To mark the occasion, BART's board president, Barclay Simpson, general manager Frank Herringer, and I, with a couple of operations staff members, went to the newly opened Embarcadero Station, where we would randomly pick our symbolic hundred-millionth passenger. BART police were also on hand to ensure crowd control. The press and broadcast media were invited to join us, and they showed up in numbers. Lights were set up. Several news cameras on tripods were at the ready, aimed at the fare gates, waiting for the signal.

We waited for the right moment. Several passengers came through before we finally pointed a finger at a lone woman exiting. Lights went on. Cameras began rolling. Two uniformed officers were standing near the gates observing. The poor woman looked absolutely terrified as Herringer and Simpson approached and presented her with a model train and a certificate commemorating the moment. She suddenly found herself surrounded by reporters with microphones asking for comment. She did not speak very good English and stammered that she was a visitor to this country. What was clear was that she was having none of the event. She tried to cover her face. Later it was suggested that she may well have been an illegal immigrant, perhaps from the Philippines, and did not understand what was happening. She thought at first she was being arrested. One of the officers happened to speak Tagalog and asked to get her name and address so that BART could send her a certificate with her name on it. She just shook her head and scooted out of there and into the wind as fast as she could, clutching her model BART train.

BART ATTRACTS A PRINCE AND A KING

The system was no stranger to VIP guests. On October 28, 1977, England's Prince Charles rode BART from San Francisco to downtown Oakland. He said he was impressed with the speed and efficiency of the train and was particularly fascinated with the control cab. On that

Left: England's Prince Charles takes a ride through the tube from San Francisco to the 12th Street Oakland City Center Station, where he was greeted by then Oakland mayor Lionel Wilson. For a few moments the prince enjoyed sitting in the operator's cab. Right: King Carl XVI Gustaf of Sweden tries a fare gate at the MacArthur Station in Oakland. He was presented with a model BART train as a memento of his visit.

occasion, operations manager William B. Fleisher and I accompanied the prince and his entourage of Secret Service and British bodyguards. On another occasion, Carl XVI Gustaf, the young king of Sweden, visited the system. He also wanted to ride the train from San Francisco to the East Bay, but because of a Muni strike that happened to be in progress at the time, with pickets on the street at downtown stations, the king would not enter the system. "He won't cross a picket line," his representative said. He was then chauffeured over to BART's MacArthur Station in North Oakland for a welcoming ceremony. Other famous visitors over the years included boxer Muhammad Ali, vice president Walter Mondale, and numerous dignitaries from around the world. Delegations from China and Japan were not uncommon. There was a great deal of international interest in the system.

A MAGNET FOR MOVIE LOCATIONS

Production teams came calling again during this time, and BART became a favorite location for movies and television shows.

Well-known Hollywood producer and director Stanley Kramer shot scenes of his movie *The Domino Principle* on BART in 1976. Most of the filming took place on the platform of the Fruitvale Station and inside a train during a Saturday and Sunday before weekend service began. BART charged a $4,000 location fee. The movie, released in 1977, starred Gene Hackman, Richard Widmark, Candice Bergen, and Mickey Rooney. Other movies would include *Predator 2,* starring Danny Glover; *The Pursuit of Happyness,* starring Will Smith; and *Fruitvale Station* (see Chapter 25). In the *Happyness* production, Will Smith portrays a true-life character based on Chris Gardner, who practically lived on BART as a homeless person with his son until he made it as a stockbroker. It is a true American, Horatio Alger story, chronicling one man's rise from an impoverished beginning to the top of the heap.

In the realm of television, numerous productions were filmed on the system, including *The Streets of San Francisco,* starring Michael Douglas, and later *Nash Bridges,* starring Don Johnson. While most movies and television shows filmed on BART had promotional value for the system, none hit the mark as well as *The Princess and the Cabbie* in 1981. The television movie starred Valerie Bertinelli as a visiting princess who yearns for independence outside her highly protected sphere. She hooks up with a young cabbie who helps her explore and learn to cope with the real world, and in the process he teaches her step by step how to use BART. Anyone watching would find it an excellent primer on accessing the system.

PATRONAGE SLOWLY INCREASES

By the end of 1977, weekday patronage was in excess of 145,000, an improvement over the previous year. Total ridership for the year was almost 39 million.

On January 7, 1978, BART inaugurated Saturday service, which was promoted by a television campaign featuring famous San Francisco attorney Melvin Belli standing on a station platform. "BART has started Saturday service," begins his monologue. Just then a train comes roaring into the station next to him. He looks at it, turns to the camera, and says, "I rest my case." Rabbi David Miller steps out of a train's double doors and says: "BART is now offering Saturday service." He then raises his hands to the heavens and says, "We've been doing it for a thousand years." These were the very first television commercials ventured by the transit district; they were created by Chiat/Day, a Los Angeles–based advertising agency. Chiat/Day later became famous in its own right for making Apple a household name with its 1984 Super Bowl commercial channeling George Orwell.

Several of BART's career critics, though, thought such advertising was a waste of taxpayer money. They tended to be the "build it and they will come" crowd. But long before, when BART was still in the embryonic stage, it was believed that marketing would someday play a significant role in the success of the system. "The reality is, we'll be competing with the automobile in a land where the automobile is king," Bill Stokes had said during the system's salad days. "After all, billions of dollars are spent each year promoting and advertising the automobile. It's an automobile culture. But if we are going to have clean air, environmentally sound land use, and conservation of energy sources, such as fossil fuels, we must attract a healthy share of the travel market. Marketing and advertising will play a significant role."

Sunday service was finally inaugurated on July 2, 1978, initially from 9 A.M. to midnight. To promote this change, we produced a television ad featuring John Madden, coach of the Oakland Raiders at the time. In the commercial, he stood on the platform of the Coliseum Station and announced folks could now take BART to the games on Sunday. "And don't forget the Snake!" he said—a reference to quarterback Kenny Stabler.

Patronage was surprisingly 18 percent higher than projected, averaging 33,000 trips. This expansion of service came about despite the onset of Proposition 13, which negatively impacted public agencies and schools across the Golden State. For BART, it meant constraints on the operating budget. To offset the funding loss, about 130 workers, mostly from professional and middle-management ranks, were laid off; in addition, 20 unfilled positions were eliminated.

On July 8, a one-day wildcat strike by train operators did shut the system down. It was never clear exactly what the issue was for the operators—some said it was a personality conflict between BART's head of operations and the union president—but in any case it was over quickly.

In 1976, a police strike was honored, albeit reluctantly, by BART's other unions. BART immediately went to the Alameda County

Superior Court for relief. Though the court declared the strike illegal, it continued for a week. The president and vice president of the BART Police Officers Association (BPOA) were then both jailed for contempt of court. Incidentally, the *San Francisco Examiner* had a banner headline on the front page of its Saturday edition proclaiming BART POLICE LEADERS JAILED. Mistakenly, the paper put my picture underneath and identified me as the vice president of the BPOA. I had held a mini press conference on the court steps right after the hearing, which is when the picture was taken. The *Examiner* front page was framed and presented to me by Herringer at a staff meeting the following Monday.

1979: A BLACK HOLE IN THE SYSTEM'S HISTORY

The last year of the decade, 1979, was an unforgettable one for BART. As 1978 ended, work was progressing on achieving close headways, which would mean adding direct service from Richmond to San Francisco. Ridership was continuing to grow, and the coming new year was full of promise and optimism. No one could have imagined the dark event about to befall BART that would prove to be one of the young system's greatest challenges and make news around the world.

After three years on the job, Frank Herringer resigned as general manager, effective December 31, 1978. During his tenure, the system had made steady progress toward reaching its full potential as a vital component of the Bay Area's transportation network. He went on to be named a vice president at the Transamerica Corporation in San Francisco and eventually rose to become president and chairman of the company. A giant in the insurance business, Transamerica also held several subsidiary companies, including Budget Rent a Car, United Artists, and Transamerica Airlines. At a farewell speech at the Commonwealth Club of California, Herringer talked about the lessons to be learned from the creation of BART. He believed the early heralding of BART as a new, cutting-edge, space-age system of the future created expectations that could not possibly be met instantaneously. "Engineers will tell you that when you have 10 percent or more new technology incorporated into a zillion moving parts, there are bound to be problems smoothing things out," he said. "But in the final analysis BART will one day be the system promised and an integral part of the Bay Area community...and even loved."

After a nationwide search for a new general manager, the BART board narrowed the prospective candidates down to six. They were from far and wide, one even from Canada. Yet again, the directors were divided. On December 19, following much heated debate behind closed doors, BART's director of planning and budget, Keith Bernard, was named the system's new general manager, effective January 1, 1979. Two of the priorities on Bernard's plate were, first, to complete the close headways program (still working with the Lawrence Berkeley Laboratory) and, second, to prepare for upcoming labor negotiations with BART's unions, which would begin in the spring. Another priority was to begin developing cost estimates for future extensions.

But just seventeen days into his new job, everything abruptly changed for Bernard, and for the entire organization, as the system was hit with one of its most pivotal events since first opening its doors for service.

THE TRANSBAY TUBE FIRE PROVES TO BE A TRANSFORMATIVE EVENT

At approximately six minutes after 6 P.M. on Wednesday, January 17, BART's train 117 was bound for San Francisco from Oakland. It was about a third of the way through the Transbay Tube when a loud noise shattered the consciousness of the passengers. No one knew what it could have been. According to some passengers, it sounded like an explosion. Then a rear car suddenly caught fire and smoke began to fill the train as the fire quickly spread to engulf the other cars. Luckily, the train was going against the normal homebound commute for that hour, and the passengers only numbered about forty; they were safely evacuated through the gallery walkway between the two trackways to the eastbound track. An eastbound train was eventually brought into the adjacent trackway to take out the passengers and a few employees from the burning train. Four of the seven cars making up the train consist were totally destroyed, at a cost of $300,000 each, and others were damaged but reparable.

An issue was made of the fact that there were passengers aboard the rescue train when it was brought in, and that they were not told the train was going into a fire area. By this time firefighters had arrived from both the San Francisco and the Oakland fire departments. As the rescue train departed to get people out, it created a horrendous vacuum that sucked toxic smoke through an open door into the gallery. Once back in Oakland, seventeen passengers, twenty-four firefighters, and twelve employees were treated for smoke inhalation. Overall it was not a smooth rescue operation. Communication and coordination problems and other complications occurred because of lack of emergency preparedness on the part of system personnel. This was a wrenchingly difficult lesson. Pundits from all corners of society came out in droves as the incident became a cause célèbre.

A critical factor was the operation of the fans and damper system in the tube that were meant to control the direction of the smoke, which was later determined to be highly toxic. The smoke emanated from the polyurethane material used in the manufacture of the walls, ceiling, and floor of the transit cars, as well as the foam in the cushioned seats. At the time, this same material was commonly used for the interior walls of airplanes and various other commercial products and had generally been given the stamp of approval by the American Plastics Council, a trade organization for the plastics industry. Polyurethane is still commonly used in a wide variety of products and is generally resistant to heat, but it does have a combustible flashpoint of around 280° Celsius.

Tragically, Lieutenant William Elliot, age fifty, a battalion chief and twenty-seven-year veteran of the Oakland Fire Department who was working in the tube, died from smoke inhalation. Elliot's death underscored the need for improved fire safety measures, wet standpipes (previously they were dry), and general equipment for fighting fires inside tunnels and the tube. It took about seven and a half hours to finally get the fire under control.

Both San Francisco fire chief Andrew Casper and Oakland fire chief William Moore were highly critical of BART's fire safety program and of the equipment made available for such emergencies. Of particular interest were the oxygen masks, which the fire chiefs felt were inadequate for fighting fires in the tube. The masks being used had only thirty minutes worth of oxygen, which was clearly unacceptable. On Sunday, January 21, 1979, in an interview with the *San Francisco Examiner*, Casper said, "I had been haggling with BART for close to a year over the purchase of new masks for firefighters who might some day have to enter the tube." He said the argument was mainly over who would pay for them. "BART has been very much remiss on this issue," Casper added. Chief Moore was on the same page, voicing his recommendation that the transit district invest in new and better equipment, including a better radio communications system.

The masks that the BART safety department and the two fire chiefs agreed on were German-made Dräger oxygen masks that would last four hours. The order would be for forty masks, but purchasing them would prove to be problematic; only six could be found in the United States, so the remaining thirty-four were ordered direct from Germany. The purchase of the masks, which cost $150,000, was the first step in what would become a full-court-press approach to making the system one of the safest fire-ready systems in the world.

BART's safety department, which was involved in the overall investigation along with the National Transportation Safety Board (NTSB) and California's Division of Occupational Safety and Health (commonly known as Cal/OSHA), also invited peers from transit systems in the East to offer their analysis and expertise. The question before them was, what happened, and how did it happen?

Several important lessons emerged from the Transbay Tube fire that six months earlier could not have been imagined. First, the California Public Utilities Commission (CPUC) ordered the tube temporarily closed for revenue service pending the outcome of the investigation into the circumstances surrounding the fire, as well as an inspection to determine whether the extreme heat had caused any damage to the tube structure. After the damaged train was removed, the initial inspection determined that there had been no damage to the tube itself. BART believed it could open up the tube again in a few days. However, several other factors had to be investigated, including a detailed review of the transit system's procedures with regard to safety, such as how well the control center personnel were trained in the operation of the fans and damper system inside the tube and tunnels.

Of particular concern as the investigation got under way was how the fire started. From the beginning it was known to be electrical in nature, but beyond that fact not much was known. Observers on the sidelines speculated about what might have happened. When interviewed, the operator of train 117 said he had heard a strange banging noise underneath the train. According to one passenger who was later interviewed, it was loud and echoed as if in a great canyon.

THE CPUC REVISES ITS ORDER

The CPUC then ordered the tube shut down indefinitely, pending the investigation's findings and the scope of what might be needed to improve the fire safety of the system. As part of the order, the CPUC made it clear that both the San Francisco and Oakland fire chiefs would have to approve the reopening of the tube. Both chiefs said they would not agree to let BART resume transby service until they were satisfied that the transit district would guarantee certain improvements in addition to the new masks. This was a shock to BART and, of course, a blow to the system's transbay commuters. What followed was a scramble to contract with various bus companies, both private and public, to take up as much of the slack as possible. AC Transit proved to be the biggest contributor in this area. It cost BART about $30,000 per day to provide transbay shuttle service. Additionally, damage to equipment due to the fire was estimated to be $2.5 million.

The work ahead included extensive testing of the polyurethane material used in the transit cars. A portion of a retired transit car was supplied for one of the primary tests at the University of California's testing lab. The material was ignited under controlled conditions with all resulting aspects measured, such as the temperature at which the material burst into flame; how quickly full involvement took place; and the toxicity level of the smoke. The film of the tests was made available to the media upon request, and it was featured at the top of the 6 P.M. and 11 P.M. television news on most Bay Area stations. The print media also published stills of the test, and the subject stayed at the top of the news for the next few months. One could only cringe at images of the tests being conducted. But, as painful as they were, the tests were of paramount importance in helping BART raise its sights regarding what material would be used in future transit cars to improve safety. Other systems were taking heed as well.

The Transbay Tube was closed for almost three months. The CPUC held a hearing on March 29 to determine whether it should allow the tube to reopen. Representatives from BART, along with a parade of interested parties, testified at the hearing. Some private citizens were for reopening, and some were against. Self-styled political parties, including the Young Communist League, demonstrated outside the CPUC in San Francisco, calling for the continued closure of the tube. In general, the goings-on were like feeding time at the monkey house.

BART was finally permitted to reopen the tube for revenue service on Thursday, April 5, after complying with certain demands of the Oakland and San Francisco fire chiefs and the CPUC, including additional training for all BART safety personnel, train controllers, and support system workers in the control center; better lighting to mark emergency doors within the tube; improved inspection procedures for the transit vehicles; a public safety program that included large emergency-information displays in the transit cars; and the replacement of all of the seat cushions in a commitment to make the system fire-ready.

The results of the investigation by BART in conjunction with the NTSB determined that the fire had been caused by a series of fluke incidents. Almost two hours before train 117 went through, train 363 entered the tube, shortly after which a loose bolt caused the cover of an undercar equipment box to come loose and then become completely dislodged, crashing onto the tracks. Between trains 363 and 117, eleven trains went through to San Francisco. When train 117 came through a little after 6 P.M., it hit the heavy metal cover, which was 2 feet wide and 6 feet long. Upon impact, the metal cover careened off the 1,000-volt direct-current third rail, knocking the rail out of alignment. Next, it hit the rear collector shoe on the last car of the train. The collector shoe, which transports power from the third rail to the train, is scored at the neck so that it can break off in such circumstances, in a fail-safe mode. Unfortunately, it did not. Instead, the flying loose cover sheared the connecting cables. The loose cables, carrying power from the third rail, then whipped around and attached to the underside of the car, thus igniting the fire.

In the aftermath of the Transbay Tube fire, BART launched a $40 million fire-safety program, beginning with the replacement of more than 32,000 seat cushions in the fleet with a new, well-tested material. BART reviewed the Southern California–based McDonnell Douglas database, containing some 400 potential materials, which were then tested at both the McDonnell Douglas lab and UC Berkeley's fire-testing lab. The material that met all of the criteria BART required was a low-smoke neoprene. Overall, the research and testing program took about five months. It was projected that the cost of the initial fire-safety program, including replacing the seats, would cost $4.2 million and be completed by the fall of 1980. Federal and state funding helped pay the bill. The full program would include the complete retrofit of all of the transit cars with new floors, walls, and ceilings, to be carried out in the early 1980s.

Once again, BART was on the leading edge of development, this time in the area of fire safety. The transit system's research and material adoption would eventually benefit the transit industry through the creation of a national databank held by the Urban Mass Transportation Administration (UMTA) and the American Public Transit Association (APTA).

HARROWING LABOR NEGOTIATIONS

No sooner did the tube reopen for service than BART turned its attention to labor negotiations with its two major unions. Talks actually began on March 16 with representatives from Service Employees International Union (SEIU) Local 390, representing about 1,500 maintenance, professional, and clerical personnel, and Amalgamated Transit Union (ATU) Local 1555, representing station agents, train operators, clerical workers, and some professional workers. More than forty bargaining sessions were held over the next three and a half months, but by the expiration of the contract at midnight on Sunday, June 30, 1979, not much progress had been made. One of the critical financial issues was the full cost-of-living adjustment (COLA) increases BART workers had enjoyed since the first contract. Full COLA meant full increases based on the quarterly Consumer Price Index, paid quarterly and compounded annually. In other words, COLA, along with regular increases, was added to every employee's base wage at the end of each contract year. The system's financial economists estimated that, with the double-digit inflation that was then occurring, continuing to pay out full COLA would drive the District into bankruptcy within a couple of years. Additionally, BART needed to bring employee wages into line, or parity, with local and national prevailing rates. Thus, COLA had to go, or at the very least be drastically modified under a scaled-back formula. The unions, of course, saw this as a major "take-away." Several other issues were on the table, including work rules, some of which the District found untenable. Historically, certain work rules, many of which came from older railroad work rules, have been the bane of management's efforts to run the system as efficiently as possible. One thing was clear: the two sides were on a potentially disastrous collision course.

BART extended the contract on a day-to-day basis so long as talks continued. Both sides met through the month of August, and by that time, a significant slow-down had been occurring in the shops as employees worked strictly by the book. Then, on the morning of Friday, August 31, only one train operator showed up for work. The rest stayed out with what they called the Blue Flu. On the one hand, a strike had not been declared and there were no pickets; on the other hand, no one was working. Only one train was operating on the entire system. In a way, it was a brilliant strategy to shut the system down without actually going on strike—everyone was still getting full pay. Later that morning, at a meeting of top management on the fifth floor of the system's Lake Merritt headquarters, BART's outside labor attorney from the San Francisco firm of Pillsbury, Madison and Sutro suddenly stood up at the end of the long conference table. He looked around as attendees were sipping coffee and ready to take notes. His fist came down on the table. "What we have here this morning is a strike," he said. "They may not be calling it a strike, but it is in fact a strike. And I believe we can defend that position."

A press conference was hastily called, and management announced the strike. The doors were then locked at all BART facilities after those union employees who had shown up for work were ushered out. The unions screamed lockout. However, the superior court in San Francisco agreed that it was a strike and certified it as such. The system was ostensibly shut down for a little over three months. In the interim, some limited service was provided courtesy of managers who had previously been train operators.

One well-publicized incident involved union members taking over the Concord shop one midnight. Led by Paul Varacalli, the executive secretary of SEIU Local 390, a group of men and women entered the shop and forcibly carried out management employees. They then locked themselves in by chaining the doors. Food was dropped to them by helicopter and picked up on the roof of the building. One of the occupiers, SEIU member Ken Holmes, was in charge of food delivery as he stood on the roof and waved the helicopter down. The protestors were in the shop for a week before a court order got them out. An agreement between the parties was finally reached on November 22, but full regular service did not begin until December 3, just in time for the Christmas season.

Various media outlets and social and political factions posed the lingering question "Was it a strike or a lockout?" San Francisco Superior Court found it to be a strike after hearing arguments from lawyers representing both BART and the unions, and as far as BART officials were concerned, that was a legal confirmation that a strike had in fact occurred. Shortly before the union members returned to work, however, an administrative law judge with the Public Employment Relations Board in Sacramento declared it a lockout. Since the administrative law judge's ruling was for the sole purpose of allowing unemployment benefits to be paid to the workers, BART did not challenge it.

A key element of the negotiations that helped to bring about the settlement became a significant issue for BART during labor negotiations in 2013. In return for the workers giving up full COLA in 1979, the District agreed to pay the employees' share of the pension fund (7 percent of base wage), phased in over a three-year period. After the slow recovery from the recession of 2008, pension-fund liabilities became an issue for states, cities, counties, and other public agencies across the nation, not to mention the private sector.

All in all, the 1970s was a tumultuous period for the still-young transit system. At the same time, it was the beginning of a new era—an era of promise and progress.

CHAPTER 20

CLOSE HEADWAYS GET THE OKAY

Finally, on June 3, 1980, after years of hearings and untold hours of technical presentations and testimony from BART engineers, lawyers, and consultants, the California Public Utilities Commission (CPUC) granted approval for closer headways. The hearing process, which began before the CPUC in San Francisco in April 1978, determined to the satisfaction of the hearing officer and commissioners that BART had adequately addressed safety issues involving the primary automatic train control system. Lifting the constraints that had been put on the system since it first opened in 1972 would now allow it to operate much as originally intended. Seven years of technical modifications—including the implementation of the sequential operating release system (SORS), which added redundancy to the primary automatic train control protection—were key to the system's long-term future.

Being able to operate at close headways was a major breakthrough. Now that more than one train at a time could make the 6-mile trip under the bay in either direction, traffic through the Transbay Tube would be significantly increased. Another key service improvement resulting from close headways was the addition of a fourth route: direct service between Richmond and Daly City. The addition of this route reduced the scheduled waiting time on the Richmond line platforms from fourteen minutes between trains to seven and a half minutes. Trains were also added to the Fremont and Concord lines during morning and evening commute periods, reducing wait times from seven minutes between Oakland and San Francisco/Daly City to four minutes. For the first time in its short history, BART published its first printed schedule. It did not list every train and was basically a "memory schedule," which meant that by remembering the intervals between trains a rider could easily figure out when his or her next train was coming through. The printed schedule has since gone through an evolutionary process, and today it lists every single train throughout each operating day, seven days a week, plus gives the amounts of inter-station fares.

In addition to the successful implementation of the close headways program, BART's two-year-old Reliability Improvement Program was beginning to show positive results in 1980. The objective of the program was to reduce or eliminate unscheduled train removals during revenue service. Having as many as fifteen trains taken out of service on any given day was simply unacceptable. The program included replacement or modification of key train and wayside components that had the most severe impact on day-to-day operations. In some cases, reverse engineering was required to determine the exact makeup of certain trouble-prone components, such as the onboard thyristor, or solid-state semiconductor, used in the transit cars' propulsion system.

Two other significant onboard modifications to the trains were implemented as part of the Reliability Improvement Program to further reduce the number of malfunctioning trains taken out of service each day. The first was called the Manual Cab Signaling system. This modification allowed a train operator to control the train manually while retaining all of the programmed safety measures operative when the automatic train control system fails. The second modification was called the Car Cut Out Program, which allowed a train to remain in service despite the failure of the braking system in one or two cars of a ten-car consist. The malfunctioning cars would simply roll free while the rest of the train operated normally with full braking capacity, thus helping to meet on-time performance objectives.

STAYING ON THE CUTTING EDGE

In the 1980s, BART general manager Keith Bernard visualized the system ten and twenty years into the future and determined that it was time to start preparing for growth both in ridership and future extensions. "BART cannot be static," Bernard said. "We must keep pushing the envelope."

In June 1980, the beginning of the new fiscal year, BART introduced the first of its short-range, five-year transit plans, which were now required by the Metropolitan Transportation Commission as part of a review of regional transportation funding needs. For BART, acquiring funding for the next step would be a major challenge. The improvement projects included completion of a third track, called the KE track (K is the letter designation for that segment of line, and E is for "express"), in an already-existing tunnel through downtown Oakland; the construction of a tail track at the Daly City maintenance and train storage facility; ninety newly designed flat-nosed C cars (which would be used as both lead and trailing cars, offering more flexibility in train makeup); and an Integrated Control System (ICS). The purpose of the ICS was to increase system capacity to include future extensions, and it also called for integrating all computer systems throughout all District facilities, from the control center at Lake Merritt to each of the shops and administration offices, tying everything to a giant mainframe. For example, a maintenance jacket for each transit car could be filed in the new computer system and then be accessed at any of the maintenance shops. The ICS's most important function would be to increase system train capacity from a current maximum of forty-nine trains to seventy-five trains, and thus meet projected ridership demands in the years to come. This particular project, however, proved to be one of the most daunting challenges ever attempted by BART. The ICS was dubbed by some as BART's Big Brain. At one point, a story went around that a woman from San Francisco was claiming BART had stolen her diseased husband's brain for its train control system.

Clearly, BART would have to apply to the federal Urban Mass Transportation Administration for capital grant money in the neighborhood of more than $500 million to accomplish several of the listed infrastructure and technical improvements. The District would use available state Transit Development Act (TDA) money combined with capital reserve to leverage the needed federal money. At the time, federal money could contribute as much as 75 to 80 percent for capital improvements. The American Public Transit Association (APTA), the industry trade group, testified in congressional hearings on the need for federal investment in the nation's rail transit infrastructure and city bus services as Congress considered the budget for the new fiscal year. However, the Reagan administration was not a major supporter of public transit and in 1982 cut UMTA's transit budget by 31 percent. With the federal grant application process in flux, BART faced a significant political challenge as it sought the needed funding for its proposed projects. President Reagan's UMTA administrator, Arthur Teele, a Florida politician and businessman, made an effort to work with the transit industry within the limits of his authority. (Teele eventually returned to his Florida roots, and several years later, in the midst of a reported scandal, he tragically took his own life in the lobby of the *Miami Herald.*)

Teele's successor at UMTA was a young man named Ralph L. Stanley. He was determined to carry out the administration's policy on the matter, which was to force state and local city governments to take an increased role in funding transit systems. When Stanley visited the Bay Area, he was quoted as saying the balkanized transportation network, with BART at the center, was like Beirut. No one knew quite what that meant, except that it seemed to be an indicator of his personal bent when it came to supporting public transit—in other words, negative. All of this meant that with the demand for scarce federal grant money from cities and transit agencies across the country, BART would have to compete hard for a share. A carefully thought-out strategy would be critical to a successful application.

THE TWO-PRONGED STRATEGY

The ball was then tossed to me, as the director of media and public affairs, to come up with a plan. I worked closely with general manager Keith Bernard and we settled on a two-pronged approach: first and foremost, to involve the business leaders of the San Francisco Bay Area as stakeholders in the system's future growth, and second, to launch a comprehensive public information program aimed at creating a top-of-mind awareness of the need to invest in the BART system to meet projected long-term ridership growth. It was important for the general public, whether they were riders or not, to understand that BART was an economic engine in the Bay Area and thus essential to everyone.

Getting the business community on board would help to harness the lobbying power in Washington of some of the nation's most powerful corporations headquartered in the Bay Area. Without question, BART was important to the region's commerce, and it had been established long before that doing business on the Pacific Rim would be a significant sector of growth for Bay Area corporations. In turn, the ability to attract top-notch people from other parts of the country and the world—people who would most likely live in the suburbs—would be enhanced if they had access to a clean, modern rapid transit system.

THE FIRST STEP

The first step was to bring in an advertising firm with a public relations arm to help put together the overall program. Cunningham and Walsh (C&W), a San Francisco–based agency, was selected. My primary contacts with C&W were Marjorie Blackwell and Adri Boudewyn, two top professionals who would work with me over the next couple of years. The initial task for C&W was to come up with a strong theme for the program. Shortly after their taking on the assignment I was invited to their office in San Francisco for a presentation in their conference room. As if right out of the television show *Mad Men,* the creative staff gathered, coffee and pastries were served, and everyone held their breath. Then one of the staff members did an imitation of a drumroll and unveiled a large placard positioned on a tripod with the proposed theme: "BART. Going Places." It was the only proposal offered. I stared at it for a long moment and then nodded. It was perfect. Those three short words said everything.

SECOND STEP

Next, I contacted a friend and colleague, Paul Cane, who was vice president of public relations for the Bechtel Corporation, and asked for his help in putting together a luncheon for the chief executive officers of all of San Francisco's major corporations. He was enormously helpful and managed to get Steve Bechtel Sr. to chair an invitation committee. Invitations were sent to all of the major companies to attend a luncheon presentation by BART at the World Trade Club on the Embarcadero. Angelo Siracusa, a prominent business leader who was president of the Bay Area Council at the time, as well as a member of the Metropolitan Transportation Commission, was also a key figure in helping put together this important event.

The purpose of the luncheon was for BART general manager Keith Bernard to present a slide show of graphics and photos depicting the system's growth potential and impact on business in the years to come, as well as the financial investment it would take to get there. Following the advice of the Bechtel people, it was to be an informational presentation only. We were asked not to say anything about seeking specific help in Washington, only that we hoped federal money could be obtained for the needed improvements. My guess was that since Bechtel was the official host of the luncheon, he didn't want the company representatives in attendance to feel they were being put on the spot. Interestingly enough, one of the CEOs at the luncheon asked what it was BART wanted them to do, and, if nothing, what was the point of the presentation? In general, the CEOs and other top company officials were more than happy to help in any way they could.

After the luncheon, Paul Cane introduced me to Steve Bechtel Sr., a gracious man in his early eighties at the time. After a brief discussion, during which he praised Bernard's presentation, he said simply, "We'll do what we can in Washington." It was not lost on us that two people who had a strong connection to the Bechtel Company were then cabinet members in the Reagan administration: George Shultz, the secretary of state, and Casper Weinberger, the secretary of defense. Whether their assistance was ever sought will probably never be known.

Following the San Francisco luncheon, an evening meeting took place in Oakland, with the same presentation given before the top people in the East Bay business community. This event was put on with the assistance of Cornell Maier, then CEO of Kaiser Aluminum, and Dick Spees, vice president of Kaiser Public Affairs, who later went on to be elected to the Oakland city council, where he had a long tenure.

BART eventually did get the critical funding it was seeking from the state and Washington for the specific named projects.

As part of the "BART. Going Places" program, a traveling-island exhibit was designed to display large photographs and text depicting the original construction years, the current system, and future projections. It was built of wood and faced with brushed aluminum to suggest a BART train. A 9-foot model of the proposed new C car was also at the center of the display, along with an animated video on a large monitor screen. The C car was BART's answer to early critics of the sloped-nosed A cars, originally designed to give the system a space-age look, which had served as a strong marketing tool. The new design called for a flat-nosed lead car that included a door at the front so it could also be placed in the middle of a train consist. As a practical matter, the C car would provide an extra measure of flexibility in the makeup and breakup of trains.

The "BART. Going Places" exhibit stood 8 feet high with a 4-foot-wide header that stretched 12 feet across the top of the two front panels, creating an arched entry into the exhibit. After being introduced at the Embarcadero Station, where it was on display for a month, it traveled all over the Bay Area, mostly to shopping malls and other BART stations. On one occasion, we took it down to Los Angeles for a transit conference. One of the visitors to the BART exhibit was writer Ray Bradbury, a major supporter of public transit. In fact, he said he'd never had a driver's license. He seemed impressed with the BART exhibit and said that one day he would love to come up to Oakland and visit the control center. I extended him an open invitation, but he never took me up on it. It was estimated that during its two-year life the "BART. Going Places" exhibit was viewed by between 200,000 and 250,000 people, most of whom took an informational brochure about the program.

BART Times was also created as a component of the program to keep the riding public informed on all matters involving the system. Published monthly, it had news, a feature column, a cartoon usually depicting the system in a humorous situation, and a calendar of events around the Bay Area that were easily accessible by the trains. The newsletter, which continues to be published and distributed on the system today, also includes stories about famous riders and would-be-famous riders, some of whom were trying to kick off their careers as entertainers or musicians by performing on the system. In the early days, musicians were not allowed to perform on the trains or in the paid or free areas of the stations. However, one guitar-playing country-style singer who called himself the Cisco Kid managed to stay one jump ahead of BART Police, using the trains as his stage. I heard him a couple of times—he was pretty good. And, of course, Cisco tin-cupped passengers for services rendered. Eventually a concert violinist who kept getting cited for playing in the free concourse area of the Civic Center Station in San Francisco sued the District for restraint of free speech. He was successful, and thereafter BART could not bar performers from the free area of the stations and plazas, although it could determine their location to ensure that passenger flow would not be impeded by their presence.

CHARTER TRAINS

Toward the end of 1981, BART began to experiment with charter trains, and we put out the word that corporations and other organizations could hire private trains for special events. A premium was charged for this service, which meant that it was a moneymaker. The nonstop charter service would only be available during evenings and weekends. One of the first customers for this new service was the National Clown, Mime, Puppet, and Dance Ministry. Roughly two hundred members, dressed in full regalia, were transported from downtown Berkeley to the Embarcadero Station in San Francisco. It was dubbed the "Clown Train" by BART workers. While snacks and *non*alcoholic beverages could be served on the charter trains, catered by the event organizers, alcohol did in fact sneak into the punch bowl now and again. On one occasion it was rumored that a teetotaling BART director joined one of the groups chartering a train and more than tasted the punch, which had been generously laced with vodka. Spies reported that he seemed to be feeling no pain before the evening was over.

PATRONAGE

The success of any transit system can usually be measured by the number of customers it attracts, and in BART's case, it can also be measured in the length of an average ride. BART system ridership is measured in trips, which are counted at the exit gates, and the length of these trips is a key factor in comparing BART with other forms of public transit in the Bay Area, such as AC Transit or the San Francisco Muni. For BART, the average trip length recorded was just over 13 miles—much longer than average trips taken on most of the other systems. This statistic is important mostly because it reflects the system's contribution to energy savings and overall environmental quality in the Bay Area's core. Also, in terms of efficiency, a ten-car train with a single operator can carry as many as 2,000 passengers (around 700 seated and the rest standing), compared to a single-occupancy automobile on the freeway. In November 1981, average weekday ridership was 176,000, roughly a 17 percent increase over the end of the previous year's 150,000 weekday average. While part of the increase could be attributed to the addition of direct service between Richmond and San Francisco, it was also an indicator that as mean time between failures grew under the ongoing Reliability Improvement Program, ridership would continue to grow.

On September 11, 1982, BART celebrated its tenth anniversary of service to the people of the Bay Area with a public cake-cutting ceremony in its Lake Merritt headquarters plaza. The system had come a long way during its first decade. Helping to underscore the occasion, movie and stage star Donald O'Connor, who had ridden BART over from San Francisco, showed up and said he hoped that some day Los Angeles would have such a system. The event not only marked ten years of service but also touted the next ten years, as the system's critical capital-improvement program was coming to fruition.

By 1982, BART's $513 million capital-improvement program was under way. On October 7 of that year, the system's board of directors approved a contract to purchase 150 of the newly designed C cars. The price tag, $279 million, or approximately $1.9 million per car, was a far cry from that first order back in 1969, which came out at $158,000 per car. In the meantime a program was launched to convert 35 A cars to B cars to create a more efficient fleet mix. Also adding considerably more flexibility to the overall operation was the completion of the third track through downtown Oakland in 1984. The $150 million Daly City tail track and storage yard facility were also ready for business by the end of 1984, and this project was an extremely important crossroad in the system's continuing evolution. It not only reduced turn-back time at the terminus station and thus augmented close headways but also helped reap savings by eliminating the need to send empty trains back to the East Bay at the end of service each night.

SUSPICIONS RAISED OVER THE DALY CITY PROJECT

The Daly City tail track and storage yard was also the proverbial "camel's nose under the tent," as political interest on the west side of the bay longed to extend the system down to San Francisco International Airport. This plan was still treacherous ground as East Bay politicians, supported by Dean Lesher's powerful *Contra Costa Times,* were suspicious of BART's expansion ambitions. Because the airport, owned by the City and County of San Francisco, lay like an island in San Mateo County, it was considered off limits. East Bay elected officials still resented San Mateo's dropping out of the original five-county District back in 1962.

Moreover, San Mateo County had not paid one dime in support of the system's construction yet was getting the benefit of the Daly City Station, which was being used primarily by San Mateo County commuters traveling to downtown San Francisco. To even consider building an extension to the airport was unthinkable. Longtime BART director Nello Bianco, from western Contra Costa County, was adamant on the subject. He pointed out that a promise had been made to Joe Silva, in that famous Martinez coffee shop meeting in 1962, that any future extensions would be built in eastern Contra Costa and Alameda Counties before expanding elsewhere—BART had to meet this commitment before going outside the District's three counties. Some believed that such a promise was pure myth. When asked years later, George Christopher, who had attended the coffee shop meeting as mayor of San Francisco, offered only a Cheshire grin and nothing more on that particular issue. Whether such a promise had been made or not may never be known. Board member John Glenn, who was now in an adversarial relationship with Bianco, often referred to the story as nonsense. Proponents of an airport extension did not consider it relevant more than twenty years later. However, the Boatwright bill of 1976 was relevant; it still stood as an impediment to any extension of the system outside of its original three counties. One thing was certain: this issue was developing legs and would spark a civil war on the BART board.

EARLY PREPARATIONS FOR AN EXTENSION PROGRAM

Even before the system's opening in 1972, extensions had been gaining traction on the staff and board's radar screen. Parallel to getting the system up, operating studies were already being conducted to identify potential corridors. During the 1980s, BART staff began to come up with preliminary cost estimates for possible future extensions in eastern Contra Costa and Alameda Counties. This was an ambitious and maybe even a fruitless endeavor considering there was little or no money for extensions, at least for the foreseeable future. At the time, a possible extension to the San Francisco airport was the only project that would be eligible for federal grant money under the UMTA formula's cost-benefit analysis. The formula required a comprehensive study of corridor density, population, and potential ridership demand in the specific area to be served.

The eastern Contra Costa and Alameda County corridors being explored for new lines did not meet the federal criteria—they were still viewed as rural areas with low population density—and could therefore receive no funding, and running an extension to San Francisco International Airport was out of the question from a legal and political standpoint. Nevertheless, BART began saving its pennies for a comprehensive extension program as work began on its capital-improvement program, which was designed not only to enhance current operations but also to support future extensions.

The BART board adopted a "First Phase Extension Program," which called for adding a total of 33 miles and ten more stations to the 71.5-mile core system. The program included an extension to the vicinity of San Francisco International Airport—the operative word being "vicinity." This policy rekindled the controversy that was always close to the surface of any discussion of extensions. How could BART spend money to extend farther into San Mateo County, which had never paid taxes to support the system? The term "vicinity" eventually created a controversy all its own, separate from the issue of whether BART should even consider such an extension before meeting its commitment to eastern Contra Costa and Alameda Counties. Impetus was given to BART's extension policy when, in March 1988, the Metropolitan Transportation Commission adopted a long-range regional transit improvement plan with emphasis on rail extensions of the BART system. This plan was crucial because it called for earmarking future state and available federal dollars for BART's extension projects.

A HISTORIC AGREEMENT IS REACHED

The beginnings of a resolution came about in early June 1988, when the board adopted a historic agreement in principle with the San Mateo County Transit District (SamTrans) that called for an extension of the BART line south from Daly City to somewhere *in the vicinity of* the airport. The key provision of the agreement was to be a payment from SamTrans of $200 million that could be applied to extensions within the original three BART counties. Politically, this was acceptable to East Bay officials with the proviso that more money would be found to build the long-promised extensions.

JOINT DEVELOPMENT

As the 1980s progressed, a new thrust emerged to get into the "joint development" business, a concept that had a great deal of promise as well as political pitfalls. While the concept was simple on the surface, putting together deals was anything but. By entering into "public/private" partnerships to develop the system's air rights on agency-owned excess property around BART's suburban stations, the system could benefit greatly both by capturing potential revenue through lease agreements and by building ridership. Even while still on the drawing board it was believed that BART stations would serve as a planning tool that would influence adjacent development. While the new system did act as a catalyst for growth along its suburban lines, initially very little development occurred specifically around the stations themselves. In fact, BART was criticized early in the game because it had not instantly attracted the promised development. As was the case with old railroad companies, whose lines stretched across America and created railroad towns that added riches to the investors' coffers, land development was to be an enrichment endeavor. Indeed, no one could dispute BART's considerable impact on the revitalization of San Francisco's Market Street corridor, where billions of dollars had been invested in new high-rise office and retail complexes. But the suburban areas were another matter.

As a public agency, BART's ambitions were more modest and tempered by the legal constraints on spending taxpayer money or public assets that could benefit private interests. However, BART eventually made a conscious decision not to take a passive role in development around its stations but to aggressively pursue it as part of a long-term strategic plan. In the words of one director at the time, "BART is more than a people mover, it is giving shape and form and economic growth to the San Francisco Bay region."

In 1984 the BART board adopted a policy to solicit private-sector interest in station development. As for the political pitfalls, some people attacked the BART board for its joint-development policy, saying that development was not the transit system's primary business and that it should be left solely to the private sector and private money.

The critical question was this: Were the taxpayers, the owners of the system, being served by BART getting into the development business? The answer, of course, was yes. Capturing land value on or about stations could only be a win-win for BART, for local incorporated cities whose tax bases would be boosted, and for the creation of jobs. This new BART board policy called for developing a general plan and an environmental impact report for each station area in partnership with local governments. A special section in the transit system's Planning Department was created to carry out the board's direction.

Historically, urban/suburban transit systems have not taken full advantage of valuable rights-of-way, as the early railroads did. For example, the telegraph lines strung along railroad rights-of-way connecting major metropolitan areas not only offered a major communication link between the East and the West but also created economic synergy between the railroad lines, communication lines, and land development that benefitted all three enterprises. It stood to reason that BART's 75-mile right-of-way was perfectly timed to accommodate outside uses, such as fiber-optic cable placement, part of an emerging telecommunications industry that would decentralize the movement of information. Coupled with joint development, fiber optics could be the conduit for the new information highway that was taking shape, linking communities and companies throughout the region and the nation. In the early 1970s, not too long after BART first opened, Fortney Stark, father of venerable congressman Pete Stark, made a presentation to the board of directors proposing that a pneumatic tube system be installed throughout the right-of-way to carry mail. The board found the idea interesting but never acted on it. After all, pneumatic systems were what you found in department stores.

WHO WOULD HAVE KNOWN?

Controversies inside the organization sometimes offered interesting and even amusing diversions from the barrage of headlines that featured BART and its surrounding swirl of agency politics. Since the opening of the system, my department had published the employee newsletter *BARTalk,* which was called *Inside Track* before a contest invited employees to submit a new name for the publication. (For a while, a parody publication, called *Outside Chance,* was secretly published from inside the organization.) *BARTalk* was edited by Sy

Mouber, the manager of public information, who worked in my department. Sy was a crusty old newspaperman whom I stole from the Metropolitan Transportation Commission, where he had worked for several years as the information officer.

Sometime in 1983, Sy came to me with an idea for an upcoming issue of *BARTalk.* It ended up involving staff member Hedy Morant, who in the late 1970s was named BART's budget director. She had emigrated from Canada, but not too much was known about her except that she was something of a financial wizard. She proved to be a very tough taskmaster within her department, running it like a drill sergeant. One of the young men who worked in her department was certain that she hated him; regardless of her actual feelings, he loathed her.

Sy wanted to invite employees who had served in the armed forces to send in pictures of themselves in their uniforms. I liked the idea and told him to go ahead. Sure enough, pictures came flooding in from all corners of the organization. I believe at that point I went on a short vacation, and on the day I returned, *BARTalk* was hot off the press—almost 3,000 copies of it—and being distributed by interoffice mail. My copy arrived on my desk first thing. I opened it and began scanning the pictures while sipping my first cup of coffee for the day. Our general counsel at the time, Malcolm Barrett, was shown in his private's uniform during World War II. Other pictures were of employees in army and navy uniforms from the Korean and Vietnam Wars. And then I saw it, and almost spilled my coffee all over my desk. At first I just stared, and then I leaned back and took several deep breaths.

There, just about in the center of the page, was a large snapshot of a young Hedy Morant in her uniform, also from World War II. Only her uniform was that of a lieutenant in the Luftwaffe. Looking bright-eyed and handsome, she was standing under the wing of a once-feared Messerschmitt. I could imagine the titter sweeping across the organization from the shops to the control center. The young man who believed Morant hated him happened to be Jewish. According to witnesses, he then went berserk. He called the Anti-Defamation League, complaining that he was working for a Nazi. Morant defended herself, saying that, like many young Germans during the war, she had been conscripted into the Luftwaffe, and that her father had been put into a concentration camp. While no one *except* the young man in her department doubted her story, the picture did raise some eyebrows. As for the young man, he quit, never to be seen again. Morant continued in her job until she fell ill and passed away a few years later.

TRACKING RIDER TRIPS IS OF VITAL IMPORTANCE

A key benefit of BART's computerized fare gates was their ability to track customer trips: specifically, where the riders entered and exited and at what times of day. The data were transmitted to a central computer, and from there sheets of trip information were extracted and analyzed for determining peak loads, train size, and scheduling to meet demand. Tracking rides also showed that average weekday ridership was continuing to grow. During the 1984–1985 fiscal year, almost 61 million passenger trips were taken, compared with 58 million the previous year. While the average weekday ridership was 211,612, tracking showed that it was evenly split between peak commute hours and midday and evening. Ridership always swelled during special events in San Francisco and Oakland, such as national business conferences, and during the five days of the 1984 Democratic National Convention, held at the Moscone Center in San Francisco, ridership jumped to 227,000 a day. Limited parking was identified as a primary constraint to long-term growth, especially considering that a major goal of the system's ongoing capital-improvement program was to increase carrying capacity by 80 percent. If potential riders couldn't park at a BART station, it stood to reason they would drive to their destinations instead. By the end of 1984, BART provided just over 23,000 parking spaces system-wide, not nearly enough to accommodate projected growth, or even to meet the demands of the current ridership. Over the next fifteen years, more than 20,000 spaces would be added with the construction of parking structures at several East Bay stations. Patrons were also encouraged to travel to the stations by carpool, bus, special shuttles, bicycles, and walking.

CHAPTER 21

THE 1980S: A DECADE OF PROGRESS AND SCANDAL

BART's expansion dreams were critical to the future of the system. For years, as the system grappled with numerous operating and technical issues, the idea of building extensions was given little more than lip service within the region, yet it always remained on the radar screen. As discussed in the previous chapter, the transit system's board had adopted a phased extension policy in 1984, though it was still not much more than a piece of paper by the late 1980s. Basically, the first phase indicated where the lines, stretching like tentacles in four directions, would go. The plan was later given impetus with the adoption by the Metropolitan Transportation Commission (MTC) of a five-year plan that put an emphasis on rail transit, specifically on BART extensions. Funding would be a key issue for some time to come. On the positive side, the five-year plan meant that certain state and federal funds under the MTC's control as the regional planning agency would be earmarked for rail transit, which included future BART extensions in Contra Costa, Alameda, and San Mateo Counties.

As for funding the various projects in the MTC plan, work was already under way to put measures on the November 1988 ballot to raise the sales tax in both Contra Costa and Alameda Counties. These important measures would support a range of transportation projects in the two counties.

There was also the potential for federal assistance. The prevailing thinking was that BART had primarily been a locally financed system, while newer systems had received 75 to 80 percent federal funding. Since BART to some degree had been an early catalyst for the Urban Mass Transportation Act of 1964, which was passed after local residents had approved taxing themselves to built BART, it stood to reason that federal money should be made available for the extension program.

"We believe our special credit should be honored by federal officials when our transit plans and requests are balanced against the plans and requests of other regions of the country," said Arthur J. Shartsis, a San Francisco attorney who was president of the BART board in 1984. Board vice president Nello Bianco, who coauthored the extension policy, continued to have serious trepidation about BART building an extension into San Mateo County, even after the voter-approved commitment of $200 million from the San Mateo County Transit Authority (SamTrans) was earmarked for East Bay extensions. From Bianco's vantage point, this deal was a cheap buy-in, without the responsibility of becoming a member of the District. By the time he became president of the board in 1986, however, he took a more global view: "For the future I see BART as the spine of a truly regional transportation system." He then included San Mateo and Santa Clara Counties when talking about future extensions.

The cost to build a line down to somewhere near the airport was estimated to be $590 million in 1987 dollars. This estimate included the possibility of two stations, one in Serramonte, in San Mateo County, and one across the 101 Freeway from the airport. "East Bay extensions must come first," Bianco said. In several editorial meetings with Dean Lesher, the publisher of the *Contra Costa Times,* East Bay extensions always took front seat in the discussions. The crusade would take a few more years to resolve as the political debate continued. Meanwhile, as BART rolled deep into 1988, a dark cloud on the horizon would soon descend on the transit district, taking the organization into a new and treacherous realm.

A SHOPPING LIST OF CLIFFHANGERS

Short of outright disaster, 1988 proved to be a year of hemorrhaging for the transit district on several fronts. The new French-built C cars were almost two years late on their contractual delivery schedule, and the cars that had been delivered were spending most of their time in the shop because of production problems. In addition, cost overruns and design problems were plaguing the Integrated Control System project, and BART would face a state audit of the project's contract. Marketing for BART would go out on a limb. The general manager would face tense labor negotiations. And the system would be faced with a huge legal scandal.

THE INTEGRATED CONTROL SYSTEM

The Integrated Control System (ICS) project, designed to allow BART to expand system capacity, had begun in 1979 under a contract with the Lawrence Berkeley Laboratory (LBL). The contract called for LBL to design a flexible train-control system to replace the original system, which was already becoming constrained in capacity as well as technologically obsolete. The ICS concept was designed to give BART the ability to expand to meet demand in the years ahead, and it centered on a computer network spanning all of the system's facilities. It was an ambitious proposal.

In May 1981, BART canceled its contract with LBL. The general feeling was that LBL had done all it could do, and there were also questions about the lab's billing practices. Then in January 1983, after an extensive search, the transit district awarded a contract to the British consulting firm Logica Data Architects, Inc. The new contract was for designing the new control system's software architecture, which was scaled back from LBL's original proposal. The following year, BART purchased six MV/10000 computers from Data General. The new computers would incorporate the ICS software for testing and eventual operation. The initial contract price tag for Logica was $2.5 million. The total project cost, including the hardware, was estimated to be $14 million. Logica came to BART with a top-notch reputation as a firm specializing in systems integration and doing business on an international scale. The software component of the ICS was due to be completed by 1986.

A NERVOUS BOARD AT ODDS OVER PROJECT PROGRESS

By 1986, however, the overall project cost, which included $18 million to Logica, had ballooned to about $40 million, and the work was far from complete. A new contract extending Logica for another year was on the table. BART board president Nello Bianco was not happy about problems with the new C car and was even less happy with the progress, or lack thereof, being made by Logica on the design of the ICS. Bianco said he had been told by unnamed BART engineers that Logica had sent a second-string team to fulfill the contract. "They must view us as small potatoes," he said at a board meeting. He then called for an ultimatum: "Either Logica sends in its top people or we should cancel the contract." Logica denied the Bianco allegation but agreed to bring in some new people. Both the board and general manager Keith Bernard felt a lot of frustration with the lack of progress. It appeared there was no less frustration on the part of Logica in regards to board politics.

Bernard was feeling the immense pressure. So was Richard Demko, his deputy general manager, who was in charge of overseeing the project as part of the transit system's $500 million capital-improvement program. Bianco called for Demko's removal from the project to make room for someone with very specific software-engineering expertise. Bianco made it clear that he was not calling for Demko to be fired, only for him to resume his primary job of overseeing maintenance and general engineering. Bianco wanted to bring back LBL.

Bianco was joined by BART director Arlo Hale Smith of San Francisco in demanding the cancellation of the Logica contract. A majority of the board was opposed. Director John Kirkwood of San Francisco was against "changing horses in midstream." "This has been a nightmare," Kirkwood said. "But it will only cost more in the long run to get another contractor." Director Wilfred Ussery of San Francisco agreed and noted it would also greatly delay the work and that Logica should be allowed to complete the job. The contract would continue, but with the proviso that regular progress reports would be made directly to the board.

Logica then brought in a fresh team from a job in Hong Kong, considered their top technical people, to complete the design work of the highly complex ICS software architecture. The work had been scaled back and divided into seven stages. The consultant's chief engineer and spokesperson was a man named John Barnes, who was in his late thirties or early forties and had a male model's chiseled features and a square jaw. In fact, he was sometimes jokingly referred to as "Mr.

Lantern Jaw." Barnes, considered a very capable engineer, gave periodic, enthusiastic, and positive reports directly to the BART board, which was becoming increasingly nervous about the progress actually demonstrated. Behind the scenes, one setback after another plagued the project while the cost escalated exponentially. Even with the setbacks, though, much was actually being accomplished with the writing of the software, and the consulting engineers continued to be positive. Others, however, believed the project was just too ambitious for the technology at the time. "Sure," said one skeptical director, regarding the engineers' optimism. "They're making money and lots of it."

Watching the project flounder year after year reminded one of gamblers at a Las Vegas craps table throwing the dice and losing, only to invest more money hoping to recoup their losses, and in the end losing more. The light at the end of the tunnel was getting dimmer and dimmer. By the following year, Bianco had pretty much had it and was becoming strident over the issue.

STATE AUDIT: A POX ON BOTH HOUSES

On Thursday, May 28, 1987, the board voted 5 to 2 to extend the contract for another two years, until May 1989. At the same meeting, Bianco, who had voted no with Arlo Hale Smith, announced that he had formally requested state senators Quentin Kopp (San Francisco) and Dan Boatwright (Concord) to order an audit of the Logica contract by the state's auditor general. This was a unilateral move on the part of Bianco. BART board members were shocked; it was the last thing most of them wanted. Margaret K. Pryor, board president for 1987 and always a force since coming on the board in 1980, said she was deeply offended by Bianco's acting on his own in the matter. BART director Wilfred Ussery exclaimed: "It will make BART a political football in the state legislature's arena." Bianco refused to back down and answered that it was a done deal. In fact, by this time the audit was already under way.

On Wednesday, December 8, 1987, Thomas Hayes, California's state auditor general, released his findings in a scathing thirty-one-page report. The report stated that the project was $25 million over budget and more than five years late (based on very early projections), and that there was no guarantee that Logica would deliver what was called for. The auditor blamed both BART and Logica for the problems, saying the project had been mismanaged by BART. Kopp was incredulous. The report was highly critical of the BART staff for preparing a contract that did not have enough built-in penalties for nonperformance. In an interview with the *Oakland Tribune,* Boatwright said the contract with Logica was "open-ended with virtually no protection for the taxpayers." General manager Bernard thanked the auditor, but said, "There's no news here. This project has given us problems every step of the way." Bianco was livid. He said, "In my nineteen years on the board this has to be the biggest scandal I've seen."

One recommendation from the auditor, which BART had done even before the report came out, was to hire (for $150,000) a consulting firm with special expertise to oversee the remaining work. The firm, LS Transit Systems, did an assessment of the work and reported some flaws but determined that the software written by Logica would eventually work. The firm also recommended that Logica be fired if the work was not completed as called for in the contract.

A HEADLINE IN *COMPUTERWORLD*

By late 1989, Logica had not quite completed the work, and the contract was coming to an end. On November 30, the company wrote a letter to BART management and the board offering to complete the work for an additional $1.1 million. Noting that the company had been paid $18 million thus far, the board took no action at its December 7 meeting, thus letting the contract lapse without an extension. Some of the media called this inaction a "pocket veto." On Friday, December 8, Logica staff walked out, prompting a headline in the magazine *Computerworld* on December 11, 1989, that read LOGICA DERAILS FROM BART CONTRACT.

The ICS project was extremely important for the transit district. It was totally separate from the train protection system but was intended to do just about everything else, from scheduling, dispatching, and tracking trains to the automatic switching of tracks for route alignments. It was critical to the future extension program to expand system capacity. To be able to operate 75 to 100 trains at one time instead of 43 trains, which had been the limit at the beginning of the project, was paramount for the long-term success of the system.

Two things then happened by the end of 1989. The MV/10000 Data General computers were replaced by Tandem computers, and several of the Logica software engineering staff were rehired by BART to complete the ICS work. That work, 99 percent of which was done under Logica, helped to support the extension program by increasing the number of trains to 55 at one time.

MARKETING MOVES TO THE FOREFRONT

Marketing the BART system was always a key to its success. Bill Stokes had made that clear long before the new baby of the transit industry opened its doors. In the early operating years, because of the various technical problems that needed to be addressed, marketing consisted primarily of getting service information out to the people. The first attempt at mass marketing—using print, radio, and television—was for the introduction of Saturday and Sunday service in the late 1970s. By the mid-1980s, however, research showed that BART was still primarily viewed as a commuter system. BART set about trying to change that and boost ridership by a modest few percentage points during the midday and evening hours, when seats were available and the system could achieve an economy of scale. At that time I made a presentation to the board for a budget to carry out a marketing strategy supported by advertising. The board approved, and a comprehensive campaign titled "BART Goes Shopping, Too!" was launched to increase system use during off-peak hours. The objective was to pump up the ratio of passenger miles to seat miles. As an added incentive, fares were reduced during the midday hours for one month.

By the end of the campaign, BART saw an increase of about 4,500 new trips a day, mostly during the midday hours. As part of the "BART Goes Shopping" program, San Francisco personality Mal Sharpe, considered the king of "man-on-the-street" interviews, established BART as a verb as he interviewed riders for the TV spots. "I don't 'take BART,'" said one young woman who was featured. "I BART to San Francisco, I BART to Oakland."

THE HENNY YOUNGMAN CAPER

During the early months of 1988, ridership slipped for several reasons, including a fare increase and construction projects around the system that caused service delays. Putting on my marketing hat, I decided we needed to do something bold, maybe even a little outlandish for a transit system, many of which had traditionally been very conservative in their promotions. But I wasn't sure what we should do. We had no outside advertising agency of record. I had severed ties with our former agency, Chiat/Day, headquartered in Los Angeles, and created an in-house agency. For collateral work, I used small creative boutique shops.

One day I had a fortuitous lunch with a well-known San Francisco public relations and advertising man named Eddie Spizel. During our conversation, he mentioned that he could get me famed comedian Henny Youngman for a campaign if I were interested. At first I rejected the idea as preposterous. But on second thought, I hired Henny to be a spokesman for a campaign we called "Take Your BART, Please!"—a takeoff on his signature line, "Take my wife, please!" (Initially Henny wanted to use his original line and simply add "and BART" to the end. I didn't feel that worked.)

When I announced at a department-heads meeting that I had hired Henny Youngman, the famous Borscht Circuit comedian, you could probably hear the guffaws reverberating throughout the building. Then suddenly everyone stopped, realizing I was serious, and stared at me as if I were crazy. "What demographic are we targeting?" asked one

The author (left) with San Francisco ad man Eddie Spizel and famed comic Henny Youngman, about to shoot a commercial for the successful "Take Your BART, Please" campaign.

department head with more than a hint of sarcasm. Youngman was eighty years old at the time. After the laughter died down, I noted for the record that I thought Youngman had universal appeal.

Later, general manager Bernard asked me privately if I really felt this was the right move. I said yes, but frankly I had a moment of doubt myself. I mean, was anybody going to pay attention to this guy? The last thing we needed at that time was a boondoggle of an ad campaign. Some board members expressed skepticism but took a wait-and-see approach. One board member was sure I had hired Rodney Dangerfield, whom she said she couldn't stand. (I assured her it wasn't Dangerfield.) Despite the doubts expressed, something, mostly my gut, told me, in the words of civil war admiral David Farragut, to go "damn the torpedoes; full speed ahead" with the idea. Youngman was still making appearances on late-night talk shows and playing clubs around the country and in Canada, so it wasn't as though we were bringing him out of retirement.

The campaign, which used radio, television, print, and outdoor display boards, took off like a rocket. It created a sensational media buzz. Excerpts of the taped video commercials were being played on

"Take Your BART, Please" billboards appeared everywhere: in stations, on trains, and on roadside displays, including one on the East Bay approach to the Bay Bridge.

the evening news of most of the television stations in the market. You simply couldn't buy that kind of exposure. Every newspaper in the Bay Area carried a headline story, some on the front page, featuring Youngman. A national magazine also did a cover story on the concept of a local transit system using an internationally known comedian as a spokesperson for its message. The publicity alone was worth the cost of the campaign, which was about $250,000.

BART SIMPSON CALLS

I was contacted in December 1989 by the producers of a new animated show that was about to be launched on the Fox network: *The Simpsons.* Since the main character was named Bart Simpson, they wanted to do a tie-in with BART. The idea sounded intriguing, until I received a copy of the show's playbook and a guide with illustrations of the characters and their characteristics, plus the basic premise of the show. Bart Simpson was characterized as an underachieving brat. I did not think BART should be associated with such a character, and so rejected the overture from the producers. I also predicted the series wouldn't last more than a season. In the words of Kurt Vonnegut: "So it goes."

BERNARD TAKES A LEAVE OF ABSENCE

In the spring of 1988, BART general manager Keith Bernard took a three-month leave from the mounting stress of system challenges and board politics, which often turned into screaming matches. The Logica work was in no small way one of his major concerns. The leave gave him some much-needed rest and time to reflect on the current status of the system and its future without having to deal with the day-to-day pressure cooker that was his office. Acting in his place was his wingman, Richard Demko, the deputy general manager for engineering and operations, who was also still under enormous pressure regarding Logica and the C car contracts. Demko had come to BART from the airline industry a decade earlier as superintendent of shops and had proved to be a strong right hand. He ascended from the shops in 1979 to become a member of an interim troika called Office of the General Manager, a three-person team put together by Keith Bernard upon being named the system's new general manager. The other members were William B. Fleisher, head of operations (field services), and William F. Goelz, BART controller.

Bernard returned with a fresh sense of how to proceed, only to be met by protracted labor negotiations with the system's unions, representing 1,700 maintenance workers, station agents, train operators, and clerical personnel. The unions threatened a strike when an agreement could not be reached by June 30, 1988. BART then proceeded to request in writing that the governor call for a sixty-day cooling-off period. But this was not a cut-and-dried process. If the governor agreed, he first had to convene an investigative panel to hear testimony from both sides, after which the panel would make a recommendation to the governor. The governor would then obtain a court order to enjoin the unions from a walkout and the transit district from a lockout during the cooling-off period.

As had become typical, negotiations dragged along during the summer months and then got serious again just before the end of the cooling-off window. In September, an agreement was finally reached at the last minute and, to the relief of everyone, the trains continued to run. Contract negotiations were always a painful time for those on both sides of the table, as well as for an anxious public, who were often held hostage to the tactics of brinksmanship. That said, problems aside, I believe the unions have, on balance, been good for BART over the years.

PAINFUL DAYS OF SCANDAL AS THE FBI MOVES IN

On Thursday, August 11, 1988, I was settling into the day's workload in my office and was about ready to have a staff meeting. My office was on the southwestern corner of the first floor, one floor above ground level at BART's Lake Merritt headquarters. Its location, directly across the large atrium lobby from the board of directors' room, was convenient, since I attended all the board of directors' meetings. My day usually started with me reviewing newspaper clips, which we published every morning and sent out for distribution to department heads with copies to the directors' mailboxes. I had just finished my second cup of coffee and was about to call the meeting when Lorraine Sandberg, my secretary, came in and told me Mr. Demko was on the phone and needed to talk to me right away. I nodded and picked up my phone.

"Dick. What's up?"

"Can you come up to my office right away?"

"Sure. Something going on?"

"I'll tell you when you get here."

When someone says they need to see you right away, it usually triggers instant anxiety. I thought some new catastrophe had befallen us. As it turned out, I was not far off.

I took the elevator up to the fifth floor and made my way to Demko's office, which was also on the southwestern corner. Larry Williams, manager of labor relations and human resources, was there. I entered and looked from one to the other. Both men had glum expressions.

"What?" I said.

"We have to take a ride out to Concord," Demko said. "We're meeting with the FBI."

"The FBI? What for?" I asked.

Demko shrugged his beefy shoulders. "We don't know," he said as he pulled on his jacket. "They wouldn't tell us, just asked us to come out for a meeting. All very hush-hush and clandestine. They specifically asked that you accompany us."

"What about Keith?" I said, referring to the general manager.

Demko just looked at me hard as we headed out the door, as if the question should not have been asked. Then he said that Bernard was attending a meeting somewhere and that his secretary would give him a message when he called in. Demko did not want to bother him or set off undue alarm while he himself was still in the dark about the purpose of the FBI's interest.

It was a warm, sunny day. We drove out to Concord in northeastern Contra Costa County, about a twenty-five-minute trip. The address was for a large office building that housed several private companies, but we did not see a listing for the FBI. Demko had been given a room number on one of the upper floors. Coming off the elevator, we made our way down a wide hallway until we found a door marked with just the number. We knocked, and after several moments the door opened and someone asked what we wanted. After introducing ourselves, we were invited in and ushered to a small conference room. An agent offered us coffee while we waited for the special agent in charge to come in and talk to us. The three of us just looked around at the Spartan surroundings and then at each other with blank expressions as we sipped our coffee. What the hell was this all about?

THE STING OPERATION

After about twenty minutes, FBI special agent Richard Held came in and announced that they had been conducting a three-year sting operation as part of an ongoing investigation into corruption at the transit district. He wanted us to know that at that very moment investigators were entering BART premises, arresting two BART managers and possibly a third manager, and confiscating their files. Warrants for searching the managers' homes were also being carried out. The three men were allegedly involved in graft and extortion by demanding bribes and payoffs from contractors for being awarded small maintenance jobs.

Dick, Larry, and I just looked at one another with our mouths hanging open in disbelief. How was this possible? Held identified the suspects as Arnold Flores, forty-five, of Richmond, a manager of plant and facilities maintenance; Hilario Frank Gomez, fifty-five, of Martinez, a maintenance manager; and Helder Simas, forty-six, of Concord, a manager of power and electrical maintenance for the transit system. Both Gomez and Flores were taken into custody at their homes rather than at work. All three managers had had the authority to let noncompetitive bid contracts under $10,000 for specific jobs in their areas not normally performed by BART staff workers. During the fiscal year of 1987–1988 alone, records showed that a cumulative $361,651 in contracts had been issued by managers Gomez, Flores, and Simas.

Held said that his team wanted to continue the investigation but they had heard that a BART employee who had been cooperating was talking to other employees about the probe. Under the circumstances, the FBI had decided to quickly shut down the investigation and go with what they had. Because BART received federal funds for various projects and took part in interstate commerce, the corruption was determined to be a federal matter, and the FBI, rather than local authorities, was given jurisdiction in the case. The FBI did partner with BART Police in later investigations of future cases.

For this case, the FBI had set up five dummy companies to seek work from the BART managers involved and then had tape-recorded conversations in which the payoffs were demanded. About twenty contracts were obtained, all of which required kickbacks, according to affidavits filed by the sting operatives who had been posing as contractors. The contracts went back as far as 1985, when the FBI first began looking into allegations that something "funny" was going on at

BART. The formal investigation began as a result of a complaint from a janitorial contractor from Dublin, in Alameda County, who had told the FBI that a kickback had been demanded if he wanted a contract.

Following our meeting with the FBI, we headed back to our Oakland office. The whole place was abuzz with the goings-on. Word went through the organization like a prairie fire. I held a staff meeting and explained what was happening, including a few more specifics than what was generally known. We carefully crafted a press release that announced the arrests and said that BART was in close cooperation with the FBI and, further, that the general manager had immediately ordered an internal investigation to review small contracts let by some twenty other middle managers at the same level as those named by the FBI.

"We want to make sure that this is an isolated case and not widespread," Bernard said.

Little did anyone know at the time what lay ahead.

The press release was reviewed by the general manager's office and by legal before being sent out to the working press by mass fax and over the Business Wire and local wire services. Once again, BART was making headline news. No sooner had the release gone out than hard-charging reporters from various news outlets, including radio, television, and print, were at the door, demanding comments about how the situation looked from BART's perspective. So early in the game, of course, we had to be circumspect, at least until the FBI filed charges with the federal prosecutor.

Helder Simas, the first manager allegedly involved, was actually the last to be charged in the extortion scheme. In an ironic twist, Flores, who had a painting company on the side, accused Richmond school trustee George Cantu of extorting money from *him* so that he could be awarded painting jobs with the Richmond Unified School District. School district records showed that Flores's company, A. T. Flores Consultants, had been given five painting jobs worth $75,000 at three Richmond schools. Flores also sat on the Richmond Planning Commission.

Meanwhile, Cantu, who owned a small maintenance company called Consolidated Cleaning Systems, was named in the FBI affidavit alleging his involvement in the BART kickback scandal. According to a newspaper report at the time, Flores had pointed the finger at Cantu, but when told of the allegations, Cantu laughed. He said that he and Flores were longtime friends and implied that the whole thing was ridiculous. It was also reported that Flores owned another side business, a limousine service called Formal Affair. Some speculated that these side businesses had been kick-started by the money gained from the contract payoffs.

Special agent David Knowlton, who was heading up the field investigation, brought in more agents because their office was now besieged with complaints pouring in from numerous contractors, BART employees, and others familiar with the now-uncovered contract caper. The complaints were primarily from small maintenance contractors in the region who had had the same experience. There was also some suspicion that some of the contractors were anxious to cover their own behinds so as not to be complicit if they had, in fact, made payoffs to secure contracts.

In September, the scandal widened to include interviewing contractors suspected of bribery. One such contractor from Santa Clara confessed to paying several thousand dollars to Flores and Gomez in bribes. In fact, one of the payoffs from this particular contractor had been captured on videotape by the FBI at a local restaurant back in July. A microphone had also been planted under the table. The FBI reported that the payoff amounted to $800 for a $5,000 contract. Flores, who cut a deal with the FBI, quit his job during the probe, and Gomez and Simas were suspended without pay pending the outcome of the charges and the findings of an internal investigation. Simas, who pleaded innocent to the charges, was ultimately convicted for accepting a $2,000 bribe from an undercover FBI agent posing as a contractor. He was sentenced to two years in prison (although he remained free on bail for more than a year) and was fined $42,000 and ordered to repay BART for losses. On December 24, 1991, his sentence was revised by federal judge Thelton Henderson, who sent Simas to a halfway house on the premise that he could then work at the new job he had managed to get to pay the required restitution. Arnold Flores pleaded guilty to accepting $16,000 in bribes and was sentenced to five years in prison, and Hilario Gomez was declared incompetent to stand trial.

BART director and board vice president Michael Bernick, a San Francisco attorney, had written a letter to Judge Henderson requesting a lighter sentence for Simas, claiming that the FBI activities came very close to entrapment. Another BART director, John Glenn of Fremont, made the letter public by bringing it up in an open session of the board as part of a discussion on information flow. Glenn's revelation fueled a long-running feud with director Nello Bianco, who then verbally attacked Glenn, accusing him of playing board politics. Glenn just laughed the accusation off. Bernick's letter to the judge, however, did outrage several of his colleagues on the BART board, who immediately expounded disclaimers. BART's board president, Erlene DeMarcus from Pleasanton, in Alameda County, said at the time that she had learned of the letter from FBI agents who were "furious about it." She also went to great lengths to make it clear that Bernick was not representing the board's view, and she sent her own letter to Judge Henderson expressing that fact. Bernick defended his letter, saying it was in the best interest of the taxpayers, who would be paid back.

NEW FRAUD LOOMING

No sooner were the headlines reporting the case of the three managers finally beginning to wane when BART was hit again, this time in its real estate department. It was learned in the fall of 1988, through an *Oakland Tribune* story, that BART real estate manager Michael M. Sharpe had been convicted of defrauding the city of Hartford, Connecticut, prior to coming west. He, too, was suspended by Bernard pending an investigation. As it turned out, Sharpe, who was thirty-seven at the time, was also being investigated by the FBI. In September the FBI raided the BART real estate offices and seized documents that recorded about $25 million in the District's land purchases. In the end, Sharpe was charged with embezzling between $125,000 and $176,000 from the transit system's coffers between March 1986 and March 1988. In one of the alleged schemes, Sharpe conspired with a building inspector, David W. Colman, to purchase a parcel of land in Oakland for BART at an inflated price and keep the extra proceeds for themselves. On August 23, 1989, Sharpe was sentenced to five years in prison.

Next, the Alameda County grand jury requested BART's financial records as part of an inquiry into the spending practices of the system's elected directors. Meanwhile, there was other sad news for the organization. BART's assistant general manager for engineering and operations, Richard P. Demko, passed away on September 29, 1988, in the midst of the system's very rocky times. This was a major blow to the organization and in particular to general manager Bernard. As his right-hand man, Demko had been expected to play a significant role in Bernard's planned reorganization. With everything that was going on at the time, a depression hung over the staff like a dark cloud. "You could feel it," said labor relations and human resources manager Larry Williams. "It was a very painful period." For some time now, the board, particularly its 1988 president, John Glenn, had expressed concern that Bernard had too many department heads reporting to him directly, and that he wasn't clamping down hard enough on key underlings and contractors whose performance was questionable. But the reorganization under Bernard was not to happen.

BERNARD RESIGNS

On Saturday evening, October 22, 1988, I received a phone call from BART board president John Glenn asking me to attend a special emergency board meeting to be held at ten o'clock the next morning. The meeting would be held in the fifth-floor conference room instead of the first-floor boardroom.

"We need to get a notice out," I said. "What's it about?"

"Personnel matter," John said. "It will be a closed meeting."

"Personnel matter?"

"Don't say anything. This can't go any further, but Keith has resigned. I received the letter today."

Five members of the nine-member board met the next day, Sunday, October 23, at 10 A.M. After a lengthy discussion, the directors sadly accepted Keith Bernard's resignation as general manager, a job he'd held for almost a decade through various turbulent periods. Despite the myriad white-knuckle problems and disappointments along the way, Bernard was held in very high esteem by the board and throughout the industry. I put out a press release, and it was headline news in Monday's papers. Here was yet another major blow to the organization. There was great concern that the general manager's resignation on top of everything else could have an adverse affect on the upcoming November 1988 vote on the omnibus measures in Contra Costa and

Alameda Counties. The measures would raise the sales tax a half cent to help pay for BART extensions along with several other projects in the MTC plan. Happily, both measures were approved by the voters.

The election returns were viewed as a thumbs-up for BART to extend farther east into Contra Costa County and east and south in Alameda County. For Contra Costa County, the vote was ironic to those who remember that the county voted against the building of BART in 1962.

Keith Bernard stayed on for a time to help prepare for a transition of his office while the board began the process of searching for a new general manager. An executive search firm was hired to begin recruiting potential applicants from across the country and Canada. Bernard left around the beginning of 1989, and general counsel Sherwood Wakeman was named interim general manager by the board. In 1990, under a contract with the Bechtel Corporation, Bernard was appointed director general of transportation for the 23.5-mile Channel Tunnel (Chunnel) project under the English Channel. Tragically, Bernard died in London in 1994 just after the opening of the tunnel. He was fifty-four at the time. A plaque commemorating his work on the project was placed on the first train to go through the Channel Tunnel from Folkestone, England, to Coquelles, Pas-de-Callais, France.

A NEW GENERAL MANAGER

On June 27, 1989, Frank J. Wilson started his new job as BART's fifth general manager. He was named by a 5-to-4 vote of the board—not considered a strong mandate, but enough for him to assume the office. Previously Wilson had worked at the Southeastern Pennsylvania Transportation Authority (SEPTA) and the Chicago Transit Authority (CTA). Coming into BART, he had two major objectives as outlined by the board: first, to reorganize the staff, and second, to push the extension program into high gear.

Wilson was beginning to move fast on both fronts when a few short months later it happened. At 5:04 P.M. on Tuesday, October 17, 1989, the Loma Prieta earthquake hit the Bay Area with a shattering rock-'n'-roll bang. BART was never the same again.

CHAPTER 22

LOMA PRIETA BECOMES BART'S FINEST HOUR

The earth shook for only fifteen seconds, but it seemed like a lifetime. And it was enough to wreak significant havoc as the San Francisco Bay Area reeled from the temblor just as the rush-hour crush was ramping up. The epicenter of the quake was in the Santa Cruz Mountains, roughly 55 miles south of the city, near the peak called Loma Prieta. It was determined to have been a magnitude of 6.9 on the Richter scale, a result of a shift in the San Andreas Fault.

The impact was felt on both sides of the bay, and transportation came to a near halt. Stoplights were snuffed out along key corridors in downtown San Francisco, and even some of the television stations were working by candlelight for a time. In West Oakland, the Cypress Street Viaduct, a key corridor connecting the Nimitz Freeway with the Eastshore Freeway, was down. Its massive structure crushed cars and killed forty-two homebound commuters when its upper deck collapsed onto its lower deck. Portions of buildings in San Francisco's Marina District collapsed, some catching fire. The third game of the World Series between the Oakland Athletics and the San Francisco Giants—a matchup sometimes referred to as the "Battle of the Bay"—was just about to get under way at San Francisco's Candlestick Park when the stadium trembled, the power went out, and panic ensued. Fans had to be evacuated and the game was postponed for ten days.

THE BAY BRIDGE

One of the greatest impacts of the earthquake was the San Francisco–Oakland Bay Bridge being knocked out of commission. A section of the upper deck of the iconic bridge gave way, landing on the lower deck, cutting off a critical transportation corridor and killing one person. Including those killed in the Cypress Freeway collapse, a total of sixty-three people died as a direct or indirect result of the quake. A swarm of aftershocks in the days that followed kept the Bay Area on tenterhooks, fearing that another strong hit was in the offing. (It never came.) Almost three decades later, the Loma Prieta earthquake is still remembered as evidence of the Bay Area's vulnerability to seismic activity.

Immediately after the quake, BART shut down while its track and structures were thoroughly inspected for any damage. Remarkably, the system was virtually unscathed. Two trains had been traveling at the time through the system's Transbay Tube 135 feet under the bay, and reportedly no one on those trains felt a thing. When questioned later, some passengers were surprised to learn there had been an earthquake when they detrained at the next station.

For several hours, power in downtown San Francisco was out, which affected the lights, fare gates, and fare collection equipment in the stations along Market Street. Battery power automatically switched on, which at least provided light to the underground stations. Third-rail power was unaffected because it is tied to a separate source, and just a few hours later, BART was up and running again. With the Bay Bridge out of commission, BART was the only game in town for direct travel between the East Bay and San Francisco. The next day, Wednesday, October 18, BART ridership jumped by about 60 percent. For the next month, while the Bay Bridge was under repair, the system operated twenty-four hours a day, seven days a week, and weekday ridership went from an average 218,000 passengers per day to more than 350,000 per day. After the bridge reopened, BART retained about 20 percent of the new riders.

Impressed with BART's performance in the aftermath of the quake, the *Los Angeles Times* wrote: "This was BART's finest hour." A few days later, while the House was in session, Congressman Don Edwards (San Jose) read a portion of that editorial into the Congressional Record, proclaiming BART's performance heroic. Meeting the challenge of

Loma Prieta was indeed an auspicious way for BART to end a decade that had seen advancements but also had been filled with disappointment and turmoil.

UNIVERSAL STUDIOS GETS INTO THE ACT

Interestingly enough, not long before Loma Prieta, Hollywood was tuned in to the region, seemingly inspired by BART. Intrigued by the idea of a major earthquake in the Bay Area, Universal Studios' theme park decided staging a mock disaster would make a great tourist attraction. At great expense, studio engineers designed and built a replica of BART's Embarcadero Station in San Francisco, complete with fare gates, platform, and train. While visiting tourists are viewing the attraction from a tram circulating through the theme park's backlot, action suddenly erupts as a fake earthquake hits and riders get the experience of an 8.3-magnitude temblor. The station goes topsy-turvy, the train upends, and water rushes in, all in a matter of a few minutes. When the tram is ready to move on to the next section of the tour (King Kong and then Jaws), the station resets itself in fifteen seconds for a new gaggle of visitors. One has to admire the incredible engineering that went into the Universal Studios earthquake attraction, which at the time captured the attention of the local and national press.

On the afternoon Universal Studios was introducing its earthquake show, I got a call in my office from Steve Rubenstein, a well-known writer for the *San Francisco Chronicle.* He told me he had been sent down by the paper to take a look and thought that it was pretty incredible. "They're calling it 'The Big One,'" he said and asked if I knew about it. "No," I said, "but it's interesting." I had sent some stock photos of San Francisco stations down to someone at the studio upon request the year before but hadn't known what exactly they were for. I thought maybe they were for a movie, since BART was popular with the Hollywood crowd.

Rubenstein thought I should go down to Universal Studios and see it for myself, which I eventually did. Even before I had experienced it in person, some of the television news stations showed me a clip of the attraction and then asked for an on-camera response. What did we think? I said it was an impressive piece of design and then suggested people come and visit the Bay Area to see the real thing themselves. The TV show *Entertainment Tonight* showed up at my office and wanted me to have a joint press conference with a Universal Studios executive. I turned it down but did consent to an interview. The earthquake attraction was closed by Universal for several months following the Loma Prieta quake.

NEW SCANDALS

In addition to the strain of operating twenty-four hours a day, seven days a week during the bridge closure, the transit district was also hit with a series of new scandals. A BART ticket scam was discovered, potentially involving millions of dollars. An investigation uncovered a small ring within the organization that was printing, encoding, and selling BART tickets at a discount on a kind of black market outside the system. It apparently had been operating for almost ten years. Three of the system's employees were arrested in the case.

Also at this time, a line supervisor who was going through a divorce in Marin County presented a list of assets and income to the court during the course of his case. His wife noted, most likely with a wink, that the $600 to $800 dollars he brought home in cash every week was not listed and demanded an accounting. When the man had no satisfactory explanation, the judge hearing the divorce proceedings sent a note to the Alameda County district attorney's office suggesting something might be amiss with said BART employee. The district attorney's office in turn tipped off BART Police. BART Police set up surveillance on the employee, who was also an elected official with Amalgamated Transit Union Local 1555, and caught him in the act of scooping up some unaccounted-for spillover bills on the floor of the fare collection machines. The employee was fired and prosecuted, while the union screamed that he'd been set up because of his earlier involvement in labor negotiations.

The next scandal began to bubble up to the surface on November 15, 1989, when BART's general manager, Frank Wilson, announced that he had suspended two high-ranking BART managers, Loren W. (Bill) Gaulter, fifty-eight, and Stanley J. Eng, thirty-eight, pending an FBI investigation into possible criminal activities tied to their respective jobs. At the time, Gaulter was assistant treasurer for the District, and Eng was chief cashier, managing all cash handling and fare collection for the transit system.

Working closely with BART Police, the FBI planted a video camera in the ceiling of Eng's office in the system's cash-handling building. The video showed clear evidence of embezzlement or outright theft of BART money, which was public money. On February 16, Gaulter and Eng were indicted in U.S. District Court in San Francisco for conspiracy, three counts of theft of BART funds, and two counts of tax evasion. It was estimated that during the time of their activities they allegedly stole somewhere in the neighborhood of $400,000. Investigators also alleged that the two men enjoyed lavish lifestyles, had started outside businesses with the money, and in general were motivated by greed. One story quoted U.S. Attorney Ben Burch as quipping that his BART fares went for "a couple of Porsches."

On March 5, 1991, both men pled innocent to the charges. It was determined that Gaulter, who in the interim had had a massive stroke, could not be tried, and he died soon after. On May 9, 1991, Eng changed his plea to guilty. On October 17, 1991, Eng was sentenced to twenty-seven months in a federal prison and ordered to repay the transit district $527,000.

A DECADE OF REHABILITATION AND EXPANSION

As BART rolled into the 1990s, it faced a new set of challenges while still trying to mop up some of the leftover problems from the 1980s. The good news was that, for the reporting period of June 1, 1989, to May 31, 1990, BART carried a total of 76 million passengers for about a billion passenger miles—the highest number of riders in its now almost twenty years of service. The ridership was 10 million more than the previous year, partly due, of course, to the Loma Prieta earthquake. The increased ridership boded well for the District's ambitious expansion program, which was finally springing to life. Also, the time between system failures had much improved, translating into generally high reliability. BART's triumphant performance during the month following Loma Prieta was also a measure of the growing importance of the system to the Bay Area.

CLOSE HEADWAYS

A cornerstone of BART's current and future operations was to ratchet up its long-standing close headways program. Headways—the distance between trains—determined the maximum level of service that could be provided; the closer the headways, the more trains operating, and thus the higher frequency of trains arriving at and departing from stations. In addition to increasing the capacity of its central computer system, BART began a program to reconfigure track circuitry as well. As noted in Chapter 13, the system's main-line tracks were divided into blocks or zones for the purposes of signaling and train protection. Because a train entering a block or zone automatically triggered a buffer zone behind it, only a limited number of trains could be operated on the system at one time. The new program involved shortening some of the blocks to allow a few more trains to be put into service at one time without compromising safety. Meanwhile, the Integrated Computer System (ICS) project was finally killed after tens of millions of dollars of expenditure.

As the C car contract came to a close with the final delivery of the 150 new cars, a major rehabilitation program was launched to rebuild the A cars from the original fleet, 20 at a time. Many of the A cars would be converted to C cars. This meant removing the sloped nose so closely associated with BART's image and replacing it with a flat nose and reconfiguring the operator's compartment. There was a move in operations to convert all of the A cars to the flat-nosed design, but the public affairs department made a presentation to the board arguing that some of the sloped-nosed cars should remain because they were such a strong symbol of the original space-age concept of the system. The board agreed, and a number of the A cars were spared and continue to operate today.

Concurrently, 80 additional cars, called C2 cars, were ordered from Morrison Knudsen Corporation, headquartered in Idaho, a manufacturer new to the transit car business. Though it had built ships during World War II, Morrison Knudsen was primarily a construction company that wanted to diversify into new markets. The company was among three bidders for the contract and got the nod after a negotiated deal was struck. The negotiation process was groundbreaking because it did not require going strictly with the low bidder; instead, the goal was to maximize deliverables on dollar investment. A promising feature of the negotiated winning bid was that the cars would be built in a refurbished factory in Pittsburg, in eastern Contra Costa County, thus creating jobs for local residents and furnishing benefits for the local economy in general. Doing the work locally was a key factor in the award of the contract to Morrison Knudsen, and it brought the price down by $51 million.

Helping to finance the new cars was a unique scheme that derived from the economic recovery act of the early 1980s. Through an innovative "sale and lease-back" program, BART sold the depreciation rights in the cars for $20 million to a Swedish company with tax liabilities, thus providing much needed capital to purchase the cars. The Swedish company (a subsidiary of General Electric called GE Credit Finans) in effect owned the cars and then was able to write off the depreciation they had purchased over a twenty-year period. As a result of the transaction, BART was millions ahead. Over the twenty-year period, the District leased the cars back for a minimal amount, and at the end of the contract period, the cars would revert to BART ownership. The first of the new C2 cars would be delivered in the mid-1990s. When the contract was completed, BART had a fleet of 670 cars.

THE FIRST PHASE OF THE EXPANSION PROGRAM

Extending the system was no longer a distant mirage. By June 1992, the first phase of the extension policy adopted by the board of directors in 1984 was becoming a reality in terms of steel and concrete. Throughout the 1990s, work proceeded on extensions, totaling 32.5 miles of new main-line track and nine new stations. The estimated cost of the program in 1992 was $2.5 billion. Sources for the funding identified so far included $523 million from the State of California, $423 million from San Mateo County, $442 million from Contra Costa and Alameda Counties, $134 million from bridge tolls, $741 million from the federal government (which would be earmarked for the planned extension to the San Francisco airport), and $107 million from BART capital reserves. Sources for additional funding needed to fill the gap would be determined later.

A NEW AD CAMPAIGN STIRS THINGS UP

On February 11, 1991, I launched a new ad campaign, primarily aimed at potential users during off-peak hours, meaning midday, evening, and weekend time periods. It included radio, television, and newspaper displays featuring comic actor and stand-up comedian Ronnie Schell. He had gotten his start in radio with the late, great Don Sherwood, who always referred to him as the "slowest rising comic in America, Ronnie Schell." I put him under contract for two years.

Born and raised in Richmond, California, just a few miles north of Berkeley, Schell was an affable staple of numerous television shows over the years. His credits included the popular *Gomer Pyle, U.S.M.C.* show, *That Girl* with Marlo Thomas, and *Good Morning, World,* in which he starred opposite Goldie Hawn. It made sense to use him as a "local boy" to be the spokesman for the new campaign. Though his brand of humor was quite different from Henny Youngman's, it was equally effective in calling attention to how BART serves the non-commute periods as well as the rush-hour ones.

A CURVE BALL

For one of the commercial spots, I wanted Schell to wear an Oakland A's jacket and hat. For several years beginning with "Billy Ball" (that is, the era under manager Bill Martin) in the early 1980s, we had partnered with the A's to promote both the games and BART service to and from the games. We put several extra post-game trains in service for the homebound crowds, and our sponsorship of the team included ads in their game programs, their game-time radio broadcasts, and their electronic displays on the field. I had worked closely with the A's vice president of marketing, Andy Dolich, for several years. He was a savvy marketer who understood that baseball had to compete hard for the entertainment dollar. We had a good working relationship and sat on the Oakland Visitors and Convention board together. But when I told him I would like to have Ronnie Schell wear an A's jacket and hat to promote BART and the A's in a television commercial, he told me he would have to charge me a logo fee. Now, granted, the fee of $100 was not all that much. But I felt there was a principle involved and so refused. The irony was that the A's stood to gain a great deal of television exposure through the BART spots, and I found it rather incredible that they wanted to charge BART for the free advertising.

The commercial spot promoting BART to the Oakland A's featured Schell coming out of a train at the Oakland Coliseum Station in a baseball uniform and tossing a baseball from hand to hand. He looks up and makes his pitch to take BART to the games. The only problem is that he is wearing an old San Francisco Seals uniform from a bygone era, instead of the A's jacket and hat that I had wanted him to wear. The last game the Seals played in the Bay Area was in 1957. Nonetheless, when I showed the commercial to the BART board at an open board meeting, it was well received. The place was teeming with reporters who were looking for a story, and they got one when board member Margaret Pryor of Oakland asked why Ronnie Schell wasn't wearing an Oakland A's uniform. Others on the board chimed in that it *was* curious.

And here's where I had some fun. I related the full account of what had happened with Dolich. Members of the board voiced agreement with my decision, and, wouldn't you know, the press loved it and made it the story of the day. It became headline news in all of the major Bay Area papers. Andy Dolich began getting press calls asking for comment. I believe he was taken aback by the whole thing. He called me, and I told him what had happened. The next day he was quoted as saying, "It's our policy to charge for use of our logo." End of story. Our relationship with the A's, of course, continued long after that bit of nonsense.

A DIRECTOR BLOWS THE WHISTLE

In April 1992, Diversified Personnel Services of Oakland was vying for a contract with BART. The contract, which called for supplying temporary help in various areas of BART's administration as needed, would be for six years and was worth $2.5 million to the successful bidder. For Diversified, this would have been a renewal or an extension of a similar contract it already had with BART that was about to expire. After a careful review of the responses to a Request for Proposal that had been sent out to several temp agencies earlier in the year, BART staff recommended another company, though at a higher rate. Diversified was owned by a prominent Piedmont woman, Lila Saks, and run by a son-in-law, Mark Unger, the company's chief operating officer. Saks was a smart and vivacious businesswoman who was also politically active in the community.

Now, it is not unusual or illegal for politicians running for office to receive campaign contributions, often from corporations or companies who want a favor down the line or a vote on an issue of interest. A well-known politician once told me: "You can buy my ear, but you can't buy my vote." BART directors are no different. They are all elected officials, and campaign contributions are the lifeblood of getting elected or reelected. At the time, director Joe Fitzpatrick, representing eastern Contra Costa County, received $1,250 in campaign contributions from Lila Saks and Mark Unger. The funds were delivered on two separate occasions in the form of two separate checks, one for $250 and one for $1,000, made out to Fitzpatrick's campaign. It was clear that they were seeking his vote for the upcoming contract. Fitzpatrick notified the FBI that he suspected the contributions were more in the nature of a bribe.

What was odd about the checks, according to U.S. Attorney Ben Burch, was that they were from a third party, and this suggested an attempt to disguise their actual origin. The FBI and the U.S. Attorney's Office began an investigation, during which wiretaps were set up, including taps on other BART board members. Other directors had also received campaign contributions from Diversified, but none was accused of any wrongdoing. In the end, the BART board went against the staff recommendation and voted to extend the contract with Diversified. Fitzpatrick also voted in favor of the extension.

After a four-year investigation, Saks and Unger were indicted on March 19, 1996, charged with conspiracy, bribery, and wire fraud, and were arraigned on April 8 the same year. Ironically, Saks was represented by a former U.S. Attorney, Joseph Russoniello.

A TRAGIC SHOOTING CAUSES A FUROR

While work on all of BART's various critical programs and projects continued to progress, the administration suddenly found its focus diverted to the tragic shooting of a young man by a BART police officer. This profoundly traumatic and shattering event was transformative for the BART Police Department and the transit agency in general. It was the first, though it would not be the last, officer-involved shooting on the system that ended in a fatality.

On Sunday, November 15, 1992, at approximately 8 P.M., Jerrold Hall, a nineteen-year-old African American man suspected of armed robbery on a BART train, was shot by a BART police officer who said he believed himself to be in peril. On the face of it, it seemed like a pretty straightforward case of justified lethal force; in fact, it was anything but straightforward. The case turned out to have deep social and political implications that still resonate today.

I got the call shortly after 8:30 on the night of the shooting. As I recall, it was a blissful fall evening and my wife, Joan, and I were sitting on our deck checking out the constellations when the phone rang. An officer on the scene, Lieutenant Gary Gee (who went on to become chief eight years later) told me about the shooting and what details were known so far.

A young African American man on a southbound train reported that he was robbed at gunpoint on the train by two young African American men. He told the train operator what had happened, and as the train came into the Hayward Station, the operator notified central control, who in turn notified BART Police. The train operator was ordered to hold the train to allow time for a police response. The victim then followed the two men off the train and again reported the incident to the station agent, who also called BART Police. A few minutes later, a BART Police canine unit arrived: a single officer accompanied by a German shepherd attack dog. The officer, who was not initially identified, stepped out of his car and looked around. At that point the man who had reported being robbed ran out of the station and pointed to the two men he had followed, who were now hanging around the parking lot near the AC Transit bus stop. He screamed that they were the ones who had robbed him and that one of them had a gun.

The officer got his pump-action shotgun and ordered the two men to lie face down on the ground, spread-eagled. One of the men, later identified as John Henry Owens, did as ordered by the officer and got down on the ground. The other man, later identified as Jerrold Hall, refused to get down. Instead, according to witnesses, as well as the officer's account, Hall demanded to know what they had done and then approached the officer and tried to grab his shotgun. The officer hit Hall in the chest with the butt of his gun. Again according to witnesses and the officer's own account, Hall then turned and began walking toward the edge of the parking lot. He was told to halt three times by the officer, who said he believed the young man was going to retrieve the gun the victim had reported having seen. Hall continued. The officer fired a warning shot into the nearby trees. Hall continued to walk away.

After a couple more warnings, the officer fired his shotgun at Hall, who was about 50 feet away at this point. One of the pellets struck Hall, sending him to the ground. The San Francisco–based *Bay*

Guardian, an alternative tabloid newspaper, reported that the dog walked beside the officer as he approached Hall, but the officer's story is that the dog, named Oden, stayed in the car until he heard the special command to pursue and attack. (A graduate of the Schutzhund Training School in Germany, the dog only understood commands in German.) At that point, the dog jumped out of the car and grabbed the wounded Hall's arm, but he then let go as Hall began to pet him, according to Gee. The dog was confused and attempted to make friends with the suspect. This was the account given by the officer, who was later identified as Fred Crabtree, a fifteen-year veteran of the force.

During our conversation that night, Lieutenant Gee told me that an ambulance had arrived to transport the wounded man to Eden Medical Center, in Castro Valley. The medics' initial statement to officers on the scene was that it looked like a chest wound made at close range. One wonders why the officers didn't also get a description of what had happened from the perspective of the involved officer. (Most likely, the involved officer was following protocol, which would advise against saying anything until he and his representative or lawyer met with internal investigators. Whenever there is an officer-involved shooting, the officer is immediately put on administrative leave and is required to turn over his weapon to the supervising officer on the scene. At some point he is Mirandized.) Meanwhile, witnesses' statements were still being collected and the other suspect was taken into custody. The alleged robbery victim disappeared. A gun was never found.

When the media began calling me later that night, requesting a statement for the eleven o'clock news and the morning papers, I reported that I was told Hall had been shot in the chest. This was an unfortunate piece of bad information. Because of the blood on Hall's chest area, the medics apparently just assumed that was the location of his wound, but they were mistaken.

At 3 A.M. on Monday, November 16, I was awakened by the phone. It was Cornelius Hall, Jerrold Hall's father, who had gotten my phone number from a reporter. He informed me that his son had died and that he had been shot in the back, not in the chest, as had been reported earlier. Mr. Hall wanted me to know what had actually happened and implied that maybe BART was trying to cover up what might turn out to be an illegal use of lethal force. I assured him that that was not the case and offered my condolences on behalf of the organization. The next day, after conferring with BART police chief Harold Taylor and general manager Frank Wilson, I prepared a press statement and held a press conference in my office to explain the error. I wanted to get out in front of the original misinformation as soon as possible.

Tim Redman, the editor of the *Bay Guardian* who was hot on the trail of the story at the time, called and set up an appointment to interview me. A lean young man with long blond-brown hair and a lot of high-test energy, Tim talked very fast. It was clear to me as he sat in my office and we discussed the case that he had an agenda. I provided as much information as I could, given that the case was an ongoing investigation and much was still unknown. His exposé, when it finally came out, was told from the point of view of the Hall family, and in that version he all but accused me of a cover-up, primarily citing the initial bad information that I had put out. (Ironically, Tim and *Guardian* publisher Bruce Brugman would be helpful to me many years later, in 2006, when I was managing media relations for former congressman Ron Dellums, who at the time was running for mayor of Oakland.)

For the next couple of months and on into the early part of 1993, BART was under siege. Representatives from various organizations—including the ACLU, the Young Communist League, and Copwatch, a Berkeley-based volunteer group—showed up at board meetings, along with grieving members of the Hall family and numerous other interested individuals. The general tone was chaotic anger, with emotions running extremely high, creating a volatile atmosphere. Sometimes it felt as though violence could break out at any moment. BART police officers were on hand to keep order. Mostly protesters were screaming that nineteen-year-old Jerrold Hall had been murdered by a white police officer, and the race issue was clearly at the epicenter of the accusations. Protesters also picketed outside the building with signs calling for justice for Hall. Radio talk shows and the eleven o'clock news examined the pros and cons of lethal force by the police in general.

The BART board scheduled a series of public hearings to respond to the outcry. Police chief Harold Taylor was ordered to give a comprehensive presentation to the board on his department's policies and the amount of training his officers were required to have. (BART police officers are academy trained and sworn California peace officers; in other words, BART police are a municipal force for a city on wheels.) One of the key issues was how complaints against officers from system riders and others were handled. In the end, the question boiled down to whether the BART Police Department should have civilian oversight by some form of a review board made up of citizens from outside the organization. The BART board maintained that the board itself was the civilian oversight body. A great deal of discussion and debate followed.

At the time, BART Police reported to the head of the safety department, who in turn reported to the general manager. Eventually the board determined that it would continue to take oversight responsibility for BART Police. The board also expressed its determination to be vigilant in keeping an eye on the department's policing and to be the court of last resort for complaints. In addition, the board ordered the general manager to have the police chief report directly to his office.

The case was still an active issue well into the spring of 1993. Officer Fred Crabtree was ultimately exonerated by the transit system's internal investigation. The case then went to the Alameda County district attorney, where again there was a finding of justifiable lethal force, and it went finally up to the Justice Department in Washington, D.C., which reviewed the case and ultimately concurred with the previous findings. It was unusual for a local case of this nature to go that high up for disposition, but its high profile and the swirl of public pressure steered the course. Needless to say, the Hall family was outraged.

While he remained on the force, Crabtree decided not to go back into the field and instead took a desk job. Friends said he never really stopped hurting from that dark Sunday night at the Hayward Station, and his own life was tragically cut short a few years later.

CHAPTER 23

A ROCKY ROAD TO EXPANSION DURING THE 1990S

The initial overall expansion plan called for building an additional 32.5 miles of main-line track in Contra Costa, Alameda, and San Mateo Counties at an estimated cost of $2.6 billion. Also on the drawing board now were eleven new stations (including a future station at Warm Springs and a possible privately funded station at West Dublin) and more than 18,000 parking spaces. With the added lines, the BART system would grow to 104 miles. This ambitious overall project would be the largest construction undertaking by BART since building the original system. Before it even got started in a serious way, however, the linchpin of the entire extension program—the planned 7.5-mile link to San Francisco International Airport from Daly City—was in jeopardy. In fact, it came within hours of going over a political precipice into oblivion. It was agreed by most that if it didn't happen then, it probably would never happen.

Almost immediately, big trouble was brewing on several fronts as different forces worked to outflank the proponents and torpedo what would become the second-largest public works project in California at the time, at least in terms of cost. Only the expansion of the San Francisco airport, complete with an air train looping over the terminals and extending out a half mile to the maintenance and parking facilities, would be considered bigger, at a cost of well over $2 billion.

The rail link to the airport, or in the vicinity of the airport, actually has roots in the original nine-county plan that was sketched out in 1956 by the Bay Area Rapid Transit Commission. That plan, which looked like a great octopus with tentacles reaching out across a map of the Bay Area, showed the line going from Daly City down through San Mateo County to Palo Alto in Santa Clara County, with a possible spur to Los Altos a little farther southwest. In those days, of course, those counties were still pretty much cow country with sparse populations. But buds of urbanization and sprawl were already beginning to sprout along the El Camino Real and U.S. Highway 101 corridors. As population density grew over the years, so did the maze of freeways, among them Interstates 280 and 380. (The latter is the short link between I-280 and Highway 101, the two major corridors serving San Mateo and Santa Clara Counties.)

EARLIER THINKING AND DISSENSION

In 1972, William J. Dwyer, the director of the San Francisco airport, strongly believed in the concept of a BART airport station, even as the new system was still preparing for its grand opening. The prevailing political thought at the time was that the airport would be the priority extension, even though this idea was disputed by the Contra Costa contingent, which was spearheaded by BART director Nello Bianco. In 1970, Lawrence Dahms was assigned by BART general manager B. R. Stokes to head up a feasibility study—at a cost of more than $371,000 and funded by the Urban Mass Transportation Administration—on how BART might expand down the peninsula to the airport. The study was called the San Francisco Airport Access Project (SFAAP), and the press interest it received may have spurred Dwyer to prepare for the possible coming of BART.

Bianco was livid, stating that a commitment had been made to Joe Silva in 1962 at that famous early-morning meeting at a coffee shop in Martinez that BART would expand first in eastern Contra Costa County before reaching anywhere outside the three-county District. "That is why BART exists today," Bianco argued. "Because of Joe's vote, when he was a county supervisor, to stay in the BART District," he said. Silva, who was also on the BART board at the time, never disputed this claim as far as anyone knew. According to Dahms, Bianco publicly called for Dahms to be fired over the airport study. Stokes

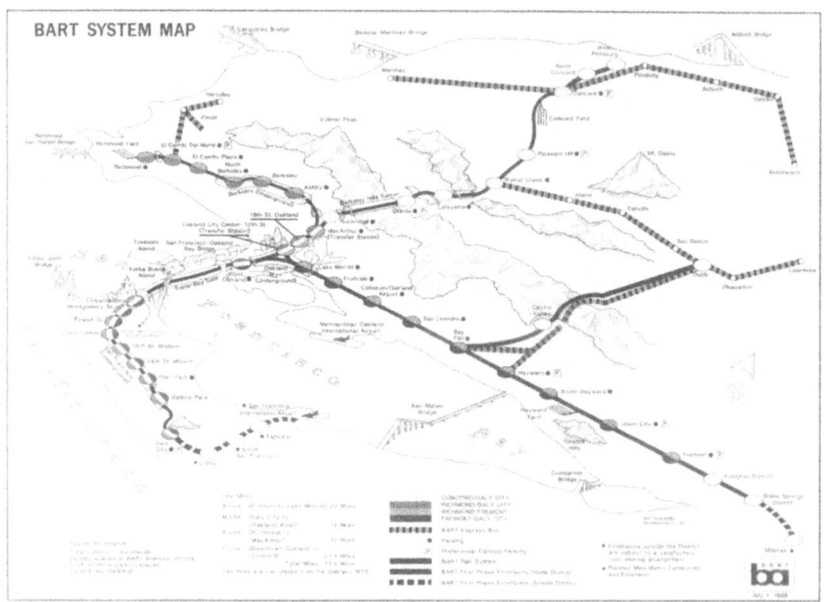

This map from 1984 corresponds to BART's potential extension program, as outlined by the BART board's policy that split the project into first and second phases.

defended the study and noted that Dahms had done a superior job in carrying out the work.

Ironically, Bianco was later a strong supporter of Dahms in 1974, when the latter was interim general manager after Stokes's departure. This kind of reversal in political relationships was not uncommon on the BART board.

When the transit system's board was first elected in 1974, Bianco, who had easily won election, was a holdover from the days when directors were appointed. He and the newly elected director from Fremont, John Glenn, were strong allies, supporting each other on various issues that came before the board. Then one day years later, out of the blue, Glenn, who at the time was chairman of the Public Affairs and Legislation Committee, announced that he was going to call on the Contra Costa County district attorney to investigate Bianco for having alleged behind-the-scenes dealings with a well-known Contra Costa developer, claiming conflict of interest. Bianco, who was sitting next to me in the fifth-floor conference room at the system's Lake Merritt headquarters, said to me out of the side of his mouth, while grimly eyeing Glenn, "What the hell is he talking about?" From that day on, the two directors were bitter enemies, often putting staff right square in the middle, each demanding personal loyalty. Bianco fought hard to prevent any consideration of an extension south to Warm Springs in Alameda County, which Glenn strongly supported. Nothing ever came of the charges Glenn had leveled against Bianco.

Meanwhile, Dwyer optimistically ordered that a "trace" be incorporated into the new United Airlines terminal, which was then under construction. The trace was, in essence, no more than a giant concrete box, but it was designed to house a future BART station, so sure was Dwyer that the extension would eventually come to pass. In later years, pillars were installed that blocked any future rail access, a move instigated by Dwyer's successor, Lou Turpen, who did not want BART to come into the airport. He and state senator Quentin Kopp feuded over that issue for some time, and when Turpen eventually departed for another job in Canada, Kopp was quoted as saying he thought the Bay Area would be healthier for it.

THE FIRST SERIOUS PLAN FOR THE AIRPORT EXTENSION

The first full-scale Draft Environmental Impact Report (EIR) and plan, including preliminary engineering, was commissioned by the Metropolitan Transportation Commission (MTC) and released for public scrutiny in March 1992. Lawrence Dahms, as executive director of the MTC, was a key initiator of the work and a prime mover in getting federal funding. A partnership that included the Federal Transit Administration (FTA), the San Mateo County Transit District (SamTrans), and the San Francisco Bay Area Rapid Transit District (BARTD) also prepared an "Alternatives Analysis" that identified a BART line stopping somewhere across the Bayshore Freeway (Highway 101), about a mile and a half outside the airport, at an estimated cost of $960 million.

Some form of bus, shuttle, or guideway people mover between the end of the line and the airport would be required, but options for filling this gap were not specifically identified. This plan showed several main-line route alignments with a locally preferred alternative, and three above-ground stations.

THE COLMA STATION

The jumping-off point for the line would be the planned Colma Station and tail track, which would create a 1.6-mile segment between the current main-line terminus in Daly City and the beginning of the airport line in San Mateo County. Construction of the Colma Station was scheduled to begin in the fall of 1992 but did not actually get started until early 1993. Before this segment could be built, the 1976 Boatwright bill, which had created the law prohibiting BART from going outside the three counties before first building the East Bay extensions, had to be amended, which it was. It was only possible because the East Bay extensions would be built simultaneously.

On Friday, February 23, 1996, beginning at 10 A.M., the freshly minted Colma Station opened with a gala celebration. BART board president Dan Richard, who became chair of the High-Speed Rail Authority many years later, presided over the morning's celebration. Honorable guests included SamTrans chairman Tom Huening, San Francisco mayor Willie Brown, state senator Quentin Kopp, state assemblywoman Jackie Speier, and congressional representatives Nancy Pelosi, Tom Lantos, Anna Eshoo, and Bill Baker. The keynote speaker for the event was then–secretary of transportation Federico F. Peña. The interior of the station sparkled like a great jewel, enhanced by the artwork *Leonardo's Dream* by artist Daniel Joshua Goldstein. The overall cost, including a 1,400-space parking garage, was $170 million, mostly funded by federal grants and SamTrans.

PASSING THROUGH THE CITY OF SOULS

The Colma Station is located near the northern edge of Colma, a small incorporated town with a population of 1,600, located in San Mateo County just south of Daly City. The extension to the airport would pass south through the rest of the city, which is sometimes referred to as the "City of Souls," for it is home to sixteen cemeteries and about 1.5 million graves. Working with the city, it was relatively easy to partially relocate a trailer park located in the path of the planned airport line, but the cemeteries presented a special challenge, since the project would require cut-and-cover construction. BART would need part of the cemetery parcels for right-of-way acquisitions, but cemeteries were exempt from eminent-domain acquisitions. Agreements had to be reached with at least eight cemeteries. The old Southern Pacific right-of-way, which ran right along the perimeter of the burial grounds, was later determined to be the optimal route for the airport extension as it wended its way south of Colma. During the 1930s and early 1940s, a streetcar line ran along that right-of-way, connecting San Francisco with San Bruno, but it was discontinued in 1942.

The cemetery grounds comprised more than 70 percent of the town's total area, and the dead far outnumbered the living. The joke at the time was "People are dying to go to Colma." In some cases, use of the right-of-way became a contentious issue when several of the cemeteries became nervous about a BART line coming through. Cemetery owners were concerned that graves close to the right-of-way might be disturbed by the planned excavations. "Those stiffs are trying to screw us," one worker was overheard irreverently joking in a local bar one night. A deal was eventually agreed upon and initially signed by all but one of the cemeteries. The lone holdout was Cypress Lawn.

In August 1997, Cypress Lawn filed a lawsuit against BART challenging the system's compliance with the California Environmental Quality Act (CEQA), a requirement that goes hand in hand with the EIR. BART officials believed the suit had no merit and that it was a blatant attempt to set forth unreasonable restrictions on construction and to force an agreement that would pay for improvements to the cemetery well beyond the scope of environmental mitigations. The court agreed, and the case was dismissed. At question was a narrow strip of land 60 feet wide and 1,000 feet long, at some distance from any gravesites. Cypress Lawn wanted $5 million for this small piece of its property, which was actually worth a fraction of that amount in terms of appraised market value. Quentin Kopp, chairman of the State Senate Transportation Committee, came to the rescue. He authored and pushed through a single-purpose bill that removed the eminent domain exemption for Cypress Lawn, which then allowed BART to move ahead with acquisition of the parcel. A more equitable deal was then agreed upon with Cypress Lawn.

From Colma south, the stations identified in the early planning were South San Francisco, Tanforan (San Bruno), and the airport station, which, under the 1992 Draft EIR, would be the southern terminus west of Highway 101, with a turn-back track stretching south to the vicinity of the town of Millbrae. Under this plan, the stations and track would be primarily at grade. One initial alternative called for tunneling beneath Highway 101 and into an underground station at the airport as it existed at the time, but this option would have been too expensive and in the final analysis was not considered. Also, the Federal Aviation Administration (FAA) had security concerns about having a rail transit station terminus in the airport. As a longtime transit advocate, Kopp was hopping mad. He immediately began a campaign to scrap the plan or modify it to take the line directly into the airport.

"It's ridiculous to spend public money to go down the peninsula to serve the airport and not go directly into the airport," Kopp said during numerous interviews on the subject. He said the initial plan as presented diminished its potential convenience and would not attract nearly the number of riders it could with a direct airport connection.

"Travelers aren't going to want to transfer to another mode of conveyance, carrying luggage, to go the rest of the way to the terminal to catch their flight," he said. "It's just not an attractive option."

TIME TO RETHINK THE PLAN

Pressure was building to take another look at the 1992 plan. The BART board eventually agreed with Kopp and directed staff to produce a new supplemental Draft EIR to incorporate a new, detailed route alignment that would take the system under or over Highway 101 and into the airport. Another few years and numerous public hearings would be required to complete the new document, which was published in 1994. The work would include a thorough analysis of seven alternatives to the proposed line, including two "no-build" options. A no-build option would make airport access dependent on cars and buses, in time squeezing its potential for growth. It was predicted that air travelers going through the San Francisco airport would increase by 70 percent over the next ten years, corresponding to development in the Bay Area in general and to emerging markets in the Pacific Rim. By reducing traffic along Highway 101 and Interstate 280, the BART line could also reduce hydrocarbons by as much as a ton and a half to two tons per day and reduce carbon monoxide by around seventeen tons per day.

In April 1995, the BART board adopted Alternative VI of the EIR, which took the line into the airport and south to an added station in

Millbrae. This plan would meet FAA concerns over having the airport station as a terminus station. It would also provide a direct connection to the Caltrain commuter line coming up from San Jose. Under the new plan, the extension would grow to 8.7 miles from the original 7.5-mile route. Meanwhile, a buzz was now growing over the prospect of BART going into the airport—but for some it was not a happy buzz.

A major hurdle during the development of the EIR and airport station plan was the San Francisco airport itself. It was like an island colony, owned by the City and County of San Francisco yet surrounded by San Mateo County. From the beginning, the airport's CEO, Louis A. Turpen, was not cooperative. He did not want a rail transit system coming into what he considered his turf, according to Kopp. Stakeholder parties—namely SamTrans, BART, and MTC officials—met with Turpen to try to reach an accord, but he was adamant in his opposition to BART on airport property, preferring instead to see BART on the west side of the Bayshore Freeway (101).

Some thought the airport was governed like a small monarchy; it had an appointed commission, but for all intents and purposes Turpen ran the show. Senator Kopp determined it was time to force the issue and put the question of a BART airport station before San Francisco's voters in the form of Measure I. At the same time, San Francisco supervisor Tom Hsieh authored an opposing measure, Measure H, which asked voters to approve a BART station outside the airport, west of Highway 101.

On June 7, 1994, San Francisco voters passed Measure I by a two-to-one margin over the competing Measure H. "I'm sure Turpen saw the handwriting on the wall and softened his attitude, albeit reluctantly," Kopp said. Though strictly an advisory vote, it was clear the voters wanted a BART station in the airport, even at an additional cost. The measure also suggested that a $3 departure charge be levied on each airline ticket to pay for it, but because of federal regulations this charge was never implemented. "This was also an important vote," Kopp said, "because even though advisory in nature it was viewed as a mandate and determined the direction on this issue for the San Francisco political establishment, and made the airport and the airport commission a partner in the proposed project."

Around December 1995, Turpen resigned his position and took a similar job at Toronto Pearson International Airport in Canada.

THE PHANTOM STATION

In 1995, when talk of a BART station at the airport was hitting the media, a woman who was prominent in the community and considered very credible came forward and told the world that in fact a station was already there inside the airport, with fare gates and all the trimmings. She swore up and down she had seen it with her own eyes. With permission from airport officials, she even talked the working press into coming with her to the airport in search of the phantom station. Ron Wilson, the airport's spokesman, maintained that no such BART station existed. He was aware of the original trace from 1972, but that was not what the woman seemed to be talking about. No such station was ever found.

THE 1996 PLAN

The new federal Draft Environmental Impact Statement (EIS) and state EIR, which one source said cost around $40 million to develop, was released for public scrutiny in 1996. Its timing was fortuitous, and in fact timing would become one of the most critical aspects of getting the proposed project under way with shovels in the ground.

After airport director Lou Turpen left in 1995, the airport's new executive director, John Martin, was ready to follow the mandate of the San Francisco voters, even committing up to $200 million toward that part of the BART project on airport property. However, there was a significant caveat: timing! In order for BART to become a legitimate project, funding had to be identified and committed. And it was all hanging by a very thin thread. The airport made it clear that it had its own plans, and if BART did not have everything in place by a specific date, it would have to go ahead without including the BART system, thus putting the entire project in jeopardy. As it happened, the timing could not have been better as Martin announced plans to build a dazzling new International Terminal in front of or west of the existing terminals. Plans for the airport expansion had been in the works for some years when Martin picked up the reins.

THE AIRPORT EXTENSION BECOMES THE CENTER OF A POLITICAL MAELSTROM

Unlike the 1992 EIR Alternatives Analysis, the new 1996 plan called for subway construction to address local concerns about an at-grade line. Two other new stations would be located in South San Francisco and the Tanforan shopping center. Future riders going to the station inside the airport would have direct access to the airport's planned Air-Train. The plan also offered a direct connection at Millbrae, south of the airport, between BART and Caltrain, the long-established peninsula commute line. But many wondered if BART could be ready in time to mesh with the airport expansion. On top of this, the new price tag for the expanded plan had escalated to $1.4 billion, which some argued was a deal breaker. In any case, the timing for getting federal funding was coming down to the wire.

Taking a step back, the process of developing this comprehensive new plan was no piece of cake. A few local community leaders drummed up well-organized opposition to the project, and anger sprouted up among a few residents along the way, with a dissident nucleus in Millbrae and Burlingame. Secret meetings were held at night, mostly to instill fear of BART. Mike Spinelli, a well-known professional photographer and a member of the Burlingame city council, was one of the chief organizers and architects of the opposition. Some were afraid that BART would bring crime to their otherwise sedate peninsula communities. According to Spinelli during a radio debate, one of the major concerns of the local opponents was the impact on Caltrain; the argument was that the coming of BART would put Caltrain out of business. Caltrain supporters hoped that the line could be upgraded—that diesel locomotives could eventually be electrified and the line extended farther into the city underground from its terminus at 4th and Townsend in San Francisco, as well as be fully grade-separated from San Jose on up the peninsula. In other words, the Caltrain tracks would somehow jump over or under the numerous grade crossings along the way. The cost for such a conversion would be enormous, with a dubious cost-benefit return, according to some analysts. And even then, the airport would not be directly served.

However, the idea had strong proponents, among whom were San Mateo County supervisors Mike Nevin and Tom Nolan. Others argued that BART would complement Caltrain and provide direct service from the peninsula to downtown San Francisco, particularly its high-employment Financial District. (The Caltrain terminus at 4th and Townsend was about a mile distant from the primary city employment destinations.) A connection between Caltrain and BART at Millbrae would be good for both systems, according to Nevin, who was chairman of both SamTrans and the Caltrain Joint Powers Board. As for the crime issue, that was a scare tactic to create hysteria in the suburbs.

The people of San Mateo County had voted to support the extension, but it was by no means a fait accompli. Numerous public meetings were held to keep locals informed, get feedback, and answer questions as part of the EIR process. The San Mateo County Civil Grand Jury issued a report following its own investigation of whether the county should pull out of the deal because it was too expensive. This report gave impetus to the plan's opponents.

Meanwhile, the 1994 national election would prove detrimental to transportation projects all over the country, as Republicans swept into Congress promising to cut federal funding. As if fighting the local battles weren't enough, ominous rumblings were coming out of Washington, and on October 31, 1995, BART received a not-so-friendly message from the House and Senate Conference Committee on Appropriations that early funding in the amount of $35 million (not part of the $750 million being sought) would be withheld pending additional work on what was viewed as environmental analysis deficiencies in the draft plan. This problem was later resolved with the help of the Bay Area delegation, with strong leadership from Republican congressman Bill Baker (Contra Costa County) and his successor, Democratic congresswoman Ellen Tauscher (Contra Costa County), along with Democratic congresswoman Nancy Pelosi (San Francisco) and Republican governor Pete Wilson. As a member of the House Transportation Appropriations Committee, Tauscher was a tireless advocate on Capitol Hill.

In 1996, a major opponent to the new plan was an establishment called Artichoke Joe's Casino, a card house located in San Bruno. Dennis Sammut, the owner, was concerned that under the BART alignment his establishment would lose a good portion of its parking. Artichoke Joe's was a very popular and extremely successful business, and parking was a critical component of its ability to accommodate clients. The city of San Bruno, which received a good portion of its revenue from Artichoke Joe's Casino, also expressed concern. Allegedly Sammut paid a reported $260,000 to a high-powered Washington law firm, Swidler and Berlin, to lobby friends on Capitol Hill on behalf of his establishment. The objective was simple: find a way to stop BART or force the transit system to change its route alignment. While it's not clear exactly what the law firm did or who was talked to on the Hill, it's a fact that language did creep into the Transportation Appropriations Bill that would halt the BART airport project if anyone brought a lawsuit against the system in San Mateo County. In essence, the language stated that during pending litigation the project would be stopped. Thus, anyone could spend a few bucks and file a lawsuit that could be in the court system for years and completely halt BART's progress.

POWERFUL COUNTERFORCES INTERVENE

Assessing the potential impact of the "lawsuit" language in the Transportation Appropriations Bill, a powerful contingent of California lawmakers suddenly jumped into the fray. These local representatives were not going to allow such an important public works project to flounder because of some phony lawsuit. Among those pressing to eliminate the lawsuit language were Senators Dianne Feinstein and Barbara Boxer, Congressman Bill Baker, and Congresswoman Nancy Pelosi. After some hardball politics behind the scenes, the language was scrapped.

The 1996 supplemental Environmental Impact Statement (EIS) and EIR included preliminary engineering and a new Alternatives Analysis. It was approved by the FTA through a device called a Record of Decision. This was a significant step toward getting the $750 million federal commitment. But the funding was by no means a done deal, as BART officials were to find out.

A CRITICAL THREAT TO THE AIRPORT PROJECT

A cliffhanger was now in the works. As plans for the BART airport line solidified, a new, very powerful threat began to emerge. First, the key financial component for the now estimated $1.1 billion project was of course the $750 million Full Funding Grant Agreement from the FTA, which is under the U.S. Department of Transportation. This agreement was a prime example of how state and local money could be used to leverage federal assistance, underscoring a partnership. The timing for the approval of this important chunk of funding was becoming more and more critical. Republican governor Pete Wilson, a strong supporter of a BART airport connection, wrote a letter to Frank Wolf, chair of the House Transportation Committee, emphasizing the idea that this was an important local, state, and federal partnership. The deadline set by airport officials was July 1, 1997. If the grant were approved, the money would be earmarked in the federal transportation-appropriations bills in increments over several years. The balance of the funding was to come from the $200 million commitment from the San Francisco airport, $200 million from the San Mateo County Transit Authority (SamTrans) as part of that county's buy-in, plus some state funding, another $10 million from the MTC, and money from BART's capital reserves. In time, the actual amounts would change.

AIRLINES BECOME AN ADVERSARY

One day in early 1994, representatives of the Air Transport Association of America (ATA), the airline industry trade and lobbying association, suddenly showed up at a BART board of directors meeting in Oakland and strongly suggested that the transit agency go back to the original 1992 plan, with a station outside the airport, west of Highway 101. If BART didn't do that, the ATA representatives, including their lawyer, threatened to pull out all the stops to keep the system from going directly into the airport. Board members expressed dismay at what they felt was the arrogance of the presentation. The ATA began underscoring its threat by spending thousands of dollars to support Measure H in San Francisco in hopes of defeating Measure I in June of that year. Measure I, of course, won, showing overwhelming support for an airport station. It seemed odd at the time that the ATA would have taken such a position, since a direct link could only benefit the airlines. The answer to that mystery became clear soon enough.

The next thing anyone knew, the ATA was pushing its "No BART in the Airport" agenda with key Republican lawmakers in Washington, including Senators John McCain and Richard Shelby. Senator Shelby, a Republican from Alabama, had just taken over as chair of the Senate Subcommittee on Transportation Appropriations from Senator Mark O. Hatfield (R–Oregon) who had retired. According to sources close to the Washington scene, Shelby didn't like the project. There was some speculation that this attitude may have been in part because the Bay Area was a Democratic stronghold. Shelby sent a note to Gordon J. Linton, the FTA administrator at the time, calling for a halt to approving the $750 million Full Funding Grant Agreement until a resolution with the airline industry could be achieved.

Shelby went so far as to threaten Linton that he would cut transportation appropriations if he went ahead and approved the funding. Since this was the single most critical piece of funding, its withholding could of course mean no project. Time was running out as the airport prepared documents to go out to bidders for its planned new International Terminal—plans that would either include or not include BART. If there were no official, approved BART airport project by the time the airport's plans were ready, the project's fate would be sealed.

What did the airline industry want that it would lobby so hard in Washington to stop such an important San Francisco Bay Area project—especially a project that would surely benefit the airlines? The concern, as it turned out, was that the industry simply did not want the airport to contribute $200 million, or any amount, to the BART project. The ATA claimed that it was illegal for airport money to be used for a non-airport project. Also, doing so would increase the airport's bottom-line expenses, which would have to be made up by increased landing fees. More important, contributing such a fee, in the airline industry's view, would set an intolerable precedent nationally as other airports considered direct rail transit connections, such as in New York and Washington, D.C.

However, on February 13, 1997, it was announced that the U.S. Department of Transportation and the Federal Aviation Administration (FAA) refuted the ATA's claims that using airport money to build a BART station in the airport was illegal and, further, that the cost-sharing plan was considered to be directly and substantially related to airport transportation. In the early spring of 1997, a meeting took place in San Francisco mayor Willie Brown's office with ATA officials led by United Airlines CEO Gerald Greenwald. Also in attendance were Congresswoman Nancy Pelosi, Senator Dianne Feinstein, and representatives from the airport, BART, and SamTrans. According to some, the airline representatives arrogantly told those in attendance that in essence it was their way or the highway (no pun intended). It was a high-stakes game with United, representing ATA, holding the aces, at least in terms of its influence in Washington.

On March 20, 1997, it was announced that a deal was finally struck that satisfied the airline people and would allow BART to build a station inside the airport. The airport would lend BART $113 million, the cost of the airport station, which would be paid back through a lease agreement with the airport. BART would pay $2.5 million a year for the next fifty years by collecting a surcharge at the airport station exit gate. Further, it was demanded that BART offer a 25 percent discount to airline employees using the system to get to work. This did not include airport workers. Overall, it was an onerous deal, but it was the only deal acceptable to the ATA, since it took the potential for increased landing fees off the table. In exchange, once the agreement was signed, the ATA would call off the dogs in Washington and support the project. Even with the accord, Shelby continued to object to the federal funding of the project, and continued his threat. His committee basically said there would be no federal funding, suggesting that a cheaper alternative be explored. FTA administrator Gordon Linton, a supporter of the project, was understandably nervous.

Now in the late spring of 1997, with the federal money still in jeopardy, the BART airport project was once again in serious peril. The deadline was fast approaching, and it appeared that Shelby was not budging on his position. While approval for the Full Funding Grant Agreement was the prerogative of the administration, Congress still held the purse strings. On June 24, 1997, the project got a boost from the House Appropriations Subcommittee on Transportation, which approved $54.8 million for the project for the federal fiscal year 1998–1999, beginning in October. More important, it approved BART's request for the long-awaited $750 million Full Funding Grant, despite the continued threat from the Senate Appropriations Committee on Transportation headed by Shelby. The Clinton administration went ahead and ordered that approval be given for the federal share of the project's funding. The new secretary of transportation, Rodney Slater, also a strong supporter of the project, then directed FTA administrator Gordon Linton to move forward with the Full Funding Grant Agreement. On July 1, 1997, the federal funding, representing 51 percent of the project cost, was approved under the federal New Starts program. It was to be a turnkey project under the Intermodal Surface

Transportation Efficiency Act. And it was approved just in the nick of time.

In order to get a jump start on construction once the funding was assured, BART had earlier sought special state legislation that would allow it to pre-qualify bidders for a "design-build" approach. On September 28, 1996, Senate Bill 1742 had authorized the transit district to pre-qualify a list of bidders in advance of awarding contracts. This proved to be a smart move to reduce the time it normally takes to vet potential bidders and conduct the evaluation process of extremely complex bids.

The challenges of actually building the new line were enormous. First on the agenda was a ground-breaking ceremony at the airport. It was held under a giant big top–style white tent with several hundred guests and numerous dignitaries in attendance. The master of ceremonies for the event was Diane Dwyer, a local television reporter and anchor, and the niece of William J. Dwyer, the former CEO of the airport. Following the ceremony on Monday, November 3, 1997, the first work on the project began with site preparation and utility relocation under a $9 million contract with Homer J. Olson, Inc., of Livermore, California. The construction market was hot, and other large projects were competing for the major contractors, which meant higher costs than originally estimated.

THE AIRPORT EXTENSION IS FINALLY UNDER WAY

The first major contracts for the airport extension were awarded on February 10, 1998. One went to a joint venture, Sverdrup Corporation and Conco out of St. Louis, Missouri, for $70.5 million for engineering and construction of the at-grade Millbrae Station and parking lot. The other went to Tutor-Saliba Corporation and Slattery Construction of Los Angeles, also a joint venture, to build the main line, including track work, three station boxes, and systems for $526 million. These two contracts would comprise 90 percent of the work. Tutor-Saliba also had the contract to build the airport's new $2.4 billion International Terminal. The AirTrain that was to provide shuttle service between the terminals and the rental car garages half a mile away would be built by Bombardier of Montreal, Canada. A fully automated people mover, it would cover a total of about 6 miles with a double loop, with the loops running in opposite directions.

From the start there were serious financial issues. Federal appropriations money was coming up short in the beginning, and BART had to obtain a $300 million line of credit backed by the Full Funding Grant Agreement in order to pay its immediate construction bills. In order to get the line of credit, it had to borrow $60 million from the MTC for seed money. In addition, environmental issues had to be dealt with in order to meet the requirements of the Environmental Protection Agency (EPA) and the California Department of Fish and Game. Since a good portion of the route alignment went through wetlands, a few species on the endangered list needed protection, including the San Francisco garter snake, the red-legged frog, and the California damselfly. Special care was taken to ensure the safety of the garter snakes by temporarily moving them to a special safe house that was lovingly called "The Snake Motel." One day I was asked by a reporter from the *Chronicle* how the snakes were doing, and I was quoted the next day in the paper saying that it was my understanding that the snakes were very happy in their new temporary habitat, which was being overseen by a specialist in the field. Two days later a very serious letter was published in the *Chronicle* slamming my quote. "How would he know whether the snakes were happy or not?" the writer asked, suggesting that I was not empathetic enough to the snakes' plight.

SNAKE BIT

Unfortunately, in April 2000, a snake that had remained in the construction zone was accidently run over by a truck. Forensic examination showed tire tracks across its back, clear evidence of a serious violation. The project was shut down by the EPA for eighteen days at a cost of over $4 million. When construction started again, trucks had to reduce their speed, thus slowing down the work. EPA operatives were onsite videotaping trucks coming in and out to record their speed. As part of the mitigation commitment, BART bought a once-operating ranch that comprised about eight acres near the coast to create a new habitat for the San Francisco garter snakes and the red-legged frogs. Interestingly, there were no reports of red-legged frogs or damselflies being seen in the construction zone during that time. Building the 8.7 miles and the four stations of the BART airport line took five and a half years.

Also at this time, a new controversy cropped up over the naming of the station at the Tanforan shopping center. Once a popular racetrack, the site had also served as a temporary internment camp for Japanese Americans during World War II, and there was concern in the Japanese community that calling it the Tanforan Station would raise some bitter memories. After some hand-wringing and a recommendation from staff, the BART board named it the San Bruno Station.

The BART San Francisco airport line opened for business with a colorful celebration on June 22, 2003. Key speakers at the event were Senator Dianne Feinstein, Governor Gray Davis, Secretary of Transportation Norman Mineta, Congressman Tom Lantos, Congresswoman Ellen Tauscher, BART Board President Pete Snyder of Dublin, and BART General Manager Tom Margro. Like the original BART project, the new airport extension was perfectly timed, in this case to mesh with the airport expansion. Any earlier or later and it would not have provided the optimal service it provides today. Out of the 400,000 trips taken each weekday on the system (using 2014 data), approximately 48,000 per day are taken on the BART airport line. While this is considered a good number, it falls short of the 1996 EIR estimated projections for Alternative VI—which predicted 68,600 trips daily by the year 2010—and yet, with the infrastructure in place, it will more than likely exceed its early projections in the years to come as gas prices soar and traffic becomes intolerable.

CHAPTER 24

THE 1990S ARE A BRIDGE TO THE FUTURE

While the lion's share of BART's expansion focus during the 1990s was on the various political machinations, lawsuits, funding, and design challenges that had to be confronted with the San Francisco airport extension, work had begun on expanding the system in the East Bay.

Anticipation of the East Bay extensions, tinged with political rhetoric, had been part of the conversation for decades, and for most it was a foregone conclusion. Roy Nakadegawa, however, who in 1992 was a new BART board member from Berkeley, made it clear from the time he took his seat on the dais that he was against East Bay extensions of the system. He began lobbing grenades at the project immediately. "They're too costly," he said. "Buses could do the job." Prior to coming to BART, he had served as a member of the Alameda–Contra Costa regional bus system (AC Transit).

As things moved ahead, it was quite a jolt to realize how much costs had escalated from the original estimates back in the mid-1980s; they were now more than twice what they had been the previous decade. The early words of Bill Stokes haunted the BART hallways—"Build it now; it will never be cheaper." Following several community meetings and public hearings seeking local input on proposed routes, station locations, and aesthetics, the work to build northeast and eastward began in earnest in the boardroom and on the drawing board.

Again, things did not go smoothly. Some of the community meetings attracted locals who were simply not all that friendly. At one such meeting in Castro Valley, the staff presenters and community relations people were met with outright hostility for a plethora of reasons. A few people always had the attitude of "not in my backyard." Some of the same old fears about BART were brought up during graphic presentations of proposed station locations and route alignments. These included concerns about potential parking overflow onto residential and city streets, increased local traffic, and aesthetics. The last of those concerns was always a major issue. Would there be enough landscaping, and would trees be planted to mask parking lots and garages? As with the airport extension, some residents expressed concerns that BART would import a criminal element to the area, and those fears were never really allayed, even with the promise of strong policing of the system. The response given to the media in reference to such concerns was always that BART is a microcosm of the society it serves and thus represents to some degree whatever happens in the surrounding streets and neighborhoods. Through it all, one of BART's newest directors, Erlene DeMarcus (representing eastern Alameda County and Hayward), who was president of the board in 1991, pushed hard to make it happen. She worked closely with community leaders to buffer their concerns.

As a result of the numerous public gatherings, BART incorporated many suggestions and demands into the Draft Environmental Impact Report (EIR) for each of the proposed new lines. Aside from the few vocal critics, overall community support for the extension program was strong. After all, residents had voted to tax themselves to help finance building the extensions.

As with securing the airport extension, the old saying "Timing is everything" was certainly spot on for the East Bay additions as well. Had BART in the 1960s been required to jump through the social, political, and environmental hoops it takes today to build any sizable public works project, it probably never would have been built. For that matter, you could not build a BART-like system overlaid on the Bay Area topography today, or even in the 1990s; the social and environmental impacts simply could not be reconciled in today's world. The new extensions would be a miracle of timing and determination.

It seems that controversy over major public works projects such as BART and California's ambitious high-speed rail endeavor is endemic to the human condition. For every proponent of progress, most assuredly a line of opponents who worship at the altar of the status quo will be waiting in the wings. Perhaps it's no coincidence that Dan Richard, the chairman of California's high-speed rail plan at the time of this writing, was an elected BART director representing Orinda during the early days of the extension program and one of the prime movers on the board. In 1996 he was president of the board and played an important role in obtaining the federal funding for the San Francisco airport project.

TAKING ADVANTAGE OF A RECESSION AND AN OFFSET DUE TO WEATHER

A recession was in full swing in the early 1990s, and the BART projects were a promising relief, particularly for the building trades. In other words, it was an excellent climate for bidding. Competition for the work resulted in better-than-hoped-for bids.

One key concern when embarking on such projects is weather patterns. BART used thirty years of National Weather Service data to plot weather patterns for certain times of the year when construction would be most advantageous. Plan though they did, the expected 40 days of rain turned out to be 221 days of wet weather over the three-year period beginning in 1992, which of course affected construction and pushed the scheduled opening dates, particularly in the case of the Dublin/Pleasanton extension, from 1995 to 1996.

WARM SPRINGS IS A BONE OF CONTENTION

A planned third East Bay extension from Fremont in southern Alameda County had also been fomenting for some time. BART prepared an Environmental Impact Report in 1991 that was certified by the BART board the following year, 1992. It called for a 5.5- to 6-mile extension south with a station in Irvington and a terminus station at Warm Springs. The planned project was conceived with a view to offering relief for southbound commuters along Interstate 880. Because Silicon Valley had become a high-employment center, Interstate 880 had become one of the most congested corridors in Northern California.

Almost a decade later, on June 26, 2003, the BART board of directors certified a Supplemental Environmental Impact Report (SEIR) and the required California Environmental Quality Act (CEQA) report in conjunction with its Santa Clara County partner, the Valley Transportation Authority (VTA), for the proposed project. But Warm Springs was put on hold, pending land acquisition, funding availability, and the resolution of long-standing political strife. This extension involved going around or under Fremont Central Park and part of Lake Elizabeth, which was smack in the middle of the adopted planned route alignment. It would require constructing a mile-long subway at greater expense as opposed to an aerial structure that was adamantly opposed by local officials. While state and local funding would eventually pay for the Warm Springs extension, it was also eligible for federal funding and so required a comprehensive review under the National Environmental Policy Act (NEPA). This was completed in 2004 with the publication of the Draft Environmental Impact Statement (DEIS) under NEPA. Yet still the plan could not get traction.

As the Colma Station was for the airport extension, the Warm Springs Station would be the jumping-off point for some day building a San Jose extension in Santa Clara County. In other words, getting to San Jose would take a two-segment approach. Strong bus advocates were vocal about their belief that an extension to San Jose was delusional on the part of the BART hierarchy, and they attended board meetings to argue their position that buses could do the job just as well. The question that was always raised was, would people take buses? It was axiomatic that trains were far more marketable for long-haul commuting.

Back in the early 1990s, BART director John Glenn was pushing hard for the Warm Springs rail extension into his district, a project he had led the charge for since first coming on the board in 1974. He was continually butting heads with his former ally and now bitter enemy Nello Bianco, a director from El Sobrante, in northwestern Contra Costa County. Sometimes the acrimony between the two reached such levels that it felt as though blows might easily follow. Whether by luck or design, it was good that they sat at opposite ends of the curved board dais. Their long-standing feud spilled over into several parochial issues, but the Warm Springs extension caused by far the most distress. (On one occasion, a developer friend of Bianco's in Contra Costa County put on a gala birthday party for him. The party was held at the Crowne Plaza Concord hotel, which is located on John Glenn Drive.

Bianco was amused by the little irony, but since the street was named after the astronaut instead of his sworn nemesis, it did not present an embarrassment.)

While Glenn was fighting for his Warm Springs extension, Bianco, who had been president of the BART board a record five times during his tenure, was fighting for an extension from the north end of the line at Richmond up along the Interstate 80 corridor, which also suffered from major congestion. Some land was purchased in anticipation of a future extension, but since there was no money to lay track, the area was turned into a park-and-ride lot on an interim basis. Meanwhile, Glenn was adamant that a Warm Springs extension was far more important than adding to the north end of the line.

As for Warm Springs, the critical question was whether an eventual extension to San Jose was truly in the offing or was just a long-standing fantasy. For years it looked as though it simply wasn't going to happen. The people of Santa Clara County voted twice to tax themselves to support such a venture, once in the year 2000 to help fund basic construction, and again in 2008 to provide for an eventual ongoing operating subsidy. Still, if there were to be no line to San Jose, then it was questionable whether Warm Springs mattered in the broader scheme of things. There was also strong support from the Silicon Valley contingent for a San Jose extension.

It would be seventeen years from the time the first EIR was certified by the BART board before ground was broken for Warm Springs on September 30, 2009. By this time, both Bianco and Glenn had long retired from the board and passed away. The 5.4-mile extension is scheduled to open in late 2016. A further extension to San Jose has been assured as plans were drawn up under a partnership between BART and the Santa Clara Valley Transportation Authority. The EIR for the first leg of a San Jose extension calls for a 10-mile line from Warm Springs to the Berryessa district of San Jose, just 6 miles short of downtown. Most of the alignment would be along the Union Pacific Railroad right-of-way at a cost of $2.3 billion, including $900 million from federal grants through the Federal Transit Administration (FTA). Strong support for the project came from Senator Dianne Feinstein, who helped lobby in Washington for the project, and from Congresswoman Zoe Lofgren (D–San Jose). It is scheduled to open in 2018.

CONSTRUCTION FINALLY BEGINS IN EASTERN CONTRA COSTA AND ALAMEDA COUNTIES

Ground was broken for the two planned East Bay extensions on October 25, 1991. During the 1991–1992 fiscal year, BART awarded $500 million in construction contracts to begin work on both the eastern Contra Costa County and eastern Alameda County extensions. It is estimated that the work generated more than 28,000 jobs in the Bay Area. The extension from the eastern Contra Costa County terminus at Concord would take the line along Highway 4 to the North Concord/Martinez Station and on to Pittsburg/Bay Point for a total addition of 7.8 miles at a cost of $506 million. The first significant challenge was the Highway 4 corridor over the Willow Pass grade, which was too steep. BART, in conjunction with Caltrans, lowered the grade to 4 percent to allow trains to climb over the Willow Pass hill.

After its basic completion, the new line went through rigorous preliminary testing that revealed a major problem with the train control: the new technology would not talk to the aging twenty-five-year-old original technology. Like a May-December arranged marriage, the communication gap was critical and had to be rectified through an integration program. The engineers went to work, and after months of adjustments and fixes, the new and old technologies were on speaking terms at last. The North Concord/Martinez Station on Port Chicago Highway in Concord opened on December 16, 1995. It would be another year before the terminus at the Pittsburg/Bay Point Station would open on December 4, 1996. It was a nice, sunny day, and good cheer seemed to be in the air as a large crowd of residents, dignitaries, and first-time riders welcomed the new station and took their trips on the first revenue BART train to come that far east into the county.

While the Pittsburg/Bay Point Station is the end of the BART extension project on that line, it also marks the beginning of a new, more daunting project, something called eBART, the brainchild of BART director Joel Keller. According to one of its principal planners, Ellen Smith, the concept of eBART, which began to take shape in 2001, was to build a connecting line from the Pittsburg/Bay Point terminus along the Highway 4 median through Antioch, eventually extending out to Brentwood. The first phase, as outlined in the EIR for the project, called for a 10-mile line terminating in Antioch in eastern Contra Costa County. The plan also called for a diesel-operated train, which would yield a considerable cost savings over using typical BART technology and trains. It would thus be a connected but separate system. The trains would be designed to look like BART trains, only narrower and smaller in length and operating over standard-gauge tracks of 4 feet, 8.5 inches. Initially each train would be a married pair, with no more than two diesel multiple unit (DMU) cars per train. The new line would have two stations in Antioch: the Pittsburg Center Station on Railroad Avenue and the Antioch Station on Hillcrest Avenue as the terminus. The BART board adopted the project in 2009 and construction began in 2011. Procurement for the first eight rail cars at a cost of $58 million was approved by the BART board on April 24, 2014. The supplier submitting the only bid was a Swiss company, Stadler Bussnang. The line is scheduled to open in late 2017 or early 2018.

A SIGNIFICANT ISSUE WITH THE DUBLIN/PLEASANTON EXTENSION

As plans revved up for the 14-mile Dublin/Pleasanton extension, a particularly sticky controversy emerged over the fate of a specific house initially destined for the scrap heap. The house in question was a Queen Anne Victorian in disrepair called the Strobridge House, which was considered a landmark in Castro Valley, an unincorporated community along U.S. Highway 580 southeast of Oakland. The venerable structure, slightly lopsided, sat on the site where BART planned to build the parking area for the Castro Valley Station on the planned new line. BART intended to raze the structure. The station itself would be located in the middle of the freeway median, with pedestrian access from the parking area through an underpass.

The house had been built in 1894 and was once the home of E. K. Strobridge, a California state senator. In 1869 his father, James Harvey Strobridge, who oversaw the building of the Central Pacific rail line (which later became the Southern Pacific Railroad), bought 500 acres of farmland in the area during the days Castro Valley was primarily rural, set in the midst of rolling hills, with a scant population of scattered settlers, mostly ranchers and farmers. At the time of the transit system's interest in the property, the house had long been vacant and boarded up. But its lines were classic Victorian, like many of the old houses in San Francisco and Oakland originally built by journeyman shipwrights between trips. A strong movement to save the old place was spearheaded by a local architect and the Castro Valley Historical Society. After all, it was one of the original houses in the area, with a lot of history associated with it.

BART RAISES THE WHITE FLAG

After several months of wrangling, and in deference to growing local concerns, BART agreed to restore the house as part of a joint-development proposal. The decision showed that the 800-pound gorilla had a soft side, or at least a pragmatic side. Bridge Housing, a San Francisco nonprofit development company, in partnership with BART, would build ninety-six low-cost housing units on the transit district's property adjacent to the new station. The project would incorporate the renovated Strobridge House as part of the overall complex, with the house's three stories turned into three separate apartments. Underscoring the shortage of low-cost housing in the area was the instant demand that flooded in for the property. By the time the housing project was completed and ready for an inaugural ribbon-cutting ceremony, it was already fully occupied, including the Strobridge House.

THE EXTENSION PROJECT MOVES AHEAD

The extension project, comprising two stations (Castro Valley and Dublin/Pleasanton), would extend eastward, branching off from the Bay Fair Station on the Fremont line in southern Alameda County through a very tricky underground segment skirting Highway 238 and then heading east along the 580 highway median. It was completed and opened for business on May 10, 1997, at a cost of approximately $517 million.

Talk of a third station to be located in West Dublin/Pleasanton was soon in the works, particularly as pressure was building on the terminus station to accommodate new riders; commuters from as far away as Tracy and even Stockton were converging on the Dublin/Pleasanton Station. Parking was an immediate issue, and eventually a parking structure was added. BART's Joint Development Department entertained proposals from private builders interested in financing a third station in return for development rights on both sides of the Interstate 580 median.

On April 9, 1998, BART entered into an exclusive agreement with LaSalle Partners (later Jones Lang LaSalle), a Chicago-based company, for the proposed building of a hotel and mixed-use development on BART property on the Dublin side of Interstate 580, as well as a convention center and hotel on the Pleasanton side. As part of the deal, LaSalle would finance a BART station in between, at a cost of $20 million. A fairly steep dip in the economy temporarily put the kibosh on the plans, but construction of the station eventually began on October 29, 2006, and the station opened on February 11, 2011, after a delay of two years due to concerns about the structural integrity of the pedestrian bridge that provided access to the station from each side of Interstate 580.

BART TANGLES WITH PG&E OVER POWER COSTS AND DELIVERY

In 1994, BART's power costs were escalating exponentially and the District was desperately looking for savings. Regenerative braking (when the motors turn into generators) offered some benefit by putting power back into the third rail, which was used almost immediately by following trains, but this was not nearly enough to offset the rising drain on the fiscal-year budget. When the power-cost issue was reported to the board, Wilfred T. Ussery, a director from San Francisco, proposed that BART begin thinking long-term about having its own power plant so the system would not be dependent on outside sources. He also put out the idea that BART could add considerably to its revenue stream by adding a "bar car" to the trains with the longest runs. "I'll bet that between San Francisco and Concord you could get in two martinis," quipped the late renowned transit writer Harre Demoro, who was covering BART for the *San Francisco Chronicle.* With several major items on the agenda that day, some involving million-dollar contracts, the bar car story simply had too much sex appeal to pass up; it made headline news, trumping those hefty contracts being considered. The wire services picked up the story, it went national, and we began receiving calls from other agencies wondering when the bar car was going into service. I had to explain that it was probably never going to happen, although there was no question that some thought it a great idea.

After months of negotiations with the Pacific Gas and Electric Company (PG&E) over power costs, BART's power gurus determined the transit district needed to seek out less-expensive sources of power to meet both immediate and long-term needs. Buying power on the open market at wholesale rates would prove to be a daunting endeavor. BART's electrical requirements could light a city the size of Alameda, which has a population of about 76,000.

In 1994 BART entered into a twenty-year contract with the Western Area Power Administration (WAPA) to provide about 7 percent of the required electrical power, about 4 megawatts. WAPA was a federal reclamation operation under the federal Reclamation Project Act of 1939. As a public agency, BART qualified as a preference entity to purchase hydropower. Wheeled through WAPA, the hydropower came from the federal Central Valley Project and would have to be delivered via the PG&E grid to the system. But PG&E would only deliver the power through one of BART's sixty-two substation connecting points, even though delivery to multiple points was needed. Some officials speculated that this was PG&E's way of slapping BART's wrists for going elsewhere for some of its power needs. In any case, the problem was solved when, on March 16, 1995, state senator Quentin Kopp, chair of the Senate Transportation Committee, authored S.B. 184, which required PG&E to deliver any power purchased by BART from third-party wholesalers to multiple locations around the system.

THE ENRON FACTOR

A year later, on May 9, 1996, the day before the opening of the Dublin/Pleasanton line, BART entered into a twenty-year contract with the Bonneville Power Administration (BPA), a nonprofit federal operation located in Portland, Oregon. BPA was created by Congress in 1936 to provide primarily hydroelectric power from the Columbia River. The deal with BART was made possible because energy leader Enron had bought out Portland General Electric and begun luring Bonneville's customers by selling power at an absolute bottom rate, which forced Bonneville to lower its prices in response. This turned out to be lucky timing for BART, since Bonneville offered power at 25 percent less than the going market rate, saving BART $9 million a year against what PG&E was charging. Prior to this arrangement, power was costing BART more than $24 million annually. Once Enron came into the picture, a surplus of power was created from Bonneville that, as it turned out, would not be available for sale to the District after June 30, 2006. When the Enron accounting debacle erupted in October 2001 and the power company went bankrupt, Bonneville eventually had to take care of its longtime local northwestern customers first. This meant BART would have to look elsewhere to meet its power demands after the 2006 cutoff date, since surplus power would no longer be available.

Today, the transit district buys less than 1 percent of its electrical power from PG&E, but it does pay the utility transmission fees. BART now gets most of its power from the Northern California Power Agency and from a power plant in Lodi, in San Joaquin County, in which the transit district has a shared ownership. With the current extensions, BART uses a total of 400,000 megawatt hours annually, or about 1,095 megawatt hours per day, according to BART's power czar, Frank Schultz. Its budgeted cost for fiscal year 2014–2015 was $38 million.

BART EXPERIMENTS WITH ELECTRIC CARS

On October 24, 1995, BART celebrated a new venture with a ribbon-cutting ceremony at its Ashby Station in Berkeley to inaugurate an electric charging station and introduce a new all-electric automobile called the City Bee. The charging station was located in the parking lot across the street from the station. Participating sponsors of the event were PG&E and Sybase, a high-tech company located in Emeryville. This event was a kick-off for a brand-new demonstration program to make all-electric cars available to riders for easy access to the system. Eventually forty of the cars would be leased from a company in Norway. In what was simply a coincidence, King Harald V and Queen Sonja of Norway were visiting the Bay Area at the time, were notified through the consulate about the event at BART, and were the guests of honor at the ceremony. The City Bee car was a grand idea, but by 1998 the program had faded from the scene.

THE GULF WAR ENTERS THE PICTURE

Looking again to be on the cutting edge of technology, BART began exploring possible advances in the state of the art that could be applied to its aging automatic train control system. On May 2, 1996, BART began testing at its Hayward test track, a 2-mile stretch running parallel to its Hayward storage yard. Engineers were assessing a new "advanced automatic train control" (AATC) prototype system that had been in the development stage for a few years. Two years earlier, on February 24, 1994, the White House announced that the transit district would receive a $19.5 million federal grant to develop the AATC. This new technology had its foundation in U.S. military satellite–based radio position locating, which was used effectively in Saudi Arabia during the Gulf War's Operation Desert Shield, which had begun on August 2, 1990. The technology was used to track equipment and troops with pinpoint accuracy. If it could do that, why couldn't it be used to track trains with the same precision? The White House and the FTA were very interested in seeing how radio positioning might be applied to ground transportation, and once again BART would become the nation's laboratory for advancing the state of the art of ground transportation technology as an outgrowth of the Global Positioning System (GPS). If it were successfully developed, BART would be the first system in the world to have a train control system of that type.

The goal, as always, was to increase the capacity of the system to accommodate additional trains through close headways by eliminating or modifying the fixed-block track circuitry. In essence, it was to be a "moving block" system, allowing trains to operate closer together during peak hours. Several companies contracted with BART to work on this project, including General Electric. Integrating the new technology with the current operating system would be an extremely challenging task, and it turned out to be one that General Electric determined it had not signed up for. The company dropped out of the project despite having already being paid almost $90 million. BART sued to recover a portion of the money and was successful in retrieving $30 million, according to Paul Oversier, BART's assistant general manager of operations and maintenance. He said the project is still viable and is being revived under the heading "Communication-Bound Trains." "Right now [in 2015] we can only operate sixty-two trains on the system at one time, [and] twenty-four trains an hour through the system's critical link, the Transbay Tube between Oakland and San Francisco," Oversier said. "We'd like to increase that to thirty trains."

By 2017, the system is expected to operate as many as sixty-four trains during peak periods.

THE GENERAL MANAGER RESIGNS

During the 1990s, general managers tended to come and go. It seemed as though the transit district's employees, numbering over 3,000, would just be getting to know the latest general manager when suddenly there was someone new. In April 1994, Richard A. White took over the reins from Frank Wilson, who left BART on January 13 to take the job as New Jersey's transportation commissioner, reporting directly to the governor. White named Dorothy Dugger, who had previously been executive manager of external affairs, to take his previous job as deputy general manager. He himself stepped into the top spot just as the latest round of labor negotiations were moving into the preliminary stages.

As spring moved into summer, White came into open conflict with the leadership of BART's two major unions, Service Employees International Union (SEIU) Local 390 and Amalgamated Transit Union Local 1555. The major bone of contention was what the unions called a work-rule issue, which involved the District's ability to transfer employees between work locations on an as-needed basis. A strike was threatened following the termination of the existing contract on June 30, 1994. Paul Varacalli, the executive secretary of SEIU at the time, worked behind the scenes to see if a satisfactory resolution was possible without hitting the bricks. Meanwhile White angrily lashed out in public at the union leadership over the impasse. After a sixty-day cooling-off period imposed by the governor, an agreement was reached to avoid a strike.

White then guided much of the extension program for the next two years. When White resigned on May 31, 1996, to become general manager of the Washington Metro system in Washington, D.C., the BART board immediately began looking for a new general manager. While normally it could take up to a year to find a new general manager who was the right fit, in this case the board didn't have to wait long. Dan Richard, president of the board in 1996, recruited a former employee of the District, and on September 30, 1996, Thomas E. Margro was named by the board of directors to succeed White as general manager.

Margro, a quiet, methodical engineer, was considered perfect for the job, not only for his demonstrated management ability but also for his political savvy. He had originally come from the Southeastern Pennsylvania Transportation Authority (SEPTA) to manage the overall extension program in the early part of the decade before leaving to take a job in the East. He was lured back to BART with the promise that he would have a semblance of autonomy in managing the District's day-to-day operations and extension program. After protracted labor negotiations for a new contract during the summer of 1997, and a sixty-day cooling-off period ordered by California governor Pete Wilson, Margro and the executive staff had to slog through a one-week strike that shut the system down. Major Bay Area corridors immediately turned into virtual parking lots. No one would dispute it was a traffic nightmare.

A BABY IS BORN ON BART

At 10:52 P.M. on Sunday, July 21, 1996, eighteen-year-old Bernadette Ortiz gave birth to a baby girl on a BART train just after it pulled into the Hayward BART Station. Ortiz and the baby's father, Steven Ehler, had boarded the train in Richmond and were headed for St. Rose Hospital in Hayward, where they were registered. Ortiz's contractions were already six minutes apart upon their departure from home. Their plan was to go to the South Hayward Station and take a cab the rest of the way to the hospital. The couple thought at first that they would get there in time, but, according to Ortiz, when they reached the San Leandro Station, still three stations away from their destination, she knew they weren't going to make it. BART's newest passenger simply was not going to wait.

Theirs was the only baby to have been born on a BART train in the system's then twenty-four-year history. Put another way, the baby was literally one in a billion, since by then the system had carried more than a billion passengers. The baby was named Stephany Ann Marie Ehler. Calling in an emergency hold at the station, train operator Ric Horrocks suddenly found himself a midwife as he helped with the delivery until paramedics arrived. Also assisting the young mother were BART police officer Don Walker and a passenger, Ignacio Aceves. Baby Stephany weighed in at 7 pounds, 2 ounces, and was soon rushed to St. Rose Hospital in Hayward.

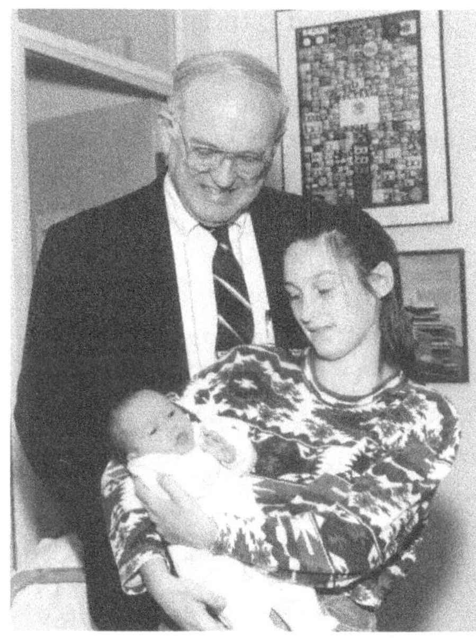

With the help of the train operator who became an instant midwife, Stephany Ann Marie Ehler was born on a BART train on July 21, 1996. Here, mother Bernadette Ortiz presents little Stephany at a BART board meeting. Director Tom Blalock of Fremont (also pictured) personally donated $500 toward Stephany's education.

On August 8, 1996, at a regular meeting of the BART board of directors, Bernadette Ortiz and baby Stephany, twenty-nine days old, were invited to be publicly congratulated by staff and board members. Everyone was excited and even moved by the event. Officer Walker and train operator Horrocks were also on hand to see the baby for the first time since her birth. On this occasion, the board approved presenting Stephany Ann Marie Ehler with a lifetime pass to the system. Since she could ride the system for free until the age of five, the pass would not really take effect until five years down the road, so for the time being, a letter signed by BART board president Dan Richard would entitle the child to the pass when the time came. The audience then witnessed something quite unexpected. In addition to receiving the lifetime pass for her daughter, Bernadette also received a personal check in the amount of $500 from BART director Tom Blalock and his wife. Blalock noted as he presented the gift to the young family that he had a granddaughter named Stephanie Ann. The board also presented Certificates of Recognition to Stephany's onboard "midwives," Horrocks, Walker, and Aceves.

PROBLEMS FOR DIRECTORS WITH THE FBI

In 1980, Margaret K. Pryor became the second woman elected to the BART board, and in 1987 she would be its first female president. During her tenure, Pryor was a strong voice for minority issues as well as for the system's expansion program, and she was always a controversial figure. On March 5, 1998, a federal grand jury indicted her, alleging income tax evasion and extortion involving a $3,000 payment from Neleco, a Boston company seeking a car-cleaning contract. A representative of the company, Paul DiBenedetti, was working with the FBI to set up a sting operation targeting Pryor. U.S. Attorney Ben Burch called the investigation, which began in 1994, "extensive." On top of that, Pryor was also in trouble with the California State Fair Political Practices Commission, and although there was no trial, Pryor was given five years probation under a plea agreement and resigned from the board, ending eighteen years as a director. On a personal note, I was saddened by her situation. Over the years, Margaret had become a friend, and we once danced, or attempted to dance, the Texas two-step at a transit conference in Houston. We may have looked silly, but it was fun.

Wilfred Ussery, a BART director from San Francisco, was also caught up in a similar FBI sting involving the same company, Neleco. He was indicted the following year by a federal grand jury for accepting a $1,000 bribe from DiBenedetti, who was working with the FBI. Again, the bribe was allegedly in return for a favorable vote on a car-cleaning contract being sought by Neleco. With a plea agreement, some other charges were dropped and Ussery was given three years probation and community service.

THE BART BABY SIX YEARS LATER

On Thursday, September 12, 2002, BART marked its thirtieth year of service to the people of the Bay Area with a cake-cutting ceremony in the board of directors' room at its Lake Merritt headquarters. Rolling the cake on a table into the large hundred-seat room and cutting the first piece to clapping and cheers was six-year-old Stephany Ann Marie Ehler,

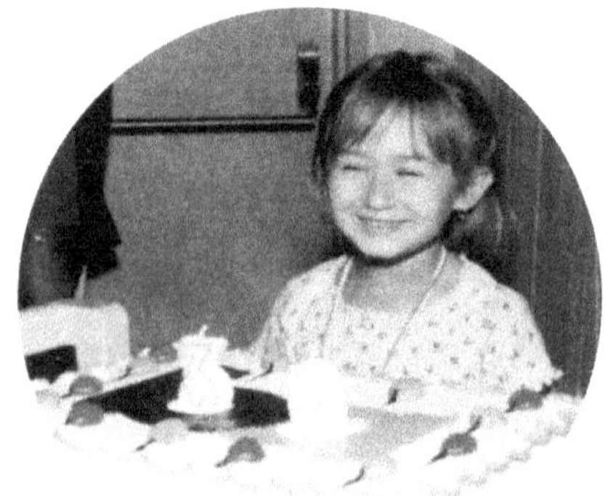

In September 2002, six-year-old Stephany Ann Marie Ehler, the only baby born on a BART train, helped BART celebrate its thirty-year anniversary by cutting the first piece of cake.

making a surprise appearance. Another surprise visitor, who had been sitting anonymously in the back, was former general manager Bill Stokes. There are still those today who would argue that if it hadn't been for Stokes, there probably would not have been a BART. Once his presence was noted, he was invited down to join the board for a photo behind the cake. It was Stokes's first visit in several years. He seemed like a beaming father coming home to see how his child was doing.

CAPITOL CORRIDOR TRAINS TAKEOVER

On August 1, 1996, Governor Pete Wilson signed Senate Bill 457, authored by Senator David Kelley (R–Idyllwild). The bill created the Capitol Corridor Joint Powers Authority (CCJPA), composed of eight counties along the corridor between Auburn in Placer County and San Jose in Santa Clara County. The other counties include Sacramento, Yolo, Solano, Contra Costa, Alameda, and San Francisco. BART, which represents three of the counties, provided management support at the inception of the CCJPA and was named to take over the management of the Capitol Corridor trains in 1998 from the California Department of Transportation (Caltrans). Caltrans, which had been managing the service since 1991, fought the move, but to no avail. The Capitol Corridor train service was operating eight trips per day, seven days a week, along 170 miles of track. Beginning in Auburn, in the Sierra Nevada foothills, the trains rolled through Sacramento, Davis, Emeryville, Oakland, and San Jose, making sixteen stops along the way. But the service had been languishing for some time. Ridership was low and didn't seem to be growing, which was creating some frustration at the state capitol, since the state was subsidizing the service. Only about 1,000 trips a day were being taken by passengers on the limited service at the time, mostly during weekends.

BART contracted with Amtrak to operate the service that had been under Caltrans. The direct connection between the Capitol Corridor trains and BART at its Richmond Station in western Contra Costa County was seen as a great opportunity to expand overall service and ridership, creating a synergy between the two systems. BART immediately set about working to increase the number of trips and, in partnership with Amtrak, launched a fresh marketing program. Two round trips were added almost immediately. Union Pacific Railroad, which had taken over Southern Pacific, owned the infrastructure and was responsible for track maintenance. By 2002, BART had doubled the ridership and was providing eighteen round trips a day. Today, under BART management, Capitol Corridor trains operate thirty round trips a day, fifteen trips in each direction. Seven of those trains go all the way to San Jose, and eight turn back at Oakland. Average daily ridership is about 4,800 per day, or about 1.76 million annually.

NEW LEADERSHIP ON THE BOARD

On December 18, 1997, James Fang of San Francisco was elected by his fellow board members to serve as president of the nine-member board for calendar year 1998, and Joel Keller of Contra Costa County was elected as vice president. This extremely important year marked the start of the San Francisco airport extension project. Fang, who was the youngest BART director in the system's history—he was twenty-eight when first elected to the board in 1990—would become the board's longest-serving member. He would also become one of the board's most influential members, much like other long-serving members, including Dan Richard (now chairman of the California High Speed Rail project) and former directors Margaret K. Pryor and Nello Bianco. These directors wielded broad influence over the course of the board and its policies, whether parochial or global in scope. And now it was Fang's time at the center of the BART universe. He was very supportive of moving forward with the Warm Springs extension and the long-proposed connector line between BART's Coliseum Station and Oakland International Airport.

Fang, a member of a politically powerful San Francisco family, is the president and publisher of *Asian Week,* which has the largest circulation of any Asian American paper in the United States. His mother, Florence Fang, was very influential in the city's political arena as well as in the Chinese community. The Fangs took over the venerable *San Francisco Examiner* from the Hearst Corporation when Hearst bought the *San Francisco Chronicle,* and they also published the *San Francisco Independent* and the *San Mateo Independent.* While seats on the BART board are nonpartisan, it is worth noting that Fang was the only Republican elected from the city of San Francisco, an otherwise solid Democratic stronghold. Board politics generally came down to who could get five votes.

Tom Blalock, who took John Glenn's seat on the board, was elected president for 1999. He would continue the fight to make the Warm Springs extension a reality.

THE HARLEM GLOBETROTTERS MAKE A PLAY

Before the close of the decade, the Bay Area was visited by the world-renowned Harlem Globetrotters basketball team. The team would be playing at the Oakland Coliseum arena (now the Oracle Arena), which is served by BART with a direct walkway connection. Thus it seemed appropriate for BART and the Globetrotters to partner up for a joint promotion. Orlando Antigua, the first non-black member of the team, would be at the center of the promotion. He became the first and only person in the world to dribble a basketball on a carpeted train floor moving at 80 miles an hour through BART's famous 3.6-mile Transbay Tube, 132 feet below the waters of the San Francisco Bay. It was a definite crowd-pleaser and made a good visual for the media.

A SENSE OF FOREBODING AS THE MILLENNIUM APPROACHES

On Friday, December 31, 1999, a lot of general nervousness was in the air as the hour of midnight approached to mark the turn of the century and the specter of the third millennium. News stories circulated that the world's computer clocks were not set to go beyond the turn of the century. Would all the computers go bonkers at one second after the stroke of midnight, as some predicted? Would automated trains suddenly stop in their tracks? Would strange messages appear from deep space? There was an aura of science fiction about the various prospects. Since it was Friday, everyone at the BART offices went over home the weekend to await the outcome. Even though there had been no reported impact on trains that Saturday and Sunday, Monday morning was still met with some apprehension, but happily, as staff employees returned to their desks, they found that the computers worked just the same and business carried on as usual.

Of course, technically the new millennium did not actually begin until January 1, 2001.

CHAPTER 25

NEW CHALLENGES IN THE NEW MILLENNIUM

Something in BART's DNA was always firing up the transit district to push the envelope, to be a prospector, forever panning for gold. The District has an institutional desire to always be on the leading edge, not only in transit technology but in every way possible, constantly looking for nuggets of innovation. Maybe it goes back to when BART was nothing more than a gleam in its early planners' eyes, the idea that this space-age train system would show the way, forever pioneer a new path, seek new initiatives. Since BART was the first all-new urban rail system to be built in the United States in sixty years, it became the nation's laboratory for the development of many modern systems we know today. And that mindset has continued through the decades.

In that same spirit, as BART's aging trains rolled generally unencumbered deeper into the new millennium, a new paradigm was beginning to take wing: the need to create a broad template for the twenty-first century. Four years before, in 1996, the BART board had directed staff to begin a process that would lead the development of such a template. We now enter the realm of strategic planning, something that had not really been tackled in any systematic way before. Plunging ahead and at the same time reacting to outside forces had generally been the modus operandi in governing the system over the decades, but now strategic planning would be a tool for shaping

BART's destiny, and for coalescing important partnerships in a very deliberate way.

Major corporations, for the most part, develop strategic plans, which usually focus on long-term growth based on predicting changes in the market, adding acquisitions to strengthen market position, and marketing with an eye to beating out competition and increasing stock value for investors. Public-sector agencies, on the other hand, do not have to worry about their stocks or whether their companies will be put into play as a prospect for takeovers or corporate taxes, yet BART saw itself operating more like a corporate entity. There was, of course, the required Short-Range Transit Plans (SRTP) published each year and submitted to the Metropolitan Transportation Commission (MTC). The STRP originally looked five years down the road, but it now morphed into a ten-year projection. These plans mostly dealt with projected ridership, maintenance of effort, equipment requirements, and financial outlooks. Eventually BART staff also developed a twenty-five-year look into the future, which estimated increases in ridership that might be constrained by limited capacity. That is, if the transit system didn't significantly increase Transbay Tube throughput (that is, the number of trains per hour in each direction) via its ambitious close headways program, there could be trouble ahead. At the time, BART's daily ridership was roughly around 300,000 on weekdays. Today that figure is now averaging more than 400,000 on weekdays and growing.

STRATEGIC PLAN DEVELOPMENT

Strategic planning was another animal altogether. In contrast to the STRP's relatively short-term range, the goal here was to develop a vision and blueprint for the long-term future in the twenty-first century. The first cut at a strategic plan was adopted and published in 1999, based on work that had begun the year earlier. The vision statement adopted is:

> To be respected as a quality regional public transportation resource and leader, with unique competencies in regional rail, indispensable to the livability and vitality of the Bay Area community.

To explain the essence of what that might mean, BART held a series of workshops with community leaders, legislators, and business representatives from around the Bay Area. The objective was to get to the heart of the matter: What did "strategic planning" look like for a fixed-rail transit system that now served four counties and would within the next few years add a fifth county? What should the big picture convey? Part of the process was for the BART board and top staff members to go on a retreat, at which a facilitator would help define long-term goals and objectives.

This question would require a magnitude of brainstorming, somewhat of a think-tank approach. Most important was defining BART's overall role in the San Francisco Bay Area transit network, which included predicting changes in market trends and the system's impact on those changes, such as, for example, high-employment centers locating in the suburbs and affecting travel patterns. If you asked the man or woman on the street what service he or she thought BART provided, the answer, of course, would most likely be "To get folks from point A to point B," punctuated with a shrug of the shoulders. True enough. And yet, could there be more to it than that? Leaders in the transit field would tell you that there is much more to BART and public transit in general than simply moving people about. For instance, the system was already improving the local information highway by leasing the space along its right-of-way to private corporations stringing fiber optic cable between San Francisco, the East Bay, and the peninsula. Fiber optic leases were bringing in $4 million, and display advertising in the stations and trains netted an additional $2.6 million, with concessions earning another $1.6 million annually.

In addition to being a key transportation provider in the Bay Area, BART also had to be viewed as an economic engine, a tool for optimum land-use planning, an instrument for environmental enhancement (it significantly eliminates tons of potential carbon emissions into the air each day), an energy saver (it reduces the need for fossil fuel), a researcher and developer of innovative technology, and a major employer, to name a few of the areas to be explored in strategic planning. Various stations, particularly the downtown San Francisco stations, served as venues for musicians performing for handouts, as well as a few homeless souls. Overall the whole idea was to position BART not only to meet new challenges but also to prospect for and take advantage of opportunities. Personally, I always saw the system as a city on wheels, assuming the role of trying to be all things to all people.

STRATEGIC GOALS

Seven goal areas were adopted by the board to be the focus of the initial strategic plan:

- Customer Experience—maximizing regional transit access and maintaining high performance standards
- Partnerships for Support—working with stakeholders to promote mass transit as a viable alternative to the automobile
- Transit Travel Demand—maximizing system utilization (seat miles vs. passenger miles)
- Land Use and Quality of Life—working with local community partners to optimize potential for attracting mixed-use developments around stations
- People of BART—striving for and maintaining a professional, caring organization dedicated to meeting customer needs
- Physical Infrastructure—maintaining the integrity of the plant through annual investment
- Financial Health—endeavoring to be guided by prudent fiscal policies, and working with regional partners to advocate for funding needs

BART, like other high-capacity people movers, is also a key player in the nation's desire for a clean-energy economy.

The subtext of the strategic plan was system expansion with a view to enhancing regional mobility, with BART as the spine of the Bay Area's core transportation network. Other elements included improving job access and system access through increased parking opportunities, adding "kiss and ride" drop-off areas, promoting feeder bus service, and developing housing in and around stations, to name a few. Providing welfare-to-work clients with access to job opportunities, child care, and training was considered a critical element, as was station-area planning to foster mixed-use development where possible. The bottom line, in a word, was growth. BART, AC Transit, and the

San Francisco Muni also began sponsoring Paratransit, which provides door-to-door bus service for elderly and disabled people within certain limited distances from stations or bus routes. The service was first launched in the late 1990s as a requirement under the federal Americans with Disabilities Act (ADA).

THE WAY TO SAN JOSE

On November 13, 2001, the BART board ratified an agreement with the Santa Clara Valley Transportation Authority (VTA) for a San Jose extension. The agreement also signaled the go-ahead for the long-awaited Warm Springs project, which would be the link between Fremont and the future new line. As part of the agreement, VTA pledged $111 million toward the planned Warm Springs extension, which had an estimated price tag of $634 million—but in fact would cost $890 million. BART director Tom Blalock of Fremont, a tireless advocate of the extension, chaired the VTA Liaison Committee. He noted at the time that the VTA agreement was a "vital and critical step toward obtaining a federal funding commitment." It not only demonstrated an inter-county partnership but also underscored the region's serious dedication to moving forward with the proposed project. The voters of Santa Clara County had already approved bond issues in 1996 and again in 2000, to be underwritten by a half-cent sales tax to help finance BART to San Jose, but not to go into effect until 2006. Meanwhile it wouldn't be until September 30, 2009, that ceremonial shovels would go into the ground to mark the beginning of the Warm Springs extension, and it would be several more years before the completion of a San Jose line. Ironically, the site chosen for the ground-breaking of the Warm Springs extension was at one time the most controversial section of the project: the Central Park area of Fremont where the subway under a portion of Lake Elizabeth would begin.

Three years later, on Thursday, April 12, 2012, construction work finally began on the San Jose extension. The ground-breaking date was triggered by receipt of $900 million under a Full Funding Grant Agreement from the Federal Transit Administration, needed to augment the bond money. A grand event under a giant tent was orchestrated to mark the historic occasion at Berryessa, just north of downtown San Jose. This location will be the end of the first phase of the planned extension, which will be 10 miles from Warm Springs.

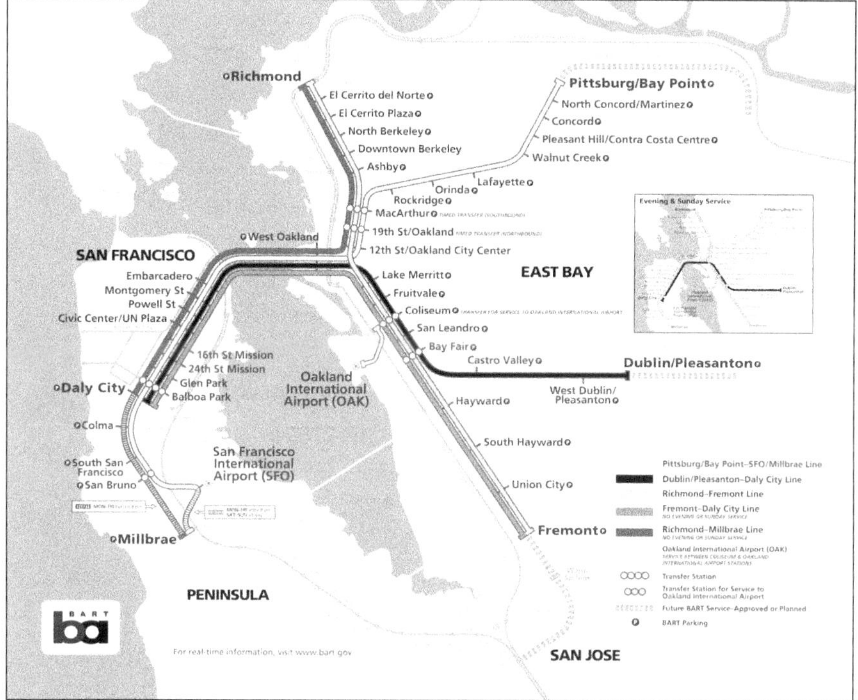

The current system map shows the extensions that have been completed and those that are under way.

Local, state, and federal elected officials and staffers were in attendance, along with Silicon Valley representatives. The project, estimated to cost $2.3 billion and be completed by the year 2018, will be the largest public works project in the history of Santa Clara County. The second phase, estimated to cost $4.7 billion and for which funding will have to be obtained, calls for a subway stretching almost 6 miles under downtown San Jose to the vicinity of the Caltrain station, scheduled for 2025. In essence this would create a transit loop, something planners had envisioned for decades.

BART LOST AND FOUND: A CURIOUS PHENOMENON

Since the 1970s, the items left on BART trains and in stations have been, and continue to be, an incredible potpourri of personal possessions. People have left laptops, phones, cameras, wallets, purses, watches, umbrellas, guitars, a copy of the Magna Carta, and even bicycles behind as they hurried off trains and out of stations.

Someone once left a prosthetic leg. On one occasion, a concert violinist forgot his violin, which he had left propped up next to his seat on a train from Daly City to downtown San Francisco. It was a priceless Stradivarius, which luckily was found and returned to its panicked owner, who was slated to play in the symphony that night. The most common items left on trains used to be umbrellas; today it's cell phones. The Lost and Found storage room is located at the 12th Street Station in downtown Oakland, where riders can go to retrieve their belongings. Anything not claimed within ninety days can be auctioned off.

BART's Lost and Found was very much appreciated when Queen Elizabeth II visited San Francisco some years ago. It happened to be raining, and the royal party was unprepared. A member of her entourage contacted BART because it was rumored to have a lot of unclaimed umbrellas hanging around. He requested fifty if possible, and emphasized they had to be black. The *San Francisco Chronicle* had earlier run a feature story about the crazy things that ended up in the system's Lost and Found storeroom, which may have been how the queen's representatives had found out about the stash. Fifty black umbrellas were dispatched to the queen's party and duly returned upon her departure.

STORAGE LOCKERS PROVED PROBLEMATIC

Strange items were often left in storage lockers as well. On one sad occasion, a woman reported hearing a faint but shrill noise coming from one of the small public storage lockers at the Powell Street Station. BART police opened it to discover a hungry week-old baby in a swaddling cloth inside, apparently abandoned. According to BART's former police chief Gary Gee, the case was turned over to the San Francisco Police Department for investigation, since the locker was in the free section of the station, a common area for both BART and Muni passengers. After the attacks on September 11, 2001, lockers in BART stations were removed for security purposes, and BART bathrooms were locked. When BART was first on the drawing board, bathrooms in stations were not included and, in fact, officials at the time were warned by others in the industry that the bathrooms would be more trouble than they were worth. Community pressure had persuaded the board and staff to add them, but as predicted, the bathrooms did become the system's albatross and a maintenance nightmare.

BIKE LOCKERS MADE FOR CHEAP HOUSING

Another area of contention was the early version of bike lockers placed at various suburban stations. These small box-like structures served their intended purpose well, but they also sometimes became cheap housing for desperate or adventurous souls. At the Lake Merritt Station, a couple of the bike lockers, measuring 4 feet wide, 6 feet long, and 5 feet high, became homes for transients. The rental cost was $35 a year. In one case, a man who called himself "Silverbone" camped in a bike locker in front of the BART headquarters building. When employees came to work in the morning, there was Silverbone, happily sitting on his sleeping bag in front of the locker, making coffee in a coffee pot he plugged into an outlet at the bottom of an adjacent lamppost. He greeted people with a friendly smile and wave as they passed him.

A couple of BART board members were not happy about Silverbone, partly because he actually had a bone going though his nose and partly because of his effrontery at positioning himself close to the entrance of the building, as if he were BART's official greeter. The funny thing was that he was generally liked by the staff. While no official action was taken by the board, the offended members asked that something be done. Eventually Silverbone's abode was moved to the other side of the Lake Merritt Station, and no one ever saw him much after that. Another issue, and one that got some press, was a locker at one of the Berkeley stations. A young couple was using it as a motel of the type that rented rooms by the half hour. Once the word got out, that activity came to a halt.

RENOVATION FOR THE AGING SYSTEM

The one-time baby of the transit industry was now getting gray hair. Capital reinvestment in infrastructure and equipment for a transit system like BART is a constant. The year before the opening of the new San Francisco airport line in 2003, BART, which had launched a $1.2 billion system-wide renovation program in 1992, marked a ten-year milestone in the work. By this time the project was 80 percent complete. It involved the replacement and/or refurbishment of 60 elevators, 99 escalators, new fare gates at certain stations, and the rehabilitation of 400 of the original fleet of transit cars, to name a few of the program's tasks. Rebuilt from top to bottom, the transit cars would be infused with twenty more years of life.

Meanwhile, by the end of June 2002, plans were drawn up for an aggressive seismic retrofit program to enhance the system's resilience in future earthquakes. While BART was originally designed using state-of-the-art technology to withstand earthquakes of the highest known magnitude, it was determined that an updated review was in order. Following the Loma Prieta temblor of 1989, during which BART performed well, several studies were commissioned to look at the system's vulnerabilities. A comprehensive review of the overall system structures was completed in 2001. The study, conducted by an acclaimed group of seismic experts in the field and at the University of California, Berkeley, recommended strengthening the aerial structures and the Transbay Tube.

The primary concern for the Transbay Tube was the potential for liquefaction to occur during a major quake. Under extreme G forces, the ballast located in bins on top of the tube that keeps it locked in place below the floor of the bay could be affected or even disintegrate. BART estimated the cost of a system-wide seismic upgrade, including the tube, to be in the neighborhood of $1.3 to $1.6 billion. Since there was no funding identified for an upgrade, the transit district would have to go to the voters to get approval for a bond measure. But first BART developed a detailed plan to upgrade those areas of the system's structure most vulnerable to earthquakes. The primary goal was, of course, to ensure rider and employee safety, but it was also important to be able to return to full operation quickly. A major information campaign was launched to keep the public apprised of what was needed.

On November 2, 2004, the voters of the three BART counties—Alameda, Contra Costa, and San Francisco—approved Proposition AA, which authorized $980 million in general obligation bonds specifically for seismic improvements. The sale of the bonds, which would begin the following year, was for the express purpose of funding the transit system's earthquake safety improvements. Some work began early on in conjunction with Caltrans, but the bulk of the effort actually did not begin until October 2008. While much of the project has been completed, the work continues as of this writing.

THE FIRST FEMALE GENERAL MANAGER

On August 23, 2007, Dorothy Dugger, who for several years had been the agency's deputy general manager, was named by the board of directors as BART's first female general manager. She replaced Thomas Margro, who left to take a new job in Southern California.

Dugger was a key staffer in getting BART's extension to San Francisco International Airport through the maze of financial hurdles and political machinations. She worked tirelessly, often well into the night. I remember going up to the fifth floor of BART's old Lake Merritt headquarters building late one night and finding her working away at the conference table in her office, papers scattered everywhere. It must have been around nine o'clock in the evening, and there was not another soul around. She was writing furiously on a yellow pad while sipping on a cold beer and smoking, both of which were prohibited in the building as a matter of policy. She looked up at me as I looked on and mockingly shook my head. "So fire me," she said, and grinned. There was no question that Dugger was a workaholic, dedicated to

A BART train enters San Francisco International Airport while the airport's Air-Train system, which connects with BART and all of the terminals, runs on the track above.

crossing all the T's and dotting all the I's before any piece of paper left her desk.

Several important projects were by this time either under way or had moved to the front burner. These included the renovation of the system, the seismic retrofit, and preparations for ordering a new fleet of transit cars. BART's cars—which originally had a life span of twenty-five years, with an additional twenty tacked on after refurbishment—were now the oldest among the nation's urban transit systems. Ten new prototype cars are expected to be delivered in 2016 for testing. Production cars are due to begin arriving in 2017.

NEW YEAR'S EVE, 2009

BART faced a major crisis with the tragic shooting by a BART police officer of a young black man named Oscar Grant III. The shooting took place at the system's Fruitvale Station in East Oakland. Grant was on his way home with friends from a New Year's celebration in San Francisco when BART police officers pulled them off a southbound train for a reported on-board fight.

Bystanders on the station's platform used their cell phones to record the incident from several angles, and many of the clips ended up on the evening news and the Internet, igniting a strong backlash from Oscar Grant's family and the community toward BART Police and the transit district in general. In Oakland, the protests started out peaceful but often became violent, taking on a life of their own. It seemed that anarchists from outside fueled the mayhem and collateral vandalism that occurred in the downtown area. The BART board, ever sensitive to community outrage, set up a special committee and hired an independent contractor to review police procedures and training. During their open public meetings, members of the board were being hammered over the issue of whether BART should even have its own police force. On one occasion a Sacramento man entered the boardroom and suddenly threw red paint on general manager Dorothy Dugger. The officer involved in the shooting, Johannes Mehserle, was charged with murder by the Alameda County district attorney. Upon a change of venue, he was eventually tried in a Los Angeles court and found guilty of involuntary manslaughter; he served two years in prison. The Oscar Grant story was later depicted in a movie titled *Fruitvale Station.*

THE OAKLAND AIRPORT CONNECTOR

On October 20, 2010, ground was finally broken to mark the construction of a rail connector system between BART's Coliseum Station and Oakland International Airport. This was an amazing event, since the "connector," as it is referred to by those in the know, had been on and off the radar screen for more than forty-five years. Some believed it was more a figment of the imagination, and some believed it shouldn't happen at all, including some BART board members, who thought that buses could do the job just as well and for a lot less money. Proponents, on the other hand, argued that once the infrastructure was in place, it would be far more efficient, quicker, and sexier in terms of market appeal than the AirBART buses it would replace. Also, travelers heading to the airport would no longer have to leave the station; they could simply access the connector from the Coliseum Station platform.

Back in 1969, well before BART even opened, the Oakland Airport Access Task Force (OAATF) was formed. It was the genesis for the future rail connector between the new rapid transit system and the Oakland airport, which had been growing since it opened. The airport had gained national attention when Charles Lindbergh presided over its official inauguration in 1927, and again when, in 1937, Amelia Earhart took off on her ill-fated around-the-world venture. The new main terminal was completed in 1962.

In 1970, a feasibility study to look at potential connector options was commissioned by OAATF. The study was done by Kaiser Engineers in 1971. At that time, a spur line directly off BART's Fremont line, beginning somewhere south of the Fruitvale Station and running along either Edgewater Drive (3.9 miles) or Hegenberger Road (3.2 miles), was thought feasible. The Kaiser plan would have been a loop, serving both southbound and northbound travelers. Hegenberger was considered the best route option and was recommended as the preferred alignment, with possible stops to serve businesses along the way. However, from an operation standpoint, a rail loop from the main line presented problems as a potential degradation of regular service. Cost estimates at the time ranged from $47 million for the loop to $172 million for a separate system; the latter was considered too costly.

But the idea remained alive. The Oakland airport wanted to be a player on the international market as well as competing for the domestic trade. A direct hookup with a major rail rapid transit system would be a key element in achieving that goal in the years to come. Eventually BART, the Port of Oakland, and the City of Oakland formed a partnership to be the sponsoring parties in conjunction with the MTC to build the connector. More studies were conducted during the 1990s, and by the end of the decade, interest in building the connector was once again on the table.

In 1993 the Intermodal Connector Project was established, but the catch was still securing funding. There wasn't any money, or at least not enough, in the coffers to begin construction. Traditional funding sources from the State of California and the Federal Transit Administration (FTA) were not yet committed, partly because of the nationwide economic downturn. Money was simply scarce. However, as the number of travelers through the airport had almost doubled over the previous twenty years, interest in the connector peaked. By 2009, BART was able to leverage funding from the state and the FTA. But there was a snag.

FEDS WITHDRAW FUNDING FROM THE OAKLAND AIRPORT CONNECTOR PROJECT

On January 15, 2010, BART and the MTC received a letter from FTA administrator Peter Rogoff informing the two agencies that corrective action had to be taken with regard to an issue that had been brought to his agency's attention. The FTA had received a formal complaint the prior September alleging that BART had not done a "service equity analysis" as required by Title VI of the Civil Rights Act of 1964, a federal requirement that is normally part of the Environmental Impact Statement (EIS) process. It requires, among other things, that a determination be made that a new project, such as the Oakland connector, does not constitute a form of discrimination with regard to its impact in the community, and that its accessibility not be prohibitive to a diverse population, particularly minorities and those at the lower end of the economic scale. An investigation by the FTA revealed that, in fact, BART had somehow not included the data required to show negative impact and thus was not in compliance. As a result, $70 million earmarked for the connector project was in jeopardy and could be withdrawn as a consequence. The money was coming from the American Recovery and Reinvestment Act (ARRA) of 2009.

A plan to bring the transit district's project analysis into compliance had to be provided on a very tight deadline, and when the outline for corrective action was submitted, everyone was on tenterhooks. On February 12, 2010, the FTA sent a follow-up letter to the MTC and to BART's general manager Dorothy Dugger that thus far BART had not been able to develop an acceptable corrective action to meet the Title VI requirements, and so informed the agencies that the plan was rejected. The money from the ARRA had to be committed to another qualifying Bay Area project before March 5 and, if the money were not disbursed by September 30, the agreement would lapse and the money would return to the U.S. Treasury. In the end, that's what happened.

Attitudes on the strict meaning of how to meet Title VI requirements seemed to change with administrations in Washington, according to some staffers. The loss of the American Recovery and Reinvestment Act money left a significant hole in the overall funding package, and BART scrambled to replace it. As it turned out, BART was able to get $25 million from the FTA under the New Starts program. The rest came from Measure B (Alameda County money for transit projects) and the State Transportation Improvement Program (STIP). But board members were still unhappy over the loss of the $70 million.

For general manager Dorothy Dugger, 2009 proved to be a donnybrook year. First the fallout from the Oscar Grant shooting on New Year's Eve; then the resignation and retirement of Gary Gee, BART's highly respected and popular police chief; followed by the Title VI fiasco—all combined to put Dugger on the political hot seat. Dugger told me that by 2011 she was in an untenable position with the board, this coming after a botched attempt to fire her in a closed session. The reported vote was 5 to 4 against her, but the action was declared illegal under the Ralph M. Brown Act by the system's general counsel. Dugger then negotiated an exit package and resigned on April 22, 2011, with many accomplishments under her belt. The politics and relationships between transit system CEOs and their boards, usually made up of businesspeople and professionals from all walks of life, is traditionally treacherous ground. Knowing how and when to duck is a prerequisite for the job.

THE BART BOARD APPOINTS A NEW GENERAL MANAGER

Following a nationwide search for qualified candidates, the board, on August 31, 2011, named Grace Crunican to be the transit system's ninth and newest general manager. Crunican came with thirty-two years of experience in the transportation field. She inherited a very long laundry list of projects that were either under way or on the drawing board, as well as an often tenuous relationship with the system's powerful labor unions. "One of the things I'm really interested in," Crunican said, "is the enormous potential that still exists for the development of partnerships with stakeholders along the BART lines, maximizing land use around stations." She also said she believes that partnerships with the communities within its sphere, such as the business community, the political community, the transit community, and so on, are a major factor in the success of a system like BART. A recent example is the mixed-use development of the Transit Village at the MacArthur Station in North Oakland. The Oakland airport connector is another good example.

The $484 million connector project is an automated guideway transit system (AGT) stretching 3.2 miles along an aerial structure between the BART Coliseum Station and the airport terminals. In other words, it has no driver and, for that matter, no engines, making it virtually

The long-awaited Oakland airport connector opened on November 14, 2014, to rave reviews. The quiet, cable-operated cars carry an average 3,300 riders a day over the 3 miles between the Coliseum Station and the terminals.

noiseless. The four three-car trains are operated by cables, similar to San Francisco's cable cars or a ski tram. The headways are around four and a half minutes. An Austrian company called Doppelmayr is the supplier of the connector system. The Oakland airport connector opened on Friday, November 21, 2014, to cheers and also astonishment at how quiet and smooth the ride was. It was estimated that it would carry about 900,000 riders to and from the airport annually. In fact the connector carried 1 million passengers during its first year.

SOME THOUGHTS

There can be no ending to the history of the San Francisco Bay Area Rapid Transit system. It's like a living, breathing organism that grows even as it regenerates itself. Today people take the system for granted, as if it has always been here to serve the populace since time began. It is such an integral part of the daily life of the region, no one gives much thought to trains whizzing up to 80 miles per hour while 132 feet under the bay between San Francisco and the East Bay communities. The marvel of how that happens is lost—as long as it gets riders from one point to another. Even delays on the system, while irritating, are pretty much taken for granted, endemic to so much moving machinery. These things happen. It is not a perfect world.

Has BART accomplished what the early planners envisioned? While it was never viewed as a panacea for all of the area's urban ills, it was always meant to be a force in the development of the region, and in that respect it has, like many of its very early predecessors, helped to shape the core Bay Area landscape, stemming sprawl and contributing to preserve and enhance urban centers, as well as the Bay Area's incredibly lush environment. Since first opening its doors for service on September 11, 1972, the system has carried almost 3 billion passengers more than 40 billion passenger miles. But what if there were no BART? Transit experts and social scientists would probably say that without BART the San Francisco Bay Area and environs would look very different today, possibly more like Los Angeles. As for its role as a planning tool for housing and commercial development, there is a great deal more to be accomplished in the years ahead.

A LETTER

On September 24, 2003, BART's then general manager Thomas Margro received an interesting letter from West Financial Group Inc., located in New York and Fort Lauderdale.

"Dear Thomas," it began. "A major company has expressed an interest in buying Bay Area Rapid Transit."

It ended with a note to please call to set up a meeting to discuss the matter further. It was signed "Kindest Regards, Steven West."

As BART was a taxpayer-owned public entity, the letter, of course, was not taken as a serious matter. But it did make one wonder what the replacement cost of the system would be in today's dollars. The three-county district's taxpayers' original investment, coupled with state and some federal funds of $1.4 billion, was considered an outrageous amount by pundits at the time. Add to that number another $9 billion, which includes the costs for all of the extensions, the Oakland airport connector, the renovation program, seismic retrofitting, new cars during the 1990s, and the San Jose extension now under construction, and you have a total of roughly $10.4 billion of capital investment over a forty-two-year period. By 2017 the basic system will have grown from 71.5 miles to 120 miles, about a 60 percent increase. BART's then board president Joel Keller speculated in 2014 that in today's dollars the worth of the system in terms of replacement value is in the neighborhood of between $35 and $40 billion. In the final analysis, it is safe to say that BART in fact was perfectly timed. Any sooner and it could not have taken advantage of developing aerospace technology. Any later and it probably would have been beyond the reach of the local taxpayers who agreed on November 6, 1962, to finance the initial construction. The project would also have faced a closed window on right-of-way acquisition and the use of freeway medians. Probably one of the great lessons of BART is the need to reduce the time it takes for giant public works projects to move from drawing board to construction.

Once again B. R. Stokes's words in the early days never rang truer: "Build it now; it will never be cheaper."

The BART story is central to the history of the Bay Area, but it is also an American story, a story of remarkable achievement in the face of great adversity, a miracle of the twentieth century and of the power of a resolute spirit. On July 24, 1997, BART was declared a historical landmark by the esteemed American Society of Mechanical Engineers for its many technical and design innovations. In 2004, BART was named the number-one transit system in the nation by the American Public Transportation Association (APTA) in Washington, D.C. These are proud achievements for the still relatively young transit system. But of course the biggest achievement of all was building it in the first place. What lies ahead for BART in the long term is uncertain. But one thing is guaranteed: the BART story will be a continuing saga, replete with successes, failures, and drama enough to fill another book in the years ahead.

ACKNOWLEDGMENTS

A book like the history of BART, with all its twists, turns, and intrigues, could not have been made without the generous help and input from numerous people with both expertise and good memories. The assistance I received also made the writing process a labor of love.

First and foremost I want to acknowledge the help I received from B. R. Stokes, BART's general manager during the construction years. He told me some very funny stories from the early days, and I believe they have helped enrich the lively BART story. Unfortunately, Bill did not live to see the publication of this book, but I was lucky enough to interview him three or four times before his passing.

Lawrence Dahms, BART's former assistant general manager and interim general manager, as well as executive director of the Metropolitan Transportation Commission, offered a few anecdotes of his own. Of particular importance was his recollection of the late Dr. Bernard Oliver's role in designing the redundant train protection device known as SORS.

Frank C. Herringer, who came to BART as general manager in 1975 from his role as administrator at the federal Urban Mass Transportation Administration, helped me with some critical facts and dates during his tenure. Frank went on to become CEO and chairman of the board of the Transamerica Corporation.

Howard Goode, the former head of BART's planning department and later a top executive at the San Mateo County Transit District, was very helpful on issues concerning the tumultuous history of the BART extension to San Francisco International Airport.

Judge Quentin L. Kopp, a longtime associate and friend, was also helpful regarding the SFO extension. Kopp, who was then a state senator and chairman of the Senate Transportation Committee, was instrumental in changing the early planned course of the extension from outside the airport to inside.

Terry Sanders, a Westinghouse engineer and project manager during the first few decades of the system's operation, was not only extremely helpful with stories concerning the early technical challenges BART faced but he also made personal files from those days available for my perusal.

Bill Moore, a former chief of the Oakland Fire Department, spent one morning with me in an Oakland coffee shop recalling the aftermath of the 1979 Transbay Tube fire, a watershed event.

Other important contributions came from the following people: former general manager Dorothy Dugger; former BART police chief Gary Gee; former budget manager Joseph Evinger; assistant general manger of operations and engineering Paul Oversier; retired general counsel for BART Sherwood Wakeman; general counsel Matt Burrows; Pam Herhold, a BART financial planner, who provided important numbers; Stacy Perkins and Mike Tanner, in capital development; Ellen Smith in planning; former head of research Ward Belding; former District secretary Phillip Ormsbee; Kerry Hamill and Alicia Trost of BART external affairs, who helped coordinate my efforts in completing the book; Frank Schultz, who was responsible for the buying power of all aspects of the operation and administration of the system; Laura Timothy, with BART's art department; Kathryn Springer, a former manager of customer service, who shared her recollections; Brenda Kahn of the Metropolitan Transportation Commission; and Judge Robert Bostick, who provided me inside information on his decision to require the Ashby Station to be below ground.

Bill Millar, former president of the American Public Transportation Association (APTA) in Washington, D.C., was most helpful in putting me in touch with B. R. Stokes. Thanks also to the late Michael Harris, a reporter for the *San Francisco Chronicle* who covered BART's early days, and to the late transportation writer Harre Demoro, whose "BART at Mid-Point" was very helpful in establishing timelines of events. Thanks to Elizabeth Adams and Bryan Hemming, who made me aware of Margaret Thatcher's visit to BART. And a special thanks to John Christian of the Hayward Historical Society, who was enormously helpful and generous with his time in searching for and providing clips from the *Oakland Tribune* archives.

INDEX

ABOUT THE AUTHOR

Michael C. Healy was head of Media and Public Affairs for BART for thirty-two years. In that capacity he was responsible for public information and served as chief spokesperson for the transit district. Marketing and customer service were also under his direction for most of that time. He is a former chair of the Washington, D.C.–based American Public Transportation Association's National Public Affairs and Community Relations Subcommittee. Upon his retirement from BART in 2005, his name was entered into the U.S. Congressional Record and he was congratulated for his service on the floor of the House. Prior to joining BART he lived on a houseboat in Sausalito and was the managing editor of *Marin Guide Publications,* a semiweekly newspaper in southern Marin County with 48,000 subscribers. He has also worked for CBS at Television City in Hollywood and as a contract writer for CBS in New York on the radio side. In the early 1970s he took time out to write a movie at Paramount Studios called *The Dirt Gang,* a raucous motorcycle film that was released by American International Pictures. During the span of his career he has written numerous articles on transportation and is currently a contributing writer for *Oakland* and *Alameda* magazines. He has also completed a novel based on his experience in Hollywood. Mike makes his home in the Montclair District of Oakland with his wife, Joan, and their dog, Bella.

About Heyday

Heyday is an independent, nonprofit publisher and unique cultural institution. We promote widespread awareness and celebration of California's many cultures, landscapes, and boundary-breaking ideas. Through our well-crafted books, public events, and innovative outreach programs we are building a vibrant community of readers, writers, and thinkers.

Thank You

It takes the collective effort of many to create a thriving literary culture. We are thankful to all the thoughtful people we have the privilege to engage with. Cheers to our writers, artists, editors, storytellers, designers, printers, bookstores, critics, cultural organizations, readers, and book lovers everywhere!

We are especially grateful for the generous funding we've received for our publications and programs during the past year from foundations and hundreds of individual donors. Major supporters include:

Anonymous (3); Advocates for Indigenous California Language Survival; Arkay Foundation; Richard and Rickie Ann Baum; Randy Bayard; Jean and Fred Berensmeier; Joan Berman and Philip Gerstner; Nancy Bertelsen; Barbara Boucke; Beatrice Bowles; Jamie and Philip Bowles; California Historical Society; California Humanities; California Rice Commission; California Wildlife Foundation/California Oaks; The Campbell Foundation; Candelaria Fund; John and Nancy Cassidy; Graham Chisholm; The Christensen Fund; Jon Christensen; Lawrence Crooks; Nik Dehejia; Topher Delaney; Chris Desser and Kirk Marckwald; Frances Dinkelspiel and Gary Wayne; The Roy & Patricia Disney Family Foundation; Tim Disney; The Durfee Foundation; Endangered Habitats League; Marilee Enge and George Frost;

Richard and Gretchen Evans; John Gage and Linda Schacht; Wallace Alexander Gerbode Foundation; Patrick Golden; Walter & Elise Haas Fund; Penelope Hlavac; Charles and Sandra Hobson; Nettie Hoge; Donna Ewald Huggins; Inlandia Institute; JiJi Foundation; Claudia Jurmain; Kalliopeia Foundation; Marty Krasney; Abigail Kreiss; Guy Lampard and Suzanne Badenhoop; David Loeb; Judith Lowry-Croul and Brad Croul; Sam and Alfreda Maloof Foundation for Arts & Crafts; Manzanar History Association; Nion McEvoy and Leslie Berriman, in honor of Malcolm Margolin; Heather McFarlin; The Giles W. and Elise G. Mead Foundation; Richard Nagler; National Wildlife Federation; The Nature Conservancy; Steven Nightingale and Lucy Blake; Northern California Water Association; Julie and Will Parish; Ronald Parker; The Ralph M. Parsons Foundation; Jeannene Przyblyski; James and Caren Quay; Susan Raynes; Alan Rosenus; The San Francisco Foundation; San Francisco Heritage; San Manuel Band of Mission Indians; Greg Sarris; Ron Shoop; Stanley Smith Horticultural Trust; William Somerville; Liz Sutherland; Roselyne Swig; Thendara Foundation; Jerry Tone and Martha Wyckoff; Sonia Torres; Michael and Shirley Traynor; Lisa Van Cleef and Mark Gunson; Stevens Van Strum; Marion Weber; Sylvia Wen and Mathew London; Valerie Whitworth and Michael Barbour; Cole Wilbur; Peter Wiley and Valerie Barth; and Yocha Dehe Wintun Nation.

Board of Directors

Getting Involved

To learn more about our publications, events and other ways you can participate, please visit www.heydaybooks.com.